Paul Rogers, Lawrence Briggs, Bryan Goodman-Stephens

Nelson

Thomas Nelson and Sons Ltd
Nelson House Mayfield Road
Walton-on-Thames Surrey
KT12 5PL UK

Nelson Blackie
Wester Cleddens Road
Bishopbriggs
Glasgow
G64 2N2 UK

Thomas Nelson (Hong Kong) Ltd
Toppan Building 10/F
22a Westlands Road
Quarry Bay
Hong Kong

Thomas Nelson Australia
102 Dodds Street
South Melbourne
Victoria 3205
Australia

Nelson Canada
1120 Birchmount Road
Scarborough Ontario
M1K 5G4
Canada

First published by Thomas Nelson and Sons Ltd 1993

ISBN 0-17-439786-0
NPN 9 8 7 6 5 4 3 2

Printed in Spain

Acknowledgements

Margaret Briggs
Gerold Deffner
Walter and Gülborg Gerecht
Pamela Goodman-Stephens
Mike Hardy
Marianne Illi
Klaus May
Jeanne McCarthy
Herbert Nagel
Josef Pogadl
Emma Rogers
Monika and Michael Schätzle
Christian Schweiger
Anna Timm
Jane Tuppen
Karen Woermer and pupils of the Gymnasium Schwarzenberg, Harburg

Tape recordings

Speakers from:
Städtisches Gymnasium, Gütersloh
organiser: Josef Ostkamp

Singers:
Ulrike Bolkart
Uwe Rösener
Ute Schmidt

Music:
Sheila Blackband
Paul Bray
Neil Ferguson
Rob Hannon

Contents

Introduction

Aims

- To provide an enjoyable and stimulating language-learning experience for students of all levels of ability.
- To develop the ability to use German effectively for the purposes of practical communication both within and outside the classroom.
- To establish the skills, language and attitudes required to promote and facilitate further study of German.
- To develop a knowledge and understanding of, and positive attitude towards, speakers of German throughout the world.
- To raise awareness of multicultural and gender issues.
- To establish an awareness of the language-learning process and thereby facilitate the learning of other languages.
- To promote a range of learning styles, including collaborative work with peers and independent learning.
- To contribute to the general education of the learners.
- To develop students' communication skills in general.
- To make a useful contribution to other areas of the curriculum, especially IT, Humanities, Health Education and Personal and Social Education.

Course components

The course consists of four stages, which encompass all aspects of the National Curriculum and Standard Grade.

Stage 1 comprises the following:

- Student's book
- Teacher's book, containing teacher's notes and transcripts
- Audio cassettes
- Copymasters
- Flashcards
- Activity box for independent learning, containing:
  activity cards
  audio cassette (duplicating master)
- video cassettes
- Computer software
- Language Master cards
- Assessment Support Pack

Core and complementary materials

The material can be broadly divided into two types: core (i.e. a common body or work which all students will follow) and complementary (providing opportunities for extension, revision and supported self-study).

All notes on complementary material in the teacher's book are indicated by boxes or by flags at three levels, GOLD, ROT and SCHWARZ (see below). Everything else, therefore, relates to core material.

The core material is:

- the first six pages and ***Auf einen Blick*** in each chapter in the students' book;
- most of the recordings on cassette;
- some of the copymasters;
- the flashcards;
- many activities explained in the teacher's notes but not involving printed or recorded materials;
- the video cassettes, if possible.

The core provides an acceptable common basis of language for each topic area, thus ensuring that students will not be asked at a later stage to build on something they have not done. This is not to say that the core would ever be enough in itself. Students need flexibility to practise, develop, revise and use what they have learned in the core. This is where the rich variety of complementary material comes into its own. It is intended that the majority of students should be able to cover the core material in each of the ten chapters in under four weeks during lesson time. Stage 1 should therefore conveniently provide a year's work.

The complementary material is:

- the *Selbstbedienung* pages towards the end of each chapter of the students' book;
- some of the recordings on cassette;
- some copymasters;
- various activities and games described only in the teacher's notes;
- the activity cards and related audio cassette;
- the computer software;
- the Language Master cards.

All complementary materials are graded to match three levels of difficulty as follows:

GOLD: simple but stimulating and attractively presented activities designed primarily with low attainers in mind but likely to appeal to all students, either for consolidation or just for fun.

ROT: interesting and imaginative materials suitable for the majority of students.

SCHWARZ: challenging material and activities for students who enjoy more demanding tasks. Some SCHWARZ activities are more difficult because they include unknown vocabulary. Frequently, however, they are more challenging because students are required to manipulate known lexis and make a logical deduction or series of deductions in order to solve a problem or puzzle.

The categorisation of activities in this way is intended to be a helpful guide for students and teachers. It is recognised, however, that perceived levels of difficulty do not always apply with equal force to all students. In certain cases, therefore, the teacher will be the most appropriate person to match students to tasks.

The students' book

The students' book is divided into ten chapters of approximately equal length. Each of these chapters is then subdivided into three related *Lernziele*.

Independent learning

The final section of each chapter is called *Selbstbedienung*. This provides a selection of additional differentiated activities for self-access, and is a springboard for other self-access extension material in the activity box. A special index to all instructions given in the *Selbstbedienung* sections is given on page 144 of the students' book. Solutions to all activities are provided on copymaster and should be made available to students.

Acquisition of vocabulary

Since great emphasis is placed upon independent learning, it is essential that students should develop good dictionary and reference skills from the outset. The students' book has an easy-to-use German–English/English–German glossary and a step-by-step approach to the presentation and explanation of grammar. Together, these help students to gradually develop the skills necessary to cope with unknown vocabulary encountered either in reading or in listening to texts required for oral or written tasks.

Students are encouraged throughout *Zickzack neu* to develop strategies to increase their word power and also to cope in situations where they are faced with unknown vocabulary. Techniques such as brainstorming, speculation and deduction are frequently used, as are games, puzzles and problem-solving activities.

A substantial part of language learning is simply the building up of vocabulary. In addition to the vocabulary taught in both core and complementary activities, *Zickzack neu* offers students another way of learning some new words associated with each topic: *Bildvokabeln*. These labelled pictures in most chapters can either be left for students to select the words they may want to use or used systematically by the teacher to introduce new vocabulary. The same pictures are provided on copymaster. These can be used to help students learn, by copying the keywords, or even for testing, as all the relevant vocabulary items are present. Why not encourage students to label as many other things in the picture as they can?

Songs and poems

In each chapter of the students' book you will find either a song or a poem. The songs are recorded on cassette. They are designed to be easily learnable and fun to sing along with. Having played the song to the class, get students to sing it line by line, either all together or in groups. If there are musicians in the class, a final stage could be to abandon the tape and let students perform it in their own way. Why not record these performances? Add actions and mime, and there are no limits to how these might be developed.

The poems in their turn are designed not only to be accessible but to stimulate students to produce their own along similar lines.

Cartoons

A cartoon strip, specially drawn for *Zickzack neu*, features in each chapter. They are not intended for detailed exploitation but to encourage students to read for their own interest. You may like to read through them together initially. Students may well be inspired by these to produce cartoons of their own.

Grammar

An awareness of structure is considered of vital importance for students of all levels of ability if they are to be able to take language encountered in one situation and transfer it to another. For many pupils a familiarity with some of the German language patterns will help them generate their own phrases or sentences by using known vocabulary and structures creatively. For these reasons, grammar is treated systematically from the beginning of the course and can be represented as follows:

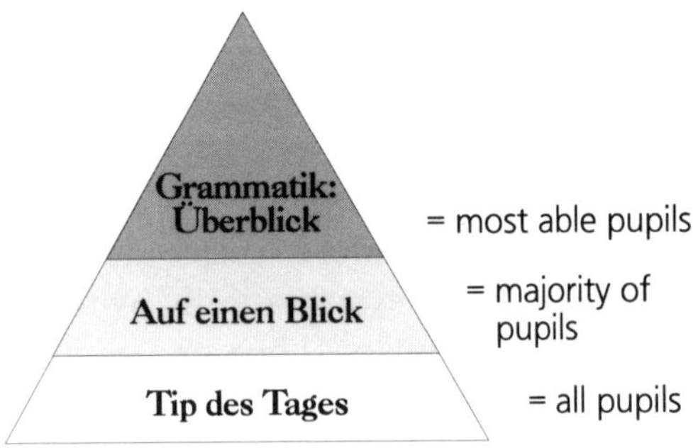

Tip des Tages: a presentation of the main structures without explanation, to support communicative activities and to focus students' attention on core language.

Auf einen Blick: a collation, without explanation, of the core structures presented in each chapter under functional headings. Students should be encouraged to begin to identify the emergence of general patterns. Since all structures are translated into English, this section clarifies meanings, supports independent learning, aids revision and serves as a point of reference if students have been absent.

Grammatik: Überblick: a summary of all the main structures in the book within a largely functional framework, with increased focus on grammatical forms. Verbs, for example, are dealt with person by person rather than in full conjugation. This has the advantage of retaining the functional context, whilst emphasising the simplicity of the patterns. This reference section is intended for those students who require more information about the way German is pieced together. All explanations are, therefore, presented clearly, and grammatical terminology is defined in simple terms before it is used.

Further practice on many points of grammar is provided on copymasters 72–82. Some relate to the individual chapters, others to sections of the ***Grammatik: Überblick***.

Differentiated activity box

The cards in the activity box contain a wealth of activities for autonomous learning. These are differentiated at the three levels of difficulty: GOLD, ROT and SCHWARZ. All the material is specially written to be directly accessible to students and to reflect their interests. Answers, where appropriate, are provided to encourage self-correction and assessment, and students should feel free to choose material at any level.

There are no teacher's notes accompanying the differentiated activity box, but the instructions to the students are unambiguous. Students may work independently, in pairs or in groups; this offers an opportunity for further development in the range of learning styles. All material is fully integrated with the core material and fun to do.

The teacher's book

Zickzack neu has been designed to expose students to the maximum amount of both spoken and written German as a normal means of communication within the classroom. To this end, a suggested sequence of language to set up each activity is provided in addition to other strategies such as mime, gesture, use of visuals, written clues and demonstration. This support is not, however, intended to be prescriptive. Indeed, many experienced teachers or teachers with German as their specialist subject may prefer to use other language or techniques to set up or practise activities.

Whilst the teacher's notes provide the language necessary to set up all activities, it is also suggested that a number of *Dolmetscher(innen) des Tages* be nominated for each lesson, through whom questions about new vocabulary can be channelled. They can be given the responsibility of looking up new words when the need arises. A card or badge designating these official interpreters can add fun to the process.

Another useful strategy, suggested at points in the teacher's notes, is to outline the task to be performed privately to one or two students in advance so that they can be part of a demonstration.

In order to convey to students the fundamental importance of using German to communicate in the classroom, it is vital that an early start be made to activities which require students to listen to and understand instructions. From there the next all-important step, of course, is for students to begin using the phrases themselves. The classroom language copymaster (1) is an essential component in this process. It should be given to students or displayed permanently, preferably enlarged on a photocopier or rewritten by the students by hand or on computer once the language shown has been encountered.

A list of suggested games to help familiarise students with classroom instructions is given on page 8. Students will enjoy frequent short-burst practice of such classroom language providing it takes the form of action or mime games and involves the use of phrases they hear regularly during lessons.

Students' familiarity with classroom vocabulary will also be greatly increased if parts of the room and items of equipment are labelled in German: *die Tür, das Fenster, der Stuhl, der Tisch, die Tafel, der Kassettenrecorder, der Tageslichtprojektor, der Vorhang, die Jalousie, der Bildschirm, die Kreide, die Filzstifte, die Bücher, die Hefte.*

Assessment material

The skills involved in each activity are clearly identified in the teacher's notes. Several activities which involve predominately oral production have been designed for use in an assessment mode once students can confidently produce the required structures and lexis without the support of written cues. When students are being assessed, the written cues on a copymaster can be either folded under or cut off and teachers can either assess students performing in pairs or conduct face-to-face interviews. Such strategies make it relatively straightforward for students and teachers to keep a continuous record of progress. This formative assessment should provide valuable diagnostic information to guide future learning and teaching.

For student self-assessment throughout the course, assessment profile sheets called *Personalakte* are available on copymasters 83–85. These relate to the topics covered in each chapter of the book, and give students the opportunity to record what they can do, which topics they enjoyed most and how easy or difficult they found them.

In addition, the separate assessment support pack provides detailed guidance on formative and summative assessment and a battery of tests in all skills. There are tests to cover the contents of each chapter, as well as more demanding cumulative tests to cover groups of chapters. Each of these tests is easy to administer and mark, and is linked to the student profile sheets.

Video cassettes

The video cassettes provide further practice in the structures and topics covered in each chapter, as well as showing the language being used in context in German-speaking countries. Full details are given in the notes that accompany the cassettes.

Computer software

Textfiles are available to run on the popular *Fun with Texts* program. These provide valuable practice at all levels and in all skills, but especially in reading and writing. Full details are available with the package.

Language Master cards

The Language Master card system is an audio-visual component which develops basic skills and encourages independent work. It offers practice in a variety of areas — for example listening, pronunciation, reading, consolidation of vocabulary and, if students are allowed to create their own cards, writing too.

Students feed the Language Master card with its pre-recorded magnetic strip into the machine and hear the recording while looking at the words. They can then record the same words on a separate track on the magnetic strip. They can listen to the master track and re-record on the student track as often as they like in order to learn the particular item on the card.

Additional practical points

- For open-ended tasks, there is flexibility over the answers. This is made clear in the teacher's notes and a range of suggested solutions is offered for reference.
- Frequent reference is made to the value of displaying flashcards and students' work. Many activities provide opportunities to produce work for display.
- Many of the games on copymaster, especially those which are graded GOLD, are best copied onto card, and if possible laminated, to make them more durable. In certain cases, especially for students with impaired vision, copymasters could be enlarged beforehand.
- When photocopying reading material, choose pastel backgrounds, preferably yellow, apricot or pink if

possible. Evidence has shown that this is the most helpful combination for slow readers.

- In many instances it can be useful to make an OHT of some copymasters, either to demonstrate activities to the whole class or to check solutions. Such OHTs could be coloured in order to emphasize and clarify.
- There are many suggestions relating to the introduction of numbers throughout the book, and each page of the students' book is numbered in figures and words in order to help the students.
- It is advisable to re-record the listening items on the activity box cassette in separate batches so that short cuts can be used to access the item they need more easily.

Games cupboard

There are many games which can be used effectively to promote language learning. The following can be used at various stages in the year to stimulate the production of a wide range of vocabulary and structures, and should be used as often as you feel suitable. Where a game is particularly appropriate to practise a specific area of language, it has also been included within the body of the teacher's notes at the appropriate point for easy reference. When selecting games, it is usually preferable to choose those which practise language recognition before those which need language production.

As a general rule in all of the games, students should be encouraged to take over the teacher's role as soon as possible. In elimination games, it is advisable to give students several lives in order to prevent those who are eliminated from losing interest.

Games to practise classroom language

Macht mit! The German equivalent of 'Simon says' — perfect for classroom commands. This game can be used time and time again when new language has been introduced. To keep the students alert, you can start or end selected commands with the key words *Macht mit!*

Zeigt auf! This also lends itself to the early stages of language acquisition, as it enables students to demonstrate comprehension without speaking. Once language has been introduced through the use of visuals, students can be expected to point quickly to appropriate cards or objects to show they have understood.

Auf die Jagd. A pretext for giving students a seemingly difficult series of directions or instructions to be followed, then marvelling at their recall. The activity can be performed using past tenses, without putting them off — for example: *Zuerst habe ich das Fenster geöffnet, dann habe ich die Tür geschlossen, den Bleistift auf den Tisch gestellt, den Tageslichtprojektor eingeschaltet und auf die Leinwand gesehen.*

Jetzt bist du dran. One student has to mime or obey an instruction without speaking, then give another instruction of their own to the next student in line. To make the activity more demanding and enjoyable, it can be made cumulative. In this case each student has to recall and carry out all the instructions given by previous players as well as that given by his or her immediate predecessor. Group support should be encouraged here to keep pace and involvement to the maximum.

Ich bin der Lehrer/die Lehrerin. An opportunity for students to assume the role of teacher and give commands or instructions to the rest of the group or class — surely irresistible, especially if they are allowed to use your chair!

Games for vocabulary learning

Englisch/Deutsch. Students make their own cards with a German word or phrase on one side and its English equivalent on the other. Tell them to choose words they find hard to remember. These cards can then be used in two ways:

1 Two or more students shuffle their cards together, then deal them out in a large circle on the table, English side up. They then take turns, starting from a given card, to say the German for each card. If they get it right they keep the card and try the next one as well, going on in this way until they get to one they can't do or get wrong. Then it is the next player's turn. Any word that a player gets wrong comes up again, of course, so there is a great incentive to learn words they don't know the first time round.

2 Alternatively, students play in pairs taking half the pack each. They take turns to lay their top card English side up, and their partner has to say the German equivalent. Each time one of them gets it wrong, he or she has to pick up the whole pile and put it under his/her other cards so that they recur later. The winner is the first player to get rid of all his/her cards.

Pelmanism. In pairs or small groups, students make, say 20 cards, writing German words or phrases on ten of them and the English equivalents on the others. This can either be prescribed vocabulary or, for revision purposes, the choice can be left to students. Once they get used to these games they will get into the habit of not choosing words their partners are likely to find too easy! The cards should be shuffled and laid face down. Each student turns over two cards and keeps them if they are a pair. If not, they are put back in place. As the focus in this game is on remembering where cards are, students can, if they wish, always help each other with the words themselves. The winner is the player who gains the most cards.

Games to practise numbers

Lotto. At its most complicated, the teacher can prepare 'lotto' cards and provide counters. At its simplest, students can write down a selection of numbers and cross them out as you call them. Students could be asked to read them back in German. This game also provides excellent practice for other vocabulary.

Platsch! Write the numbers to be practised on the board in the form of stepping stones across a river, for example:

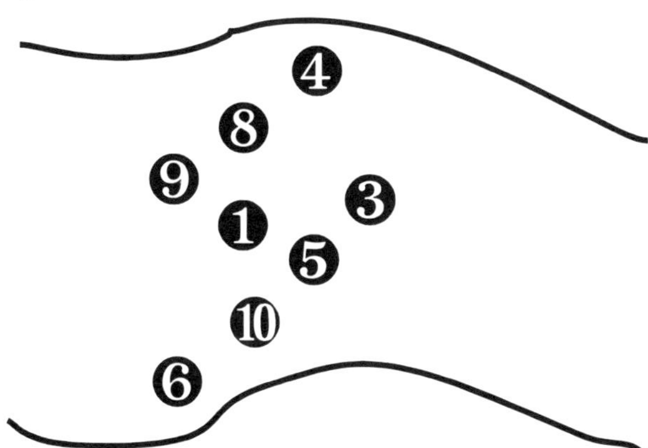

Ask a volunteer to 'cross the river' using the stepping stones. A sequential route could be included, but students are free to choose their own path. If there is a hesitation or a mistake, the rest of the class shouts *Platsch!* as the volunteer 'falls in the river'.

Zuviel/Zuwenig. Think of a number and ask the class to guess it. The only clue you give them is whether the number they have suggested is *zuviel* or *zuwenig*. This game works best with a wide range of numbers.

Welche Zahl? Write the numbers haphazardly all over the board. Divide the class into two teams and ask a representative from each one to come to the board. Call out a number, and the first one to circle it with a piece of chalk wins a point for his/her team.

Dirigent. Divide the class into two teams: '*vorwärts*' and '*rückwärts*'. Call out a number. The '*vorwärts*' team always has to give the next number, the '*rückwärts*' team always has to give the previous number. Play one team against another, giving a point for a correct response.

Zählt mal so. Start by saying *Zählt mal so*, and begin to count in a particularly way — for example: forward; backward; alternate numbers; or in multiples of 2 or 3 etc. Students join in as soon as they can with the right sequence, and are out if they give a wrong number. Change the sequence at intervals by saying *Zählt mal so* and beginning again. A group version of this can be played in which you point at a specific group to count. If the group makes a mistake, or fails to join in after the first three or four numbers are called, they are out. Students may assume the role of caller once they are familiar with the rules.

Wach auf! Give each student a number or a word at the beginning of a week. At any time during the lessons for that week call out a number or word and wait for the correct student to stand up. Students could be divided into teams and awarded points for correct responses.

Abwischen. Write numbers in random order on the board. Then invite two students to come to the front. The first student to rub out the number you call earns a point. You can also play this by just pointing at the next student or at groups or teams of students. In the latter case, it is advisable to write two sets of numbers on each half of the board and provide two board rubbers. If the numbers are required for further practice, they could be ringed in coloured chalk instead of being rubbed off.

This game can also be played with other vocabulary, for example pictures of objects or a series of words.

Würfelspiel. Students can throw dice in pairs or groups and say aloud the total number. They could also add up their scores over a series of five or six throws.

Die Leiter. Draw two or more six-rung ladders with a number on each rung. Each team or group throws a dice and reads out the number. If it is the next on the ladder, it is crossed off and the team moves up to the next rung. This game can also be used to practise new vocabulary.

Quadratzahlen. Draw a square like the one on page 10 on the board or OHP. Students have to say the numbers against the clock, incurring a five-second penalty for any incorrect number. This could be played with pictures or symbols to practise other vocabulary.

	A	B	C	D	E
Anfang →	5	15	61	27	84
	55	30	13	60	99
	43	12	100	8	11
Ziel	26	48	18	90	72

Games using flashcards

Making and using flashcards.

Students generally respond well to visuals, and home-made flashcards can inject humour and increase motivation and comprehension. Cut-outs from magazines, simple line drawings, symbols and photographs can all make good flashcards. Pictures may be glued onto card or put into plastic wallets to make them more durable.

Various types of flashcard design:

- A picture on one side only with the text on the other.
- Related pictures on both sides, for example *er ist glücklich/traurig.*
- Related pictures on one or more flashcards, for example a sequence of events. This sequence can be described in the present or past.
- Folded cards with one part hidden when folded.
- A card with a flap which can be used to change the picture. *Normalerweise komme ich zu Fuß nach Hause. Heute aber fahre ich mit dem Rad.*
- A concertina of pictures which can be used to tell a story.

Flashcards can be used to cue a wide range of vocabulary and structures. The activities below can be used at any stage during the course.

Flashcards can be used to encourage creative use of language — for example, to see how many sentences relating to one picture the class can make up in a limited time. A kitchen timer can be used to set the time. Encourage the class to compete against itself and to try to improve on its previous best score. Flashcards can help with reading and writing. Display several flashcards, clearly numbered for all students to see. Write on the board a number of sentences, one relating to each card but in a different order. The students then write down the number of each card and the sentence which relates to it.

Richtig oder falsch? A group game. One student has a pile of flashcards. At random he/she picks up a card and says something about it. The others decide if it is *richtig* or *falsch.*

Gedächtnisspiel. Blu-tack ten flashcards to the board and write a number next to each. Remove the flashcards one at a time and call out, for example, a sentence relating to a missing flashcard and ask the students to say the correct number. Later this process can be reversed by calling out a number and asking students to make an appropriate comment.

Was waren das? Show about ten related cards and then ask the class to try and remember what they were. When they can remember all of them, remove one and ask them which is missing.

Ohne Worte. Show a picture of an object and ask a student to mime it for others to guess.

Die Hälfte der Klasse weiß Bescheid. Once the students know which cards you have in your hands, select one card and show it to half of the class. The other half must then ask questions to find out what it is.

Fünf Fragen. Hold a card so that the class cannot see it. Give a clue, for example *Ich habe ein Animal.* Students have five attempts to guess which animal it is.

Das stimmt nicht. Show four cards. Ask the students to decide which is the odd one out. This game is useful for the revision of vocabulary from other areas.

Was war drauf? Challenge students by showing a card for a split second only. Then ask them to describe the picture, for example:

Teacher: *Was war drauf?*

Student: *Ein Mann.*

Teacher: *Ein Mann oder zwei Männer?*

Allow the students to speculate before showing them the card properly. Such speculation can also be encouraged by blurring slides of overhead transparency drawings and inviting students to work out what is depicted. The image should only be brought into focus when each stage of questioning has been exhausted.

Was ist das? A game to be played with any group of flashcards depicting nouns. The flashcards are shuffled and a plain piece of paper placed on top to hide the image. The caller looks under the paper to see what the top card is and asks: *Was ist das?* Other students reply: *Das ist ein(e) ...* , and the student who guesses correctly comes out and acts as caller. He removes the top card and looks at the next before asking: *Was ist das?*

Was machst du? This game is similar to the above, using flashcards depicting actions.

Eins, zwei, drei. Display a large number of flashcards depicting a range of vocabulary areas. Point to a student, who should point to three related flashcards as fast as possible and say, for example: *ein Kaffee, eine Limonade und ein Orangensaft; eine Katze, ein Hund und ein Goldfisch.*

Richtig oder falsch? This is a version of 'Simon Says'. From a pile of flashcards, pick one and show it to the group, making a statement about it in German. If the statement is *richtig*, everyone repeats it, but if it is *falsch* they keep quiet. Anyone speaking in the wrong place, or failing to repeat a true statement, is out. The winner takes over the role of caller.

Other games

Das ist falsch! A game played by two teams. Each team has ten cards. A student in one team says what is on his/her card. The other team say whether they think this is true or false. Points can be awarded.

Ja und nein. A student comes to the front of the class and the teacher asks him/her questions. The student has to answer without simply using the words *ja* or *nein*. A score can be kept of the number of questions each student manages to answer. As well as being fun, this game helps familiarise students with phrases like *hoffentlich, das stimmt, selbstverständlich, klar.* Questions like *Trinkst du gern Cola?* can be answered with *Ich trinke sehr gern Cola.* A good way of catching students out is to ask a question that requires a factual answer, and then to repeat their answer for confirmation — for example:

Teacher: *Wann hast du Geburtstag?*

Student: *Am vierzehnten Juli.*

Teacher: *Am vierzehnten?*

Student: *Ja.*

Schlachtschiffe. The game of battleships can be adapted to practise various items of language. In its simplest form, give students the area of vocabulary to be practised — for example, parts of a verb, numbers, days of the week — or put a set of flashcards on display as a reminder. Each student writes down any three of the alternatives. Each in turn guesses what his/her partner has written, and if the guess is correct the partner must cross it out. The first one to eliminate all three of his/her partner's items is the winner.

Woran denke ich? The basic guessing game in which someone thinks of a word within a given range for others to guess by asking *Ist das ein(e) ... ?* This can also be played by asking *Woran denke ich? Das beginnt mit B ...* to provide alphabet practice as well.

Im Rampenlicht. A group game in which students take it in turn to answer for 30 seconds any questions fired at them. Initially the questions to be used can be written on the board.

Unser Geheimnis. Select a student in advance of the lesson with whom you agree a secret code. For example, when you point to the chosen item, it might be the next item after you point to, say, *die Katze*, or something black or green, etc. A number code can be used referring to a set sequence so that 3529 would indicate that the 3rd, 5th, 2nd and 9th in any 'go' is the correct answer.

During the lesson, appear to select that student at random and ask him/her to leave the room. The others then choose an object or flashcard in the room. When the student returns, say the name of an object or flashcard around the room and ask, for example, *Ist das?* The student replies *Nein.* Continue in this way until you use the secret code to indicate the selected object, at which point the student can readily appear to guess the item.

How long you continue before revealing the secret code is a matter of discretion. Once one technique has been revealed (or guessed), switch to another using a different student.

Flüstere es mir. Students must pass a message along a row of players. Each student must remain seated, and only a quiet whisper is allowed. The message can be an instruction to do something, and the student at the end of the row carries out the instruction. This is best done as a race between rows.

Bist du wach? Give each student in the class a number or a word at the beginning of the week, and write a full list on a notice at the side of the blackboard. At any odd time during the German lessons for that week, call out a number and word, and the correct student should stand up. If not, he/she is out and crossed off the list. At the end of the week those left on the list could perhaps be given a team point.

Kannst du einen Satz bilden? A particulary good game for practising word order and/or conjugation of verbs. Divide the class into two equal teams. Write a selection of words (see below for examples) on plain paper, making two copies of each group of words, one for each team. Before the game begins these can be used to demonstrate the word order/conjugation point being practised, by sticking them in various combinations to the board and pegging them in a line, or by getting pupils to stand in front of the class holding them.

The students physically change places when a new component forces a change to the word order, and this helps make the point graphically — similarly with inversion for questions.

In order to play the game, distribute one set of word-cards to each team. A good, clear space will be needed in the classroom. Say a sentence in English. The aim is for each team to compose the sentence in German by getting students with the appropriate word-cards to stand in a line in front of the class. The first team to compose the sentence correctly gets a point. The game can become rather frantic, of course, but in order to arouse in students a passionate desire to get word order right this seems a fair price.

Below is an example of 15 wordcards (two sets of which would serve a class of 30) that could be used to practise both conjugation and word order. You can quickly manufacture your own sets of workcards to suit the occasion.

NB In order to get all students involved, it is advisable to write a list of words used and tick them off as they are required.

A variation of this is to have two-sided workcards, thus increasing the possibilities — and the panic!

Useful addresses

Austrian Government Tourist Office:
30 St George Street, London W1R 9FA

German Government Tourist Office:
61 Conduit Street, London W1R 0EN

Swiss Government Tourist Office:
1 New Coventry Street, London W1V 8EE

Austrian Embassy:
18 Belgrave Mews, London SW1X 8HU

German Embassy:
23 Belgrave Square, London SW1X 8HW

Swiss Embassy:
16–18 Montagu Place, London W1H 2BQ

Lufthansa: 23/28 Piccadilly, London W1V 0EJ

CILT (Centre for Information on Language Teaching and Research): 20 Bedfordbury, London WC2N 4LB

Goethe Institut:
50 Princes Gate, Exhibition Road, London SW7 2PH

CBEVE (Central Bureau for Educational Visits and Exchange): Seymour Mews House, Seymour Mews, London W1H 9PE

List of Flashcards

The following flashcards are provided for use with *Zickzack neu*. Some are not needed until stage 2.

Pets

1 dog (with lead)
2 cat
3 budgie
4 horse (with saddle)
5 mouse
6 guinea pig
7 hamster
8 goldfish
9 rabbit
10 tortoise

Housing

11 Wohnung
12 Reihenhaus
13 Einfamilienhaus
14 Doppelhaus
15 Bungalow

Breakfast and other meals

16 rolls; Schwarzbrot; loaf of bread
17 jar of marmalade/jam; jar of Nutella; jar of honey
18 packet of cornflakes; muesli packet
19 glass of milk; packet
20 cup of coffee; cup of tea; cup of cocoa
21 carton of orange juice; apple juice
22 cheeses
23 platter of cold meats
24 butter (packet); margarine (tub)
25 boiled egg; box of eggs
26 Quark; yoghurt
27 chips; mayonnaise
28 sugar (granules + cubes)
29 onions; red/green peppers
30 salt; pepper
31 cut of beef; any other meat
32 bottle of cooking oil
33 noodles; spaghetti
34 (cooked) chicken
35 bottle of coca cola; bottle of lemonade
36 rissoles
37 potatoes
38 tomatoes (tinned + fresh)

Activities

39 watching TV
40 computer
41 record player; radio; cassette player
42 football; basketball
43 friends meeting/greeting
44 tennis; table tennis
45 cycling; rollerskates
46 going shopping
47 eating at table at home
48 homework
49 guitar; flute; clarinet; recorder; piano
50 comic; book
51 chess board + pieces
52 Jugendzentrum
53 Disco; gymnastics/dance
54 cooking
55 cinema
56 strolling
57 slouching on a sofa
58 stamp collection

More food and quantities

59 Hamburger
60 (Brat)wurst; tube of mustard; curry sauce
61 ein belegtes Brot (cheese + ham)
62 crisps
63 Schaschlik
64 crate of beer; litre of wine
65 carton/box (of chocolates); bag of sweets; (Mars) bar
66 100 Gramm/200 Gramm/500 Gramm/1 Pfund

In town

67 Dom
68 Rathaus
69 Schloß; Stadtmauer
70 Restaurant; Café
71 Stadthalle
72 office blocks; high-rise flats
73 swimming pool (indoor + outdoor)
74 sports stadium
75 post office (main)
76 campsite
77 Verkehrsamt
78 harbour
79 railway station
80 hospital
81 car park
82 bank
83 museum

Shops

84 Metzgerei (backed with meats: Wurst, Schinken etc.)
85 Bäckerei (backed with bread)
86 Drogerie (backed with toothpaste, cosmetics etc.)
87 Apotheke (backed with medicines)
88 Konditorei (backed with pastries)
89 Buchhandlung (backed with books)
90 Sportgeschäft (backed with sports equipment)
91 Schuhgeschäft (backed with footwear)
92 Kleidergeschäft (backed with clothes on rails)

93 Warenhaus (backed with floor plan, records, consumer goods etc.)

94 Supermarkt (backed with tins, washing powder, biscuits etc.)

95 Markt (backed with fruit and vegetables etc.)

Purchases

96 postcard; stamps
97 T-shirt
98 souvenirs (doll, beer mug etc.)
99 writing block; writing paper; envelopes
100 purse/wallet
101 rubber; pencil; pen; ink
102 flowers; plants

Means of transport

103 on foot
104 bicycle
105 mofa; motorbike; moped
106 car
107 bus
108 tram
109 train (S-Bahn)
110 underground
111 ferry
112 aeroplane

List of copymasters

No.	Title	Level
1	Wie sagt man?	
2	Zahlendomino	GOLD
3	Die Hitparade — eine Woche später	ROT
4	Bildvokabeln: Im Klassenraum	GOLD
5	Europa	ROT
6	Finde die Städte	ROT
7	Ich komme aus Österreich. Ich wohne in Linz	GOLD
8	Wie heißt dein Partner?	ROT
9	Wie heißt dein Partner?	ROT
10	Ich habe eine Schwester	GOLD
11	Und du? Wie heißt du?	ROT
12	Lieber oder Liebe?	GOLD/ROT
13	Tiere	GOLD
14	Lauter Tiere	ROT
15	Tierisch kompliziert	SCHWARZ
16	Bildvokabeln: Ungewöhnliche Tiere	GOLD
17	Wo wohnen sie?	ROT
18	Welches Zimmer ist das?	GOLD
19	Was für Zimmer habt ihr?	SCHWARZ
20	Bildvokabeln: Im Haus	GOLD
21	Die Uhrzeit	GOLD
22	Zeitdomino	ROT
23	Martina beschreibt ihren Alltag	ROT
24	Das Verb bleibt sitzen	SCHWARZ
25	Geburtstagsumfrage	ROT
26	Was ißt man zum Frühstück?	GOLD
27	Zum Frühstück	ROT
28	Interviews	ROT
29	Ißt du gern Süßes?	ROT
30	Bildvokabeln: Zu Tisch!	GOLD
31	Welches Fach ist das?	GOLD
32	Schuldomino	GOLD
33	Kreuzworträtsel	ROT
34	Stundenplan-Lotto	ROT

35	Die Klasse 7c	ROT
36	Bildvokabeln: In der Schule	GOLD
37	Freizeitaktivitäten	GOLD
38	Computerpartner	SCHWARZ
39	Was machst du gern? Was machst du nicht gern?	ROT
40	Jugendzentrum Pinneberg	SCHWARZ
41	Im Fernsehen	GOLD
42	Wann ist die Sportschau?	ROT
43	Bildvokabeln: Musikinstrumente	GOLD
44	Sechs Unterschiede	ROT
45	Hast du mein Portemonnaie?	ROT
46	Was ißt du gern?	GOLD
47	Billig oder teuer?	SCHWARZ
48	Bildvokabeln: Im Wilden Westen	GOLD
49	Wetterspiel	GOLD
50	Telefongespräche	ROT
51	Ich fahre nach ...	ROT
52	Ein Brief über Ferienpläne	ROT
53	Schmeckt das?	ROT
54	Fernsehen und Radio in Großbritannien	ROT
55	Bildvokabeln: Am Strand	GOLD
56	Namenlied	
57	Alphabetlied	
58	Wo ich wohne	
59	Alter Mann	
60	Steh auf!	
61	In meiner Freizeit	
62	Welt ohne Geld	
63–67	Selbstbedienung: Lösungen	
68–70	Dictionary skills	
71	Dictionary skills: Answers	
72–79	Grammatik: Übungen	
80–82	Grammatik: Lösungen	
83–85	Personalakte	

List of cassette recordings

Kapitel 1 (Cassette A: side 1)

Hallo!
Im Sportklub
Fotoquiz
Namenlied
Feuer!
Was läuft?
Die Hitparade
Wie heißt du? Wie alt bist du?
Wie alt sind sie?
Wie sagt man das? Das Alphabet
Internationales Leichtathletikfest
Das Alphabetlied

Kapitel 2

Auf dem Campingplatz
Wo ich wohne
Zungenbrecher
Wo wohne ich?
Das liegt im Osten
Richtig oder falsch?

Kapitel 3

Wie heißen sie?
Wieviel Geschwister hast du?
Mein Stammbaum
Wie sind die Namen?
Hast du ein Haustier?
Ich habe einen Hund
Hast du kein Haustier?

Kapitel 4 (Cassette A: side 2)

Ich wohne in einem Dorf
Wo wohnen sie?
Das ist das Wohnzimmer
Krabbi
Meine Adresse
Computerliste
Alter Mann

Kapitel 5

Es ist ein Uhr
Entschuldigung. Wieviel Uhr ist es?
Wann beginnt der Film?
Martina beschreibt ihren Alltag
Wann hast du Geburtstag?
Wann ist es?
Ein Geburtstag in der Familie
Steh auf!

Kapitel 6 (Cassette B: side 1)

Das Frühstück bei der Familie Braun
Die Frühstückspalette
Was ißt du gern zum Mittagessen?
In der Pizzeria
Was heißt ‚gesund essen'?

Kapitel 7

Welches Fach ist das?
Welche Fächer hast du heute?
Interviews über Schulaufgaben
Eine gute Ausrede
Deutsch ist mein Lieblingsfach
Sag mal
Eine schlechte Note

Kapitel 8

Interviews nach der Schule
Was machen sie nach der Schule?
Computerpartner
Beste Freunde
Welche Sendung?
Ich sehe gern fern
Wie findest du Trickfilme?
Streit
Wann ist der Film?
Sonja und Max
Was für Musik hörst du am liebsten?
In meiner Freizeit

Kapitel 9 (Cassette B: side 2)

Geld
Wieviel Geld haben sie dabei?
Auf der Bank
Welt ohne Geld
An der Eisbude
Einmal Vanille
Was nimmst du?
Ich gebe mein Geld für CDs aus
Sechs junge Leute
Wofür sparst du dein Geld?
Billig oder teuer?
Kommst du mit zum Jahrmarkt?

Kapitel 10

Schönes Wetter
Drei Telefonate aus den Ferien
Wieviel Grad ist es?
Wo fährst du hin?
Wir fahren nach Spanien ans Meer
Was paßt zusammen?
Häuser und Wohnungen
Schmeckt das?
Fernsehen und Radio in Großbritannien
Das Fernsehprogramm
Die Schule in Großbritannien

Outline of contents and grammar

Kapitel 1 — Hallo! Wie heißt du?

Lernziele

1 Hallo! Ich heiße ... (Greetings and giving your name)
2 Wieviel? Eins bis zwanzig (Counting to 20)
3 Wie alt bist du? (Saying your age and using the German alphabet)

Language/Grammar

- greetings
- ich/du
- Ich bin ... Jahre alt.
- Wie alt bist du?
- Wie schreibt man das?
- numbers 1–20

Kapitel 2 — Wo wohnst du?

Lernziele

1 Länder in Europa (Some countries in Europe)

2 Wo ich wohne (Saying where you live)

3 Wo liegt das? (Saying where places are)

Language/Grammar

- Ich komme aus ... /Woher kommst du?
- Ich wohne in ... /Wo wohnst du?
- aus + country/town
- Wo liegt das?/Das liegt ...
- im + Norden/Nordwesten, etc.
- In der Nähe von ...

Kapitel 3 — Meine Familie

Lernziele

1 Hast du Geschwister? (Talking about brothers and sisters)

2 Das ist meine Familie (Introducing your family)

3 Hast du ein Haustier? (Talking about pets)

Language/Grammar

- Ich habe ... /Hast du ... ?
- plurals: Brüder/Schwestern/Geschwister
- Wie heißt ... ?
- der/die/das
- Das ist ...
- einen/eine/ein
- mein/meine/mein
- kein/keine/kein
- er/sie/es heißt ...

Kapitel 4 — Bei mir zu Hause

Lernziele

1 Ich wohne in ... (Saying where your house or flat is)

2 Die Zimmer (Rooms in the house)

3 Telefonnummern und Adressen (Telephone numbers, addresses, numbers 21–100)

Language/Grammar

- Wie ist ... ?
- Was ist ... ?
- Wir haben
- in einer/einem/der; am
- groß/klein/modern/alt
- von meinem/meiner/meinen

Kapitel 5 — Mein Alltag

Lernziele

1 Wie spät ist es? (Telling the time)

2 Tagesroutine (Daily routine)

3 Daten und Feiertage (Dates and special celebrations)

Language/Grammar

- Wie spät ist es?/Wieviel Uhr ist es?
- Wann ... ?
- Es ist + time
- um + time
- am + date
- Ich esse/frühstücke/verlasse/mache/gehe/gebe
- separable verbs: Ich stehe auf/sehe fern
- reflexive verbs: Ich wasche mich/treffe mich
- Word order — verb in second place

Kapitel 6 — Wie schmeckt's?

Lernziele

1 Was ißt du zum Frühstück? (Breakfast)

2 Mittagessen und Abendessen (Midday and evening meals)

3 Gesundes Essen (Healthy eating)

Language/Grammar

- inversion of subject and verb in questions: Ißt du ... ?/Trinkst du ... ?
- Wie oft ... ?
- gern
- numbers over 100
- sehr oft/oft/manchmal/selten/nie
- Man sollte ... + verb
- mit (+ Dative)

Kapitel 7 — Schule

Lernziele

1 Schulfächer und Schulaufgaben (School subjects)

2 Lieblingsfächer (Likes and dislikes of subjects; opinions)

3 Der Schultag (School day and routine)

Language/Grammar

- Wie lange ... ?
- Mein Lieblingsfach ist ... /Meine Lieblingsfächer sind ...
- ... gefällt mir gar nicht.
- toll/super/interessant/langweilig/es geht
- in der ersten/zweiten/dritten Stunde

Kapitel 8 — Meine Freizeit

Lernziele

1 Sport und Hobbys (Sports and hobbies)
2 Fernsehen (Expressing opinions about television programmes)
3 Was machst du am liebsten? (Favourites)

Language/Grammar

- Was machst du am liebsten in der Freizeit?
- Wie findest du ... ?
- Ich spiele + sport
- expressing opinions
- gern/am liebsten

Kapitel 9 — Was kostet das?

Lernziele

1 Geld und Preise ((Money and prices; changing money)
2 Ich habe Hunger! (Snacks, drinks and ice creams)
3 Was machst du mit deinem Geld? (What you spend your money on or are saving up for)

Language/Grammar

- Was kostet/kosten ... ?
- Was nimmst du?
- Wofür gibst du dein Geld aus?
- Wofür sparst du?
- Fährst du gern mit ... ? + Dative
- einmal/zweimal/dreimal
- Ich möchte ...
- Ich hätte gern ...
- Ich gebe mein Geld für ... aus/spare für ... + Accusative

Kapitel 10 — Wie schön!

Lernziele

1 Wie ist das Wetter? (The weather and the seasons)
2 Was machst du in den Ferien? (Holidays)
3 Meint ihr uns? (Agreeing/disagreeing with German young people's impressions of Britain)

Language/Grammar

- Wie ist das Wetter?
- Wieviel Grad ist es?
- Wo fährst du hin?
- Mit wem?
- Es + weather conditions
- im + seasons
- Wir fahren ans Meer/aufs Land/ins Gebirge/nach + country/town
- mit + Dative
- Ich wohne in/bei + Dative
- agreeing/disagreeing

Key to icons

Icon	Meaning
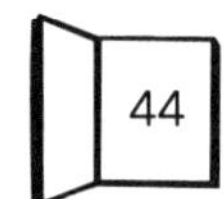	Students' book page 44
	Copymaster 20 — complementary material at level GOLD (for example)
	Flashcards 11–15
	Cassette recording
	Board/OHP
	Complementary material at level SCHWARZ (for example)
	Pairwork/*Partnerarbeit*
	IT suggestion

1 Hallo! Wie heißt du?

Main teaching points

Lernziel 1: Saying what your name is and greeting people

Grammar presented:

Imperatives
Greetings

Personal pronouns (*ich, du*)
Interrogatives (*wie? wieviel? was?*)

First, second and third person singular present tense (*sein, heißen*)

Vocabulary presented:

das Beispiel	*Guten Morgen!*	*Ich heiße ...*	*rot*	*schwarz*
der Buchstabensalat	*Guten Tag!*	*das Lernziel*	*der Schlüssel*	*der Tip des Tages*
gold	*Hallo!*	*der Name*	*schreib(t) ... auf*	*wie heißt du?*
Grüß dich!	*Ich bin ...*	*die Nummer*	*das Spiegelbild*	*die Zahl*

Lernziel 2: Counting to 20

Grammar presented:

Numbers 1–20

Third person singular present tense (*laufen*)

Vocabulary presented:

null	*fünf*	*zehn*	*fünfzehn*	*zwanzig*
eins	*sechs*	*elf*	*sechzehn*	*Feuer!*
zwei	*sieben*	*zwölf*	*siebzehn*	*Hits der Woche*
drei	*acht*	*dreizehn*	*achtzehn*	*oder*
vier	*neun*	*vierzehn*	*neunzehn*	*was läuft?*

Lernziel 3: Saying your age and using the German alphabet

Grammar presented:

Third person singular present tense (*sagen, schreiben, fehlen, fangen, gehen*)

Third person plural present tense (*sagen*)
Interrogative (*welcher?*)

Vocabulary presented:

aber	*das Heft*	*der Klassenraum*	*richtig*	*Wie alt bist du?*
das Alphabetlied	*Ich bin 14 Jahre alt*	*der Kuli*	*der Saal*	*Wie schreibt man das?*
die Antwort	*in*	*die Landkarte*	*der Schüler*	*der/das Wort*
Bildvokabeln	*internationales*	*die Lehrerin*	*die Schülerin*	*das Zahlenrätsel*
der Buchstabe	*Leichtathletikfest*	*die Mappe*	*die Selbstbedienung*	
die Frage	*jetzt bist du dran*	*die Partnerarbeit*	*die Tür*	

Before beginning work on this chapter, check where the video material, Activity Box cards and Assessment Support Pack tasks will be most appropriate.

Welcoming the class

Presentation
Listening
Speaking

Welcome the class using German from the very beginning. Initially this will require a lot of mime and gesture. Teach also: *Wie geht's?* and the answers: *Danke, gut* and *Nicht gut.*

Teacher: *Kommt bitte 'rein. Setzt euch. Guten Morgen. Guten Tag. Wie geht's? Gut? Nicht gut?*

Encourage the students to repeat the greetings chorally and then individually.

Wie sagt man?

The copymaster of classroom language is intended to set the scene for the consistent use of German by everyone from the outset. Poster-size versions of the key expressions should be displayed around the room to support all activities. You will need to keep referring the students to the expressions until they become completely familiar with them.

Introductions

Listening
Speaking

Introduce yourself to the class, starting with individual students.

Teacher: *Guten Morgen/Tag. Ich bin Frau/Herr ... Und du?* (whisper) *Ich bin ...*

Student: *Ich bin Jane.*

(**NB** All women teachers in Germany are addressed as *Frau*, irrespective of marital status.)

Partnerarbeit

Consolidation
Listening
Speaking

Encourage pairs to greet each other and give their names. This could be done as a chain activity, with the student who answers the first question asking the next question and so on. Pairs who perform well can come to the front of the class to perform the dialogue. Use lots of praise from the outset.

Teacher: *Kommt nach vorne. Ja, du Ann, und du, Hari. Du und du, kommt! Gut/Sehr gut/Fein/Prima/(Fantastisch!)*

Use *Sch/Ruhe*, if required.

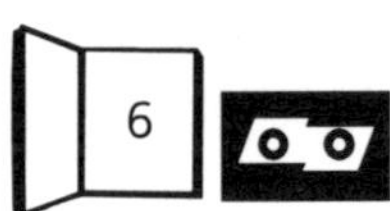

Hallo!

Listening
Practice

Play the recording straight through, then repeat item by item, using the first item as an example. Elicit that it is a group of German teenagers introducing themselves.

Teacher: *Hört gut zu. Ist das Anne? Ja oder nein?*

Student: *Ja.*

Teacher: *Ja richtig. Das ist Anne. Sehr gut.*

Play the recording again, using the pause button.

Explain the use of *Was sagt?*

Teacher: *Sagt Anne ‚guten Morgen'? Ja oder nein?*

Student: *Nein.*

Teacher: *Richtig. Was sagt Anne?*

Student: *‚Hallo!'*

Teacher: *Prima!*

 **Hallo!**

1 — Hallo! Ich bin Anne.
2 — Hallo! Ich bin Renate.
3 — Grüß dich! Ich bin Paul.
4 — Hallo! Ich heiße Uschi.
5 — Grüß Gott! Ich bin Martin.
6 — Grüß dich! Ich bin Oliver.
7 — Guten Tag! Ich bin Frau Meyer.
8 — Guten Morgen! Ich heiße Stefan.

Follow up this activity by practising pronunciation of the names and the greetings with the whole class.

Teacher: *Wiederholt. Anne. Hallo. Grüß dich. Grüß Gott. Guten Tag. Guten Morgen. Ich bin. Ich heiße.*

Wie heißt du?

Listening
Speaking

Ask the students to say their own names. Encourage them to take over the teacher's role as soon as possible.

Teacher: *Wie heißt du?*

Student: *(Ich heiße/bin) Michael.*

Hier ist dein Deutschbuch

Listening
Speaking
Reading

Hand out students' books in preparation for the following activities.

Teacher: *John, hier ist dein Deutschbuch. Susan, bitte schön. Mark, hier bitte.*

Teach *Danke.* Then teach the pronunciation of the book title. Give the students time to look through the book.

Teacher: *Wiederholt: Zickzack Neu. Schlagt das Buch auf. Seite sechs.*

Demonstrate and write the page number on the board/OHP. You might also practise a tongue-twister with the class.

Teacher: *Ein Zungenbrecher: Zickzack Neu — Lernziel eins.*

Partnerarbeit

Listening
Speaking
Reading

Play the recording of ***Hallo!*** once more. Ask the students to look at the speech bubbles. Then they can repeat and do role-play in pairs. You could also ask them to question each other about what each person says. Perform a model dialogue and write it up.

Teacher: *Hört gut zu. Lest Seite 6 und wiederholt.* (Point to speech bubbles:) *Und jetzt — Partnerarbeit.* (To one student) *Was sagt Anne? ‚Hallo! Ich bin ...‘*

Student: *‚Hallo! Ich bin Anne.‘*

Teacher: *Prima. Und was sagt Renate? ‚Hallo! Ich bin ...‘*

Student: *‚Hallo! Ich bin Renate.‘*

Teacher: *Toll! Arbeitet jetzt mit einem Partner/einer Partnerin! Stellt einander Fragen. Partner/in A fragt: ‚Was sagt Anne?‘ Partner/in B antwortet: ‚Hallo! Ich bin Anne.‘*

Im Sportklub

Listening

Members of a sports club introduce themselves. Ask the students to look at the pictures and listen to the recording. They must decide the order in which the people speak and write down their names.

Teacher: *Seite 6.* (Write on board/OHP:) *Seht euch die Bilder an. Das sind Teenager aus einem Sportklub. Hört gut zu. Wie ist die richtige Reihenfolge? Schreibt die Namen auf.*

Zum Beispiel —

(Play the cassette and complete the first one with the class:) *Wer ist das? Sven? Martin? Oder Boris? Hört jetzt gut zu und macht weiter!*

Im Sportklub

1 — Guten Tag! Ich heiße Boris. Ich spiele gern Tennis.
2 — Guten Tag! Ich bin Sven. Ich bin Schwimmer.
3 — Hallo! Ich heiße Martin. Ich spiele Fußball.
4 — Grüß dich! Ich heiße Elke. Ich spiele Fußball.
5 — Tag! Ich heiße Gabi. Ich spiele Tischtennis.
6 — Hallo! Ich bin Barbara. Ich spiele Badminton.

Solution:

1 Boris **2** Sven **3** Martin **4** Elke **5** Gabi **6** Barbara

Fotoquiz

Listening
Reading
Practice

Ask the students to look at the group photograph and the baby pictures. Ask them to listen to the teenagers introducing themselves.

Teacher: *Seite 7. Seht euch die Fotos an. Hier sind sechs ...* (Using your fingers count up to six and repeat:) *sechs Teenager: Christa, Bernd usw. Hört gut zu.*

Fotoquiz

1 — Ich heiße Christa.
2 — Ich heiße Susi.
3 — Ich bin Lutz.
4 — Ich bin Sven.
5 — Ich bin Brigitte.
6 — Ich bin Bernd.

Ask the students what each of the teenagers says.

Teacher: *Was sagt Christa? Und Lutz, Susi?* etc.

Partnerarbeit. Wer ist das?

Presentation
Practice

Refer the students to the baby photos and ask them to work in pairs to match the photos to the teenagers. First teach *Wer ist das?* and *Das ist ...*

Teacher: *Partnerarbeit. Wer ist das?*
(Perform a model dialogue with a student:) *Nummer eins. Wer ist das? Ist das Lutz?*

Student: *Nein, das ist Susi.*

Solution:

1 Susi **2** Brigitte **3** Bernd **4** Lutz **5** Sven **6** Christa

These are the correct answers, but obviously the students will find room for doubt or speculation!

Namenlied

A song to practise the pronunciation of greetings and names. The students can have a lot of fun singing the song to this tune, an adaptation of 'The dance of the Hours' (from *La Gioconda*) and possibly known by some as 'Hello Mother, Hello Father'.

Teacher: *Hört gut zu und singt mit.*

Namenlied

Hallo Mutter, hallo Vater!
Tag Andreas, Tag Renate!
Hallo Thomas, hallo Tina!
Grüß dich Georg, grüß dich Grete, grüß dich Gabi!

Students may now attempt the *Lernziel 1* activities in the *Selbstbedienung* section on page 12 of the students' book. See page 28 of this book for more details.

Presentation of numbers 1 to 20

Listening
Speaking

Introduce orally the numbers 1 to 20.
Teach the numbers in groups of three with the students repeating after you. Spend some time on pronunciation work, e.g. *zwei, drei, fünf, acht, zehn, elf, zwölf.* Differentiate between *vierzehn* and *fünfzehn* when spoken at normal speed.

Teacher: *Hört gut zu und wiederholt. Eins–zwei–drei, vier–fünf–sechs,* etc.

Practise numbers using some of the games suggested in the Introduction on page 9.

Feuer!

Listening
Speaking
Reading

Play the recording, then ask the students to count backwards, using the visual on page 8. Real countdowns are sometimes stopped because of failures. Here a mistake in pronunciation has the same effect. If the countdown is successfully completed, the students can shout *Feuer!*

Feuer!

ZEHN–NEUN–ACHT–SIEBEN–SECHS–FÜNF–VIER–DREI–ZWEI–EINS–NULL ... **FEUER!**

The students could go through the countdown again in a chain activity.

Teacher: *Kettenspiel.*
(To one student:) *Du beginnst mit ,zehn',*
(to another student:) *dann sagst du ,neun', und so weiter.*

Partnerarbeit. Was ist das?

As preparation for the pairwork activity, write the numbers on the OHP/board and call out any of the numbers at random. Students must come to the front and point to the appropriate number. This should help them to focus also on the differences between the continental forms of 1 and 7. The numbers are also shown in handwriting in the students' book for reference and for the pairwork activity.

Teacher: *Acht … wo ist die Zahl acht?*
(To a student:) *Komm nach vorne. Zeig mir die Zahl acht.*

As a lead-in to the pairwork activity, perform a model dialogue as in the students' book, using one of the numbers on the board.

Teacher: *Jetzt Partnerarbeit.*

Was läuft?

Listening
Speaking
Reading
Writing

Ask the students to listen to the conversation and to write down the order in which the films are mentioned. Complete the first one with the class as an example, and write up the answer.

Teacher: *Schlagt euer Buch auf Seite 8 auf. Hört gut zu und schreibt die Saalnummern in der richtigen Reihenfolge auf.*

Zum Beispiel: (play the first part of the dialogue) *das ist Saal* 7 (write it up).

 **Was läuft?**

— Gehen wir ins Kino?
— Was läuft denn?
— *Fantasia* im Saal sieben.
— Hmm, was gibt's sonst?
— *Der Tunnel* läuft im Saal zwei. Das ist ein Krimi.
— Was läuft denn im Saal fünf … *Simon Sez in New York.* Oder *Superman* im Saal sechs?
— Nee.
— *Feuer*?
— Was!?
— *Feuer* im Saal acht.
— Und im Saal eins?
— *Bambi*? Toll, nicht?
— Was! *Bambi*! Was gibt's sonst noch?
— *Tom und Jerry* im Saal drei, oder *Tarzan* im Saal vier.
— Tja. Was meinst du? *Simon Sez*?
— OK. Gehen wir in Saal fünf.

Solution:

7–2–5–6–8–1–3–4–5

This could be adapted as a communicative activity. One student could have the book open and give the film titles, while the other tries to remember the number.

Teacher: *Partnerarbeit. Partner A sagt zum Beispiel ‚Tarzan' und Partner B antwortet ‚Saal 4'.*

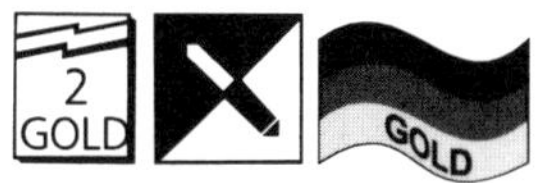

Zahlendomino

Reading

A domino game providing reading practice. The students can complete the sequence individually or in small groups. Demonstrate, preferably using the board/OHP.

Teacher: *Zahlendomino. Das ist ein Dominospiel. Wie ist die richtige Reihenfolge?*

Solution:

1–sieben; 7–vier ; 4–zwei; 2–fünf; 5–siebzehn; 17–elf; 11–fünfzehn; 15–drei; 3–zehn; 10–neun; 9–sechzehn; 16–zwanzig; 20–zwölf; 12–sechs; 6–dreizehn; 13–vierzehn; 14–neunzehn; 19–achtzehn; 18–acht; 8–eins

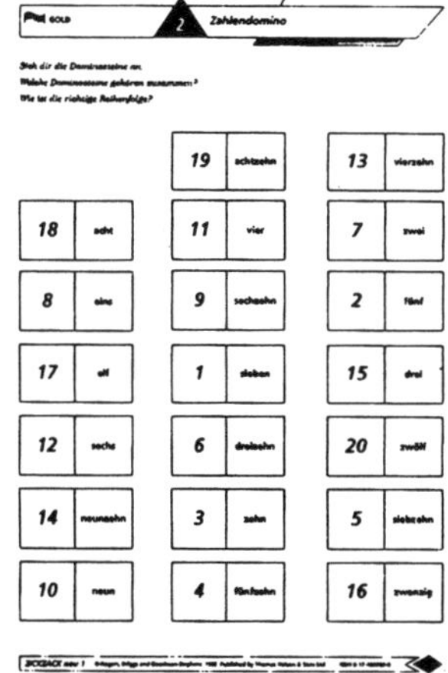

2 Zahlendomino

		19	achtzehn	13	vierzehn
18	acht	11	vier	7	zwei
8	eins	9	sechzehn	2	fünf
17	elf	1	sieben	15	drei
12	sechs	6	dreizehn	20	zwölf
14	neunzehn	3	zehn	5	siebzehn
10	neun	4	fünfzehn	16	zwanzig

Die Hitparade

Listening
Speaking
Reading

Refer the students to *Hits der Woche* on page 9 and play the recording of the disc jockey announcing the week's Top 20.

At this point they just need to follow the text.

Teacher: *Schlagt eure Bücher auf Seite 9 auf. Hört gut zu!*

Die Hitparade

— Auf Platz zwanzig: *Sieben Tage* von Feuerwerk.
Platz neunzehn: *Schwarz Rot Gold* von Lola Lace.
Platz achtzehn: *Einmal ist keinmal* von Frei.
Platz siebzehn: *Broken Dreams* von Insomniacs.
Platz sechzehn: *Susi ist erst siebzehn* von Hbf.
Auf Platz fünfzehn: *Blitz* von Evi Bamm.
Platz vierzehn: *Die Sonne scheint* von Karussell.
Platz dreizehn: *Queen of Hearts* von The Gamblers.
Platz zwölf: *Toll Toll Toll* von O Weh.
Platz elf: *Grüß dich!* von Hanno H.
Auf Platz zehn: *Komm mit!* von Prima.
Platz neun: *Teenage Rock* von Head Bangers Inc.
Platz acht: *Anne* von Hallo.
Platz sieben: *Mann oh Mann* von Ozean.
Platz sechs: *Ich geh ins Bett* von Serpentine.
Auf Platz fünf: *Telefonliebe* von Britta Tell.
Platz vier: *He, du da* von Ede Funk.
Platz drei: *Wie geht's?* von Simon Sez.
Platz zwei: *Gute Nacht* von Elegy ...
Und auf Platz eins ist diese Woche: *Wie heißt du?* von Polizei.

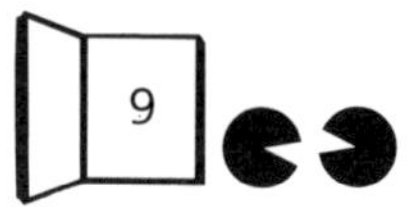

Partnerarbeit

Speaking Practice

Practise the pronunciation of the titles in the pop chart and the pairwork dialogue in the book, before asking the students to conduct their own dialogues. This activity can become a memory test or communicative game, if you tell one of each pair to close the book.

Teacher: *Wiederholt, bitte: ‚Wie heißt du?' von Polizei, usw.*

Teacher: *Partnerarbeit.*
(To one student:) *Du sagst: Was ist auf Platz sechs?*
(To another student:) *Und du antwortest: ‚Ich geh ins Bett' von Serpentine.*

Die Hitparade — eine Woche später

Listening Speaking Reading Writing

An 'information gap' activity based on the same song titles as in ***Die Hitparade***. Tell the students that they have between them the position in the charts for the following week of all of the songs in the hit parade. Ask them to fill in the gaps on their respective sheets by questioning each other. Perform one or two examples to illustrate.

Teacher: *Partnerarbeit. Hier ist Blatt A, und hier ist Blatt B. Auf Blatt A sind 10 Titel in der richtigen Reihenfolge und 10 Titel in der falschen Reihenfolge.*
(Point to the unnumbered songs underneath:) *Auf Blatt B sind diese 10 Titel nochmal,*
(point again to the jumbled songs on sheet A) *aber nun in der richtigen Reihenfolge. Partner A fragt ‚Was ist auf Platz 2?' Und Partner B antwortet ‚He, du da'. Partner A schreibt ‚He, du da' hier.*
(Write it up and point to the place on the copymaster.)

If necessary, ask one of the students to explain in English how the activity works.

Teacher: *Wie geht das auf englisch?*

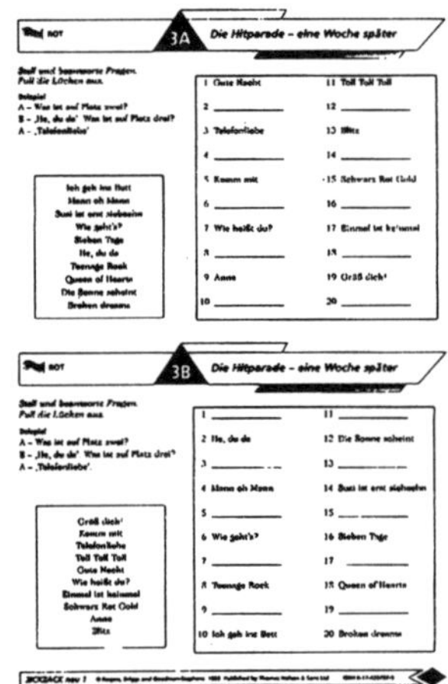

IT suggestion

As a follow-up to this, students could word-process a similar list of the Top 20 charts for the UK, along with their own forecast for the following week's charts. This will reinforce the use of numbers, and of the word *von*. Perhaps a small prize could be awarded to the student whose forecast proves to be the most accurate!

As a further follow-up activity you could obtain a recent Top 20 singles chart from a German magazine and use it to practise the language from the pairwork activity.

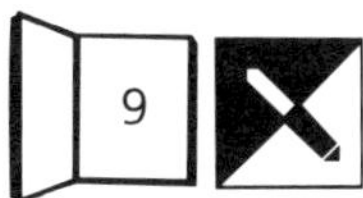

Zahlreich

Listening
Speaking
Reading
Writing

A straightforward activity to enable consolidation of numbers. Ask the students to look at the drawings and say or write the numbers each time.

Teacher: *Seht euch die Bilder an. Nummer eins — wieviel ist das?*

Solution:

a acht **b** sechs **c** drei **d** zehn **e** neunzehn **f** vierzehn

Students may now attempt the *Lernziel 2* activities in the *Selbstbedienung* section on pages 12–13 of the students' book. See page 28 of this book for more details.

Wie heißt du? Wie alt bist du?

Listening
Speaking
Reading
Writing

Prepare the students for this activity by drawing a cake with, for example, 12 candles on it. Use it to demonstrate how to ask and answer the question *Wie alt bist du?* Then, when the students are ready, play the recording and ask them to note down the names in the correct order. Then play the recording again and ask them to add the ages.

Teacher: *Hört gut zu und schreibt die Namen in der richtigen Reihenfolge auf.*
(Play first dialogue:) *Ist das Anja oder Anne?*

Student: *Anja.*

Teacher: *Gut.* (Write it up)

... and so on.

Once the students have completed the list of names, ask them to add the ages.

Teacher: *Hört nochmal zu. Wie alt ist Anja?*
(Play the first dialogue again.)

Student: *Zehn.*

Teacher: *Richtig.* (Write up Anja, 10.)
Jetzt macht weiter.

Wie heißt du? Wie alt bist du?

1 — Wie heißt du?
— Anja.
— Und wie alt bist du?
— Zehn.

2 — Und du? Wie heißt du?
— Sven.
— Ja, und wie alt bist du?
— Ich bin zwölf.

3 — Wer bist du denn?
— Ich bin Asaf.
— Wie alt bist du, Asaf?
— Ich bin vierzehn Jahre alt.

4 — Heißt du Thomas?
— Ja, ich heiße Thomas.
— Wie alt bist du?
— Dreizehn.

5 — Du bist Anne, ja?
— Ja, ich heiße Anne.
— Und wie alt bist du?
— Ich bin siebzehn.

6 — Und du? Wie heißt du denn?
— Fatima. Ich bin neun Jahre alt.

7 — Wie heißt du?
— Ich heiße Paul.
— Und wie alt bist du?
— Ich bin acht Jahre alt.

8 — Und wie heißt du?
— Ich bin Karin.
— Wie alt bist du, Karin?
— Ich bin elf Jahre alt.

Solution:

1 Anja, 10 **2** Sven, 12 **3** Asaf, 14 **4** Thomas, 13
5 Anne, 17 **6** Fatima, 9 **7** Paul, 8 **8** Karin, 11

Partnerarbeit. Was sagen Asaf und Anne?

Refer the students to the talking heads. Practise reading the dialogue out loud. Then ask individuals: *Wie heißt du?* and *Wie alt bist du?* Practise the expanded forms: *Ich bin zwölf* and *Ich bin zwölf Jahre alt.* Encourage the students to ask the questions as soon as possible. Practise in a chain game, or as pairwork in which the students give their own names and ages.

Teacher: *Partnerarbeit.*
(Point to the visuals:) *Zum Beispiel:*
(Read the dialogue aloud and ask the students to practise it in pairs:) *Jetzt seid ihr dran. Lest den Dialog ... Ja, und du? Wie heißt du? Wie alt bist du?*

The students could now make up conversations between any pair from the photograph on page 10. Make sure the list of names and ages is still available for reference.

Teacher (to a student): *Wähl einen Namen ... Wie heißt ,wähl' auf englisch? Richtig* — 'choose' ... *also, wähl einen Namen, zum Beispiel Anja, Paul ...*

Student: *Paul.*

Teacher: *Gut, du bist Paul.*
(To another student:) *Wähl einen anderen Namen.*

Student: *Sven.*

Teacher: *Gut. Du bist Sven.*
(To both students:) *Partnerarbeit. Macht einen Dialog: ,Wie heißt du?' usw.*

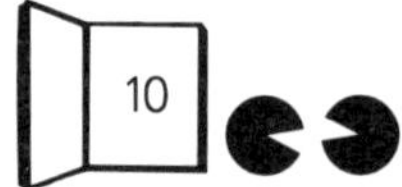

Partnerarbeit. Was sagen sie?

Listening
Speaking
Reading

A spaghetti diagram providing further practice of names and ages. The students work in pairs, taking it in turns to ask each other what the teenagers say.

Teacher: *Partnerarbeit.*
(To one student:) *Stell deinem Partner/deiner Partnerin die Frage: ,Was sagt Nummer eins?'*

Student A: *Was sagt Nummer eins?*

Student B: *Ich heiße Frank. Ich bin zwölf Jahre alt.*

Partnerarbeit. Wie alt sind sie?

Listening
Speaking

A speculation activity. Ask the students to look at the photographs of the five young people and say how old they think they are.

Teacher: *Seht euch die Fotos an. Wie alt ist Detlev? Was meint ihr? Vierzehn? Fünfzehn?*

Student: *Sechzehn.*

Teacher: *Ja, vielleicht, oder?*
(To the rest of the class:) *Stimmt das? Fünfzehn? Sechzehn?*

Teacher: *Jetzt Partnerarbeit.*

After the students have asked each other questions like these, play the recording for them to check if they are right or wrong.

Wie alt sind sie?
— Ich bin Detlev. Ich bin 16 Jahre alt.
— Ich heiße Lisa. Ich bin 12 Jahre alt.
— Ich bin Florian. Ich bin 13 Jahre alt.
— Ich heiße Heike. Ich bin 14 Jahre alt.
— Ich bin Markus. Ich bin 11 Jahre alt.

Wie sagt man das? Das Alphabet

Presentation

Some students may find the suggested transcription useful as a guide to pronunciation. Play them the recording, pausing for repetition after three or four letters each time.

Teacher: *Hört zu und wiederholt.*

Wie sagt man das? Das Alphabet

A	ah	B	bay	C	tsay
D	day	E	ay	F	ef
G	gay	H	hah	I	ee
J	yot	K	kah	L	ell
M	em	N	en	O	oh
P	pay	Q	koo	R	air
S	ess	ß	ess-tset	T	tay
U	ooh	V	fow (like *now*)	W	vay
X	eeks	Y	oopsi-lon	Z	tset

You may also wish to provide examples of vowels with umlauts.

Wie schreibt man das?

Listening
Speaking
Reading

A cartoon dialogue presenting spelling in German. Start by reciting the German alphabet in blocks of three letters, and ask the students to repeat them.

Teacher: *Hört gut zu.*
(Write up the letters in the blocks as you go.)
Wiederholt: A – B – C.

Students: *A – B – C.*

Teacher: *D – E – F ...*

Students: *D – E – F ...*

Then see how far the students can get on their own, taking it in turns to pronounce successive blocks of three letters.

Teacher: *Und jetzt ein Kettenspiel.*
Du sagst: A – B – C (pointing to the first student).

Student 1: *A – B – C.*

Teacher: *Und du sagst: D – E – F* (pointing to a second student).

Student 2: *D – E – F.*

Teacher: *Und so weiter.*
(pointing to a third student:) *G – H* ...
Jetzt fangen wir an. Also, du (pointing to the first student:) *A* ...

Student 1: *A – B – C.*

Student 2: *D – E* ...

Now ask the students to read the cartoon dialogue and look at the ***Tip des Tages***, and then to practise in pairs spelling their own names in German.

Teacher: *Seht euch ‚Wie schreibt man das?' an und wiederholt.*

Jetzt Partnerarbeit. Partner/in A fragt: ‚Wie heißt du?' Partner/in B antwortet, zum Beispiel: (choose a student's name). *Partner/in A fragt: ‚Wie schreibt man das?'* etc.

You can provide further practice by beginning to spell out the names of students in the class and ask who will be the first to work out whose name you have chosen.

Internationales Leichtathletikfest

Listening
Speaking
Reading

Ask the students to look at the pictures of the athletes giving their names to the official recorder before the 100-metres event, and to listen to the recording. The students could try to complete some of these names themselves. The first one is given as an example.

Teacher: *Hört gut zu! Schreibt die Namen fertig.*
(Demonstrate number 1.)

Internationales Leichtathletikfest

Recorder:
— Also. Nummer eins. Ihr Name, bitte.

Athlete:
— Mayer.

— M – E – I – ...?
— Nein, M – A – Y – E – R.
— Also, M – A – Y – E – R, Mayer. Danke.

— Nummer zwei. Ihr Name, bitte.
— Smith.
— Wie schreibt man das?
— S – M – I – T – H.
— Also, S – M – I – T – H, Smith. Danke.

— Nummer drei. Ihr Name, bitte.
— Jacquemart.
— Wie schreibt man das, bitte?
— J – A – C – Q – U – E – M – A – R – T.
— Also, J – A – C – Q – U – E – M – A – R – T, Jacquemart. Danke.

— Nummer vier. Ihr Name, bitte.
— Nixon.
— N – I – X – O – N?
— Richtig.

— Nummer fünf. Ihr Name, bitte.
— Lundqvist.
— Wie schreibt man das, bitte?
— L – U – N – D – Q – V – I – S – T.
— Also, L – U – N – D – Q – V – I – S – T, Lundqvist. Danke.

— Nummer sechs. Ihr Name, bitte.
— Piaget.
— Wie schreibt man das, bitte?
— P – I – A – G – E – T.
— Also, P – I – A – G – E – T. Danke.

— Nummer sieben. Ihr Name, bitte.
— Becker.
— B – E – C – K – E – R?
— Richtig.

— Nummer acht. Ihr Name, bitte.
— Waldorff.
— Wie schreibt man das, bitte?
— W – A – L – D – O – R – F – F.
— Also, W – A – L – D – O – R – F – F. Danke.

> As a follow-up activity, the students could practise in pairs giving the athletes' names. Ask them to take it in turns to ask and answer the question.

Teacher: *Partnerarbeit. Stellt einander die Frage: Wie schreibt man ‚Becker'? usw.*

IT suggestion

As a follow-up activity, pairs of students could use word-processing software to make a list of some real athletes' names (some difficult to spell), and dictate them for another pair or for the whole class to guess.

Welcher Buchstabe fehlt?

Listening
Speaking
Reading

Ask the students to work out the only letter of the alphabet which does not feature in the athletes' names in ***Internationales Leichtathletikfest***. Conduct the exercise in the form of a chain game, in which successive students ask their neighbour if it is letter A, B, C, etc.

Teacher: *Welcher Buchstabe fehlt? Du — ist es A?*

Student: *Nein.*

Teacher: *Richtig. MAYER: M – A. Ist es B? ...*

Solution: Z

Students may now attempt the *Lernziel 3* activities in the *Selbstbedienung* section on page 13 of the students' book. See page 29 of this book for more details.

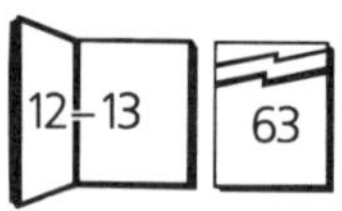

Solutions are also provided on copymaster 63 for the students to use themselves.

63 Selbstbedienung: Lösungen

Kapitel 1

Buchstabensalat

1 hallo
2 guten Tag
3 grüß dich
4 heiße
5 guten Morgen
6 nein

Spiegelbild

1 Susi
2 Sven
3 Paul
4 Anne
5 Bernd
6 Uschi

Wieviel ist das?

a sechs und eins – das ist sieben
b fünf und drei – das ist acht
c vier und zwei – das ist sechs
d drei und sechs – das ist neun
e zwei und zwei – das ist vier
f sechs und fünf – das ist elf
g eins und vier – das ist fünf
h fünf und fünf – das ist zehn
i zwei und eins – das ist drei
j sechs und sechs – das ist zwölf

Welche Zahl ist das?

siebzehn

Zahlenrätsel

1 Hallo
2 Wie heißt du?
3 Wie alt bist du?

Frage und Antwort

Wie sagt Paul?	Grüß dich
Was läuft im Saal zwei?	Der Tunnel
Was ist auf Platz sieben in der Hitparade?	Mann, oh Mann
Wieviel ist das?	Neun
Wie alt bist du?	Ich bin zwölf

Kapitel 2

Länderquiz

1 Dänemark	6 Österreich
2 Italien	7 Frankreich
3 Deutschland	8 England
4 Irland	9 Schottland
5 die Schweiz	10 Wales

Die Hauptstadt von Italien ist Rom

1 Italien – Rom
2 Schottland – Edinburg
3 Deutschland – Berlin
4 Frankreich – Paris
5 Schweiz – Bern

Das Auto kommt aus ...

1 D = aus Deutschland
2 F = aus Frankreich
3 DK = aus Dänemark
4 LUX = aus Luxemburg
5 A = aus Österreich
6 CH = aus der Schweiz

Purzelwörter

1 LUXEMBURG	5 WALES
2 SCHWEIZ	6 DÄNEMARK
3 DEUTSCHLAND	7 FRANKREICH
4 BELGIEN	

Zahlenrätsel

1 sechs 2 zwei 3 acht

Alphabeträtsel

Wie schreibt man das?

Wo liegt Grasdorf?

(Pairs of towns can be either way round.)

Grasdorf liegt im Nordosten in der Nähe von Strandburg.
Hirschdorf liegt im Nordwesten in der Nähe von Bergstadt.
Hügeldorf liegt im Westen in der Nähe von Seeburg.
Sandbach liegt im Osten in der Nähe von Flußstadt.
Steindorf liegt im Südwesten in der Nähe von Feldstadt.
Waldburg liegt im Südosten in der Nähe von Hafenstadt.

ZICKZACK neu 1

Lernziel 1

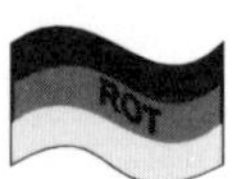

Buchstabensalat

Jumbled words for the students to write out correctly.

Solution:

1 hallo **2** guten Tag **3** grüß dich **4** heiße **5** guten Morgen **6** nein

Spiegelbild

Mirror-images of names for the students to write out correctly.

Solution:

1 Susi **2** Sven **3** Paul **4** Anne **5** Bernd **6** Uschi

Lernziel 2

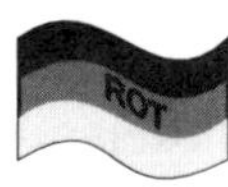

Wieviel ist das?

A domino activity requiring simple addition.

Solution:

a sechs und eins — das ist sieben
b fünf und drei — das ist acht
c vier und zwei — das ist sechs
d drei und sechs — das ist neun
e zwei und zwei — das ist vier
f sechs und fünf — das ist elf
g eins und vier — das ist fünf
h fünf und fünf — das ist zehn
i zwei und eins — das ist drei
j sechs und sechs — das ist zwölf

Welche Zahl ist das?

A gap-filling activity requiring deduction.

Solution: siebzehn

Lernziel 3

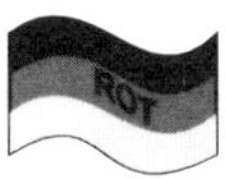

Zahlenrätsel

Words hidden in a numerical code.

Solution:

1 Hallo **2** Wie heißt du? **3** Wie alt bist du?

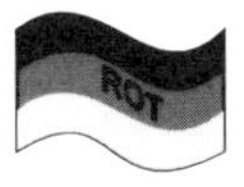

Frage und Antwort

A matching activity involving questions and answers.

Solution:

— Was sagt Paul?
— Grüß dich.

— Was läuft im Saal zwei?
— *Der Tunnel.*

— Was ist auf Platz sieben in der Hitparade?
— *Mann oh Mann.*

— Wieviel ist das?
— Neun.

— Wie alt bist du?
— Ich bin zwölf.

Bildvokabeln

Im Klassenraum

Reading
Writing

The illustration is not intended for detailed exploitation, but provides the students with the opportunity to expand their vocabulary. A version of the students' book drawing is provided on copymaster 4 for the students to label and colour.

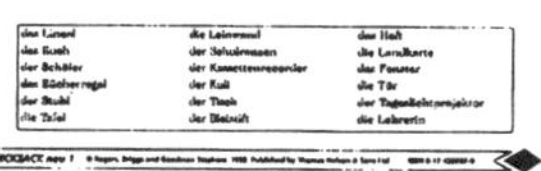

Das Alphabetlied

Listening
Speaking
Reading

The songs in *Zickzack Neu* are designed to be easily learned and fun to sing along with. Play the song to the class and ask the students to sing it line by line, either together or in groups. A final stage could be to let the students perform it in their own style and make their own recording.

Alphabetlied

A B C D, so fängt's an.
E F G H geht es dann.
I J K
L und M,
So geht das Alphabet.
So geht ...
das Alphabet.

N O P Q, hör gut zu.
R S T U, ich und du.
V W X
Y Z,
So geht das Alphabet.
So geht ...
das Alphabet.

Grammar exercise 1, on copymaster 72, is based on the material in this chapter.

After completing work on this chapter, check whether any further reinforcement is appropriate from the video material, Activity Box cards and Assessment Support Pack tasks.

2 Wo wohnst du?

Main teaching points

Lernziel 1: Countries in Europe

Grammar presented:
Separable verb 2nd person singular present (*ansehen*)
Interrogatives (*welches? wer? woher?*)
1st and 2nd person singular and 3rd person plural present (*kommen*)

Vocabulary presented:

das Alphabeträtsel	*diese*	*Irland*	*Paris*	*die Schweiz*
ansehen	*Edinburg*	*Italien*	*die Person(en)*	*der Teenager*
auf Urlaub	*Europa*	*das Land (Länder)*	*Rom*	*von*
Bern	*Frankreich*	*das Länderquiz*	*richtig*	*wer spricht?*
der Campingplatz	*die Hauptstadt/städte*	*der Lückentext(e)*	*Salzburg*	*Wien*
Deutschland	*ich komme aus*	*München*	*Schottland*	*woher kommen sie?*

Grammar revised:
Imperatives
heißen and *sein* (first person singular present tense)

Lernziel 2: Saying where you live

Grammar presented:
First person singular present tense (*wohnen*)
Indirect questions /statements (*wo ich wohne/du wohnst*)

Vocabulary presented:

andere	*es*	*ja*	*meine*	*war*
das Auto	*das Foto*	*jung*	*nein*	*was machst du?*
das Bild(er)	*halt!*	*kannst du?*	*der Ort*	*die Welt*
(eine) Deutsche	*hier*	*los!*	*Purzelwörter*	*wiederhol*
doch	*der Junge(n)*	*das Mädchen*	*die Symphonie*	*der Zungenbrecher*

Grammar revised:
Interrogatives and imperatives
heißen and *sein* (first person singular present tense)

Lernziel 3: Saying where places are

Grammar presented:
Third person singular present tense (*liegen*)
Prepositions (*im* + points of compass, *in der Nähe von*)
First person singular and plural and third person singular present tense (*sprechen*)

Vocabulary presented:

das Alphabeträtsel	*im Nordosten*	*im Westen*	*nicht nur ... sondern*	*die Tabelle(n)*
Amerika	*im Nordwesten*	*in der Nähe von*	*auch*	*überall*
auch	*im Osten*	*Mitglied der Ami-*	*nochmal*	*wir sprechen deutsch!*
das Dorf (Dörfer)	*im Süden*	*schen Gemeinschaft*	*oder*	*wo liegt das?*
falsch	*im Südosten*	*die Muttersprache*	*Rußland*	*wo spricht man*
im Norden	*im Südwesten*	*Norditalien*	*schon lange*	*deutsch?*

Grammar revised:
Imperatives
Interrogatives

Before beginning work on this chapter, check where the video material, Activity Box cards and Assessment Support Pack tasks will be most appropriate.

Europa

Listening
Speaking
Reading

Present (some of) the countries of Europe using the map in the students' book.

Teacher: *Seht euch die Landkarte an. Das ist Europa. Das ist Frankreich/Deutschland/die Schweiz*, etc.

Partnerarbeit. Welches Land ist das?

Follow this up by using the model dialogue in the students' book and a selection of the language games described below.

Teacher: *Welches Land ist das?*
(Begin to spell a country and ask the students to guess it as soon as possible:) *F – R – A* ...

Student: *Frankreich.*

Teacher: *Fantastisch!*

Students could continue the game in pairs or groups once they feel confident.

1 Ich denke an ein Land

Ask the students to guess the country you are thinking of as quickly as possible. Encourage them to take over your role as soon as they can.

Teacher: *Ich denke an ein Land. Welches Land ist es?*

Student: *(Ist es) die Schweiz?*

2 Länderlotto

Ask students to write down three to five names of countries, which they must tick if you call them out. The first student to tick all the countries calls out *(Länder)Lotto!*

3 Buchstabenquiz

Call out a number and ask the students to say a country which has that number of letters.

Teacher: *England hat sieben Buchstaben.*
(Write *England* on the board, spell it out *E – N – G – L – A – N – D* and count each letter.)

Welches Land hat ... Buchstaben?

For a SCHWARZ follow-up, ask the students to continue the activity in pairs. Write up the question form: *Welches Land hat ... Buchstaben?*

4 Was hast du geschrieben?

Another guessing game, this time involving writing. Demonstrate with individual students in front of the class before asking them to work in pairs.

Teacher: *Andrew, schreib etwa drei Länder in dein Heft, zum Beispiel: England, Frankreich, Belgien. Zeig mir nicht, was du schreibst!* (Cover your eyes as he/she writes them down.) *Fertig? Gut. Was hast du geschrieben? Dänemark? Ja oder nein?*

Student: *Nein.*

Teacher: *Frankreich?*

Student: *Ja.*

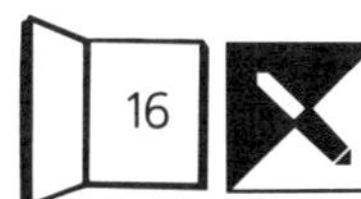

Was ist die Hauptstadt?

Listening
Speaking
Reading

If you wish, you could, at this point, focus on a few of the capitals of the countries shown on the map in the students' book and introduce the notion of capital cities.

Teacher (point to London on the map): *Das ist London. London ist die Hauptstadt von England. Wie heißt Hauptstadt auf englisch? Wiederholt jetzt Paris, Berlin, usw.*

Teacher: *Was ist die Hauptstadt von Belgien?*

Student: *Brüssel.*

Teacher: *Richtig.*

Once the students are confident, introduce a variant:

Teacher: *Die Hauptstadt ist Edinburg — welches Land ist das?*

Student: *Schottland.*

Partnerarbeit. Buchstabenrätsel

Listening
Speaking
Reading

A simple game of logic. The students work in pairs, taking turns to choose a country and to write down the initial letter of that country and of its capital. The chooser gives his/her partner one of the answers and sees how quickly he/she can give the other. Perform one or two examples, writing them up.

Teacher (write up 'F' and 'P'): *F ist Frankreich, was ist P?* (Or: *P ist Paris, was ist F?*)

To make it more demanding, you could ask the students simply to work it out from the two letters without further clues.

Teacher: *I, R — was ist das?*

Student: *Italien und Rom.*

Europa

Writing

A blank map of most of Europe for students to complete and colour, if they wish. The names of the countries and their capitals are listed at the foot of the copymaster.

Finde die Städte

Speaking
Writing

A map of Germany, Austria and Switzerland showing the main towns as numbered dots. A menu of names appears at the bottom.

Talk the students through the pronunciation of the towns shown as numbered dots.

They then practise pronouncing the names in pairs. When they are reasonably confident about the pronunciation, ask them to match the numbers and the towns and to write them out.

Teacher: *Das ist eine Landkarte von Deutschland, Österreich und der Schweiz. Hier sind die Städte. Was ist Nummer eins?* etc.

Teacher: *Jetzt Partnerarbeit: stellt einander Fragen. Was ist Nummer eins, zwei, usw?*

(Or without the copymaster:) *Jetzt Partnerarbeit: Partner/in A sagt eine Stadt und Partner/in B sagt das Land. Zum Beispiel, ich bin Partner/in A.*
(To a student:) *Köln. Welches Land ist das?*

Student: *Deutschland.*

Teacher (for the written activity): *Schreibt die Antworten in euer Heft.*

Solution:

1 Berlin **2** Hamburg
3 Bremen **4** Kiel
5 Lübeck **6** Rostock
7 Neubrandenburg
8 Potsdam **9** Magdeburg
10 Hannover
11 Osnabrück
12 Dortmund **13** Essen
14 Düsseldorf **15** Köln
16 Bonn **17** Halle
18 Erfurt **19** Leipzig
20 Dresden **21** Kassel
22 Frankfurt **23** Mainz
24 Saarbrücken **25** Karlsruhe **26** Stuttgart
27 Nürnberg **28** Augsburg **29** München
30 Innsbruck **31** Salzburg **32** Linz **33** Wien **34** Graz
35 Genf **36** Bern **37** Basel **38** Zürich **39** Luzern

A map of the German-speaking lands also appears on page 21 of the students' book. This can be used for reference at any point.

Städte und Länder (Galgenspiel)

Practice
Speaking

Play hangman with the class using towns and countries. Encourage students to take over the teacher's role as soon as they guess the correct answer.

Teacher: *Jetzt spielen wir das Galgenspiel.*

Student: *A?*

Teacher: *Nein.*

Student: *E?*

Teacher: *Ja* (write up 'E').

Auf dem Campingplatz

Listening
Speaking
Reading

Six teenagers on a campsite in Germany introduce themselves and say where they come from. Ask the students to listen to the cassette, and identify the order in which the teenagers speak and where they come from.

Teacher: *Hört zu. Wer spricht? ... Woher kommt Nicole — aus Manchester?*

Student: *Nein, aus der Schweiz.*

Teacher: *Gut. Und Hugh?*

(For the pairwork:) *Jetzt Partnerarbeit. Wählt eine Person und stellt die Frage: ‚Wer bin ich?'*

Auf dem Campingplatz

1 — Hallo, wie heißt du?
— Nicole.
— Woher kommst du?
— Ich komme aus Bern in der Schweiz.

2 — Grüß dich! Wie heißt du?
— Alastair.
— Bist du Engländer?
— Nein, Schotte. Ich komme aus Schottland.
— Oh, pardon.

3 — Hallo, wie heißt du?
— Derya.
— Woher kommst du?
— Aus Deutschland.

4 — Tag! Wie heißt du?
— Hugh.
— Hugh?
— Ja, ich komme aus Wales.
— Ach so.

5 — Hallo! Wie heißt du?
— Michael. Ich komme aus Österreich.
— Aus Österreich?
— Ja.

6 — Grüß dich! Wie heißt du?
— Kuldip.
— Woher kommst du?
— Ich komme aus England.

Solution:

1 Nicole. Aus der Schweiz **2** Alistair. Aus Schottland
3 Derya. Aus Deutschland **4** Hugh. Aus Wales
5 Michael. Aus Österreich **6** Kuldip. Aus England

Focus students' attention on *ich komme aus* by asking them to introduce themselves to their partners or to the rest of the class, as if they were strangers.

Teacher: *Michael sagt ‚Ich komme aus Österreich.' Wie heißt das auf englisch? Gut. Ich komme aus ...*
(To a student:) *und du?*

Student: *Ich komme aus ...*

Teacher: *Kettenspiel.*
(To the first student:) *Du beginnst — ‚Hallo! Ich heiße ..., (ich) bin ... Jahre alt, und (ich) komme aus ...'*
(To the second student:) *Und du — ‚Hallo, ich ...'*

Partnerarbeit. Wer bin ich?

Listening
Speaking
Reading

A game of deduction based on ***Auf dem Campingplatz***. Students choose to be one of the people shown on the map, and ask their partner to work out who they are. Demonstrate one or two examples.

> Students may now attempt the *Lernziel 1* activities in the *Selbstbedienung* section on page 22 of the students' book. See page 38 of this book for more details.

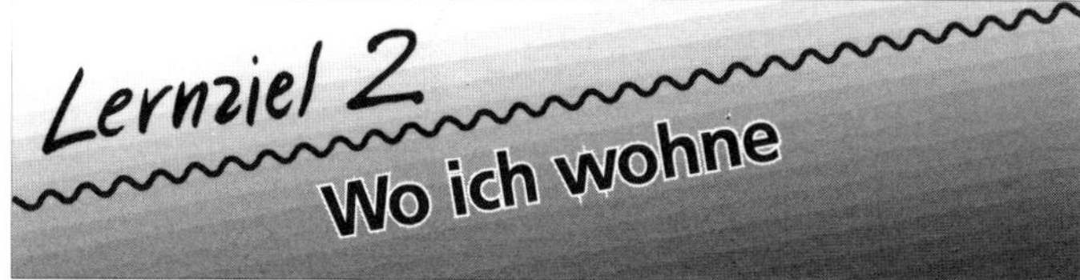

Presentation of language (Ich komme aus/Ich wohne in)

Listening
Speaking

Introduce the topic of saying where you live using examples from the local area. Ask the students to follow your example.

Teacher: *Ich komme aus England. Ich wohne in Manchester.*
(To a student:) *Und du?*

Student: *Ich komme aus England. Ich wohne in Sale.*

To add variety and interest you can ask students to choose their own details from any of the maps, places and names shown in the students' book. They can then exchange their information. The copymaster which follows enables students to use this language in a communicative context.

Ich komme aus Österreich. Ich wohne in Linz

Listening
Speaking
Reading

A communicative activity for the whole class, in which students are given a country and a home town and have to find someone else who lives in the same town as they do. In order to make sure that every student has a card, you may need to make several copies of the copymaster. You should distribute at least two copies of each card.

Demonstrate the procedure by questioning one or two students in front of the class.

Teacher (reading from your card): *Ich komme aus Österreich. Und du?*

Student: *Ich komme aus Deutschland.*

Teacher: *Ich komme aus Österreich, und du?*

Student: *Ich auch!*

Teacher: *Gut! Ich wohne in Linz. Und du?*

Student: *Ich wohne in Wien.*

... etc.

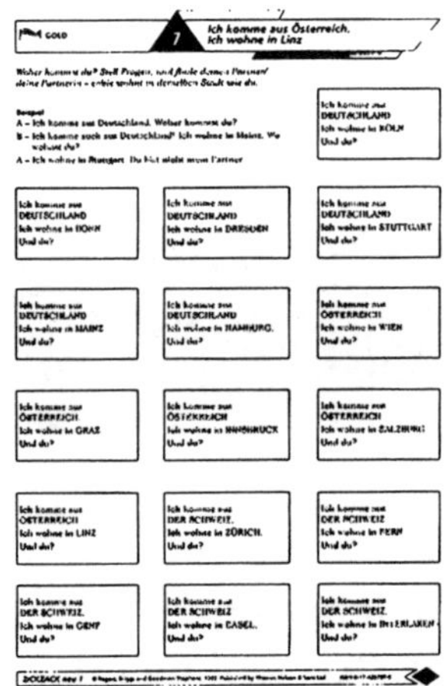

GOLD 7 Ich komme aus Österreich. Ich wohne in Linz

		Ich komme aus DEUTSCHLAND Ich wohne in KÖLN Und du?
Ich komme aus DEUTSCHLAND Ich wohne in BONN Und du?	Ich komme aus DEUTSCHLAND Ich wohne in DRESDEN Und du?	Ich komme aus DEUTSCHLAND Ich wohne in STUTTGART Und du?
Ich komme aus DEUTSCHLAND Ich wohne in MAINZ Und du?	Ich komme aus DEUTSCHLAND Ich wohne in HAMBURG. Und du?	Ich komme aus ÖSTERREICH Ich wohne in WIEN Und du?
Ich komme aus ÖSTERREICH Ich wohne in GRAZ Und du?	Ich komme aus ÖSTERREICH Ich wohne in INNSBRUCK Und du?	Ich komme aus ÖSTERREICH Ich wohne in SALZBURG Und du?
Ich komme aus ÖSTERREICH Ich wohne in LINZ Und du?	Ich komme aus DER SCHWEIZ. Ich wohne in ZÜRICH. Und du?	Ich komme aus DER SCHWEIZ Ich wohne in BERN Und du?
Ich komme aus DER SCHWEIZ. Ich wohne in GENF Und du?	Ich komme aus DER SCHWEIZ Ich wohne in BASEL. Und du?	Ich komme aus DER SCHWEIZ. Ich wohne in INTERLAKEN Und du?

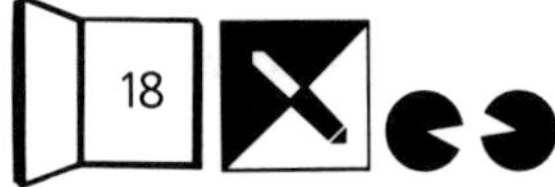

Partnerarbeit. Ich wohne in Köln

Listening
Speaking
Reading
Writing

Ask the students to work in pairs and take it in turns to ask the question provided in the students' book. By following the lines students will find the answers. Talk students through the example in the book.

Teacher: *Seht euch die Fotos und Bilder an. Was sagen die Jungen und Mädchen?*
Beispiel: Nummer eins: Was sagt Michael?

Student: *‚Ich heiße Michael. Ich komme aus Deutschland. Ich wohne in Köln'*

Teacher: *Gut. ‚Ich heiße Michael. Ich komme aus Deutschland. Ich wohne in Köln.'*
Jetzt Partnerarbeit.

The students could now write down all the information.

Teacher: *Und jetzt schreibt alles in euer Heft.* (Write up the first one on the board/OHP to illustrate.)

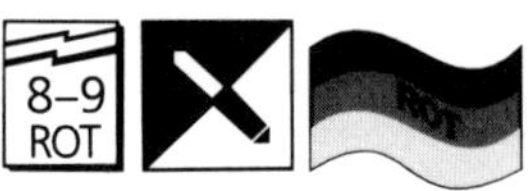

Wie heißt dein Partner?

Listening
Speaking
Reading

In this communicative activity the aim is for the students to find out the name of their partner. Each student is given a card bearing his/her name and the place he/she comes from, plus the name of the town his/her partner comes from. By asking one person after another where they come from, each student should eventually find their own partner and so discover his/her name.

Deliberately false hopes are raised by having usually two or more people coming from each town. Cut off the number of 'cards' you need for the class. Altogether there are enough for eighteen boys and eighteen girls. One sheet is for the Germans, and one for their British or Irish partners. The 'real' partners are in the same place on each sheet, so count the number of boys you have, cut up half that number of cards from the British sheet and then the corresponding cards from the German sheet. Do the same for the girls. This will ensure that everyone finds a partner. Distribute the cards randomly.

Make sure you practise the pronunciation of the names (including the towns), which could be written up for reference purposes at the start. Check that the students understand what information they have on their cards, and tell them that they are going to have to work out who their partner is by where he/she comes from and so find out his/her name. When a pair have found each other, they should report to you. Go through a few typical dialogues with pairs in front of the class as an example.

Teacher: *Seht euch diese Namen an und wiederholt ...*
Findet euren Partner/eure Partnerin. Stellt einander Fragen. Zum Beispiel:
(demonstrate with a student) *Woher kommst du?*

Student: *Aus Bremen in Deutschland. Und du?*

Teacher: *Aus Newcastle in England.*

Student: *Du bist nicht mein Partner. Tschüs!*

Checklist on pairs

Boys

English:	*German:*
Andrew Gray	Dieter Braun
Nick Adams	Michael Dau
Mike Thomas	Jörg Mehde
Ian Scott	Peter Vogel
Paul Pike	Andreas Schnabel
Martin Wilde	Bernd Hollweg
Anthony Farrell	Lars Kröner
David MacBride	Lutz Meier
Simon O'Brien	Thomas Weber

Girls

English:	*German:*
Sarah Pope	Gabriele Gellhorn
Mandy Grace	Renate Bauer
Catherine Fuller	Sabine Müller
Susan Burke	Kirsten Langer
Maureen Haddon	Monika Klein
Sharon Smith	Claudia Bach
Kate Murray	Barbara Fischer
Tina Fletcher	Merle Schwarz
Julia Lyle	Stefanie Adenauer

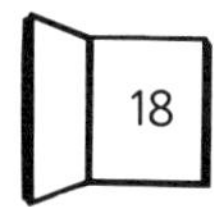

Steffi

Reading

The cartoon is intended for interest only and not for detailed exploitation.

Wo ich wohne

Listening
Speaking
Reading

This song emphasises that, in spite of all our differences, we all inhabit the same place — the world. Use mime and gesture, and/or visuals (world map or globe), to support the students' understanding. Ask them to refer to the glossary to work out the meaning of the refrain *Doch ich ...*

Play the song to the class and ask the students to sing it line by line, either together or in groups. A final stage could be to let students perform it in their own style, possibly using mime and gesture also. They could also make their own recording.

Wo ich wohne

1 Ich wohne hier,
Du wohnst da.
Ich sage ‚Nein',
Und du, du sagst ‚Ja'.

Doch ich wohne
Im selben Ort, wo du wohnst,
Und er heißt die Welt,
Er heißt die Welt.

2 Ich sage ‚Komm!'
Du sagst ‚Geh!'
Ich schreibe A,
Und du, du schreibst B.

Doch ich wohne ...

3 Ich bin jung,
Du bist alt.
Ich sage ‚Los!'
Und du, du sagst ‚Halt!'

Doch ich wohne ...

Wer ist das?

Listening
Speaking
Reading

A short cartoon depicting Wolfgang Amadeus Mozart, aged 7, being asked some personal questions. Some students should be able to guess who he is. Write up the answer once his identity has been established. The following additional information may also be of interest:

- born in Salzburg 1756
- began composing at the age of 5
- made several European tours giving concerts
- died at the age of 35 in 1791
- the cause of his death is controversial

Some students might be able to produce a brief display about Mozart, containing this and any additional information they discover as a result of research (possibly in co-operation with members of the music department).

Teacher: *Seht euch das Bild und die Fragen und Antworten an. Wer ist das? Wie heißt er?*

Zungenbrecher

Listening
Speaking
Reading
Writing

Tongue-twisters for fun. Play the cassette version and ask the students to repeat, and possibly record, the sentences. Some may be able to produce their own versions, using a word processor.

Teacher: *Zungenbrecher. Hört gut zu, und wiederholt. Könnt ihr diese Zungenbrecher schreiben?*

Zungenbrecher

— Doris ist Deutsche, und kommt aus Dortmund.

— Erich und Friedrich kommen aus Zürich.

— Konrad, Karin, Kirsten und Kurt kommen aus Köln.

— Gerold und Berthold kommen aus Detmold.

IT suggestion

Students could produce their own versions using word-processing software.

Students may now attempt the *Lernziel 2* activities in the *Selbstbedienung* section on pages 22 and 23 of the students' book. See page 39 of this book for more details.

Presentation of language (location of towns)

Listening
Speaking

Introduce the topic — the geographical location of towns — using examples from your local area.

Then help the students to fix on the location of major towns in the UK by marking them on a simple outline map on the board or OHP (e.g. Manchester, Edinburgh, Glasgow, Birmingham, Cardiff, Bristol, Dublin, Belfast, London, Southampton, Harwich).

Teacher: *Ich wohne in Manchester. Das liegt im Norden.*

Introduce other points of the compass by asking where various towns in the UK are situated. The outline map will make this explicit. You may also need to teach *in der Mitte* if your town is situated in the centre of the country.

Teacher: *Schaut auf die Karte. Manchester liegt hier.* (Write in the name.) *Im Norden.*
Was liegt hier im Süden? (Point.)

Student: *London.*

Teacher: *Ja, richtig. London liegt im Süden. Was liegt hier im Osten?*

Student: *Harwich.*

Teacher: *Gut. Das ist Harwich. Was liegt hier im Südwesten?*

Student: *Bristol.*

Teacher: *Richtig.*

... etc.

Encourage students to take over the teacher's role as soon as possible.

Wo wohne ich?

Listening
Speaking
Reading

Consolidation of points of the compass. Refer the students to the visual and the map showing eight towns covering eight points of the compass. Ask them to listen to the recordings and work out the name of the town in which each speaker lives. Complete the first example with the class.

Teacher: *Seht euch die Karte an. Hört zu. Wo wohnen die acht Jungen und Mädchen?*
(Play the first recording.) *Wo wohnt Andrea?*

Wo wohne ich?

1 — Hallo, mein Name ist Andrea. Ich wohne im Süden. Wo wohne ich?

2 — Guten Tag, ich heiße Lutz und ich wohne im Osten. Wo wohne ich?

3 — Hallo, ich heiße Kadir. Ich wohne im Westen. Wo wohne ich?

4 — Morgen! Ich heiße Monika. Ich wohne im Norden. Wo wohne ich?

5 — Hallo, ich bin Stefan. Ich wohne im Nordosten. Wo wohne ich?

6 — Guten Tag! Ich bin Fatma. Ich wohne im Südosten. Wo wohne ich?

7 — Grüß dich, ich bin Christa. Ich wohne im Südwesten. Wo wohne ich?

8 — Hallo, ich bin Alia. Ich wohne im Nordwesten. Wo wohne ich?

Solution:

1 München **2** Dresden **3** Bonn **4** Kiel **5** Rostock
6 Passau **7** Freiburg **8** Emden.

Partnerarbeit

Speaking
Practice

The students could now complete the pairwork activity in the students' book. Ask them to take it in turns to choose a town and ask their partner to work out which town they have chosen. Talk students through the model dialogue in the book.

Teacher: *Jetzt Partnerarbeit. Partner/in A wählt eine Stadt und beantwortet Fragen mit ‚Ja' oder ‚Nein'.*
(Demonstrate with a student.) *Wähl eine Stadt: Dresden, Bonn ... Fertig?*

Student: *Ja.*

Teacher: *Wohnst du im Norden?*

Student: *Nein.*

Teacher: *(Wohnst du) im Süden?*

Student: *Ja.*

Teacher: *Wohnst du in München?*

Student: *Ja. Jetzt bist du dran.*

Das liegt im Osten

Listening
Speaking
Reading
Writing

Tell the students that you are going to play a recording of some German speakers talking about where they live. The students must listen each time for the name of the speaker, the name of the town and its location. Refer them to the menu of names and places in the students' book. Students could write their answers or give oral responses, whichever is more appropriate. For oral responses, pause the cassette after each person has given the relevant details, and check whether the students have understood. Collate the results on the board/OHP.

Teacher: *Schlagt die Bücher auf Seite 20 auf. Seht euch die Tabellen an. Jetzt hört ihr sechs Personen. Sie sagen, wo sie wohnen. Sagt/Schreibt auf: den Namen, die Stadt und wo das liegt. Zum Beispiel:* (demonstrate using the first one).

Das liegt im Osten

1 — Ich heiße Alima, und ich komme aus Deutschland. Ich wohne in Hamburg. Das liegt im Norden.

2 — Ich bin Peter. Ich wohne in Deutschland — in München. Das liegt im Süden.

3 — Ich heiße Jutta. Ich wohne in Chemnitz. Das liegt im Osten.

4 — Ich heiße Martin. Ich wohne seit einem Jahr in Saarbrücken. Das liegt im Südwesten.

5 — Ich bin Heidi. Ich wohne in Berlin. Das liegt im Nordosten.

6 — Hallo! Ich heiße Kasimir. Ich wohne in Köln. Das liegt im Westen.

Solution:

1 Alima, Hamburg, im Norden **2** Peter, München, im Süden **3** Jutta, Chemnitz, im Osten **4** Martin, Saarbrücken, im Südwesten **5** Heidi, Berlin, im Nordosten **6** Kasimir, Köln, im Westen.

In der Nähe von ...

Listening
Speaking

Introduce the concept of *in der Nähe von* ... using local towns and villages as examples.

Teacher: *Ich wohne in Sale im Norden. Das liegt in der Nähe von Manchester*, etc.

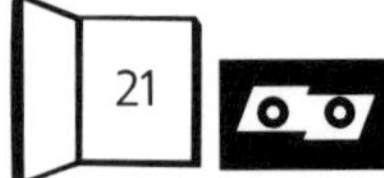

Richtig oder falsch?

Listening
Speaking
Reading
Writing

Ask the students to look at the map and to listen to the recordings. They must decide who is telling the truth and who is lying, and write *richtig* or *falsch* accordingly.

NB The only errors included relate to the names given, and not to the details of location.

Teacher: *Schlagt euer Buch auf, und seht euch die Karte an.* (Play the first recording and ask:) *Stimmt das? Ist das richtig oder falsch?*

Student: *Richtig.*

Teacher: *Ja gut. Rudi wohnt in Rellingen. Rellingen liegt in der Nähe von Hamburg. Ihr schreibt ‚richtig'.*

Richtig oder falsch?

1 — Hallo! Ich heiße Rudi. Ich wohne in Deutschland — im Norden. Ich komme aus Rellingen. Das liegt in der Nähe von Hamburg.

2 — Guten Tag! Ich komme aus Freital in der Nähe von Dresden. Mein Name ist Dirk.

3 — Grüß Gott! Ich komme aus Österreich. Ich heiße Ulli, und ich wohne in Peggau in der Nähe von Graz.

4 — Hallo! Mein Name ist Britta. Ich wohne in Zirl in der Nähe von Innsbruck.

5 — Also, ich heiße Stefan, und ich wohne in Siegburg. Das liegt in der Nähe von Bonn.

6 — Grüß dich! Ich bin Petra. Ich wohne in Gommern in der Nähe von Magdeburg.

7 — Hallo, ich heiße Maria. Ich wohne in Baden in der Nähe von Zürich.

Solution:

1 richtig **2** richtig **3** richtig **4** falsch (Name) **5** richtig **6** richtig **7** falsch

Partnerarbeit. Wo liegt Zirl?

Listening
Speaking
Reading
Writing

Pairwork consolidation of the language of the previous activity. Ask students to refer to the map and to test each other with questions about the countries, towns and people. Demonstrate with the students and write up (some of) the questions to support the activity.

Teacher: *Jetzt Partnerarbeit.* (To a student:) *Wo liegt Zirl? In Deutschland oder ...*

Student: *In Österreich.*

Teacher: *Ja. In der Nähe von Wien?*

Student: *Nein, in der Nähe von Innsbruck.*

Teacher: *Wo wohnt Dirk?*

... etc.

(Write up the questions and then tell the whole class:) *Jetzt seid ihr dran. Stellt und beantwortet Fragen.*

Students could write down the details of one or two dialogues to consolidate further the vocabulary and structures.

Students may now attempt the *Lernziel 3* activities in the *Selbstbedienung* section on page 23 of the students' book. See page 39 of this book for more details.

Selbstbedienung

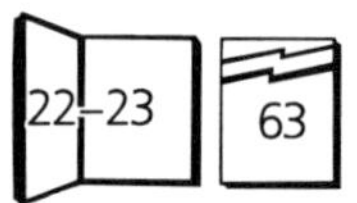

Solutions are also provided on copymaster 63 for students to use themselves.

Lernziel 1

Länderquiz

A puzzle for practising the names of countries.

Solution:

1 Dänemark **2** Italien **3** Deutschland **4** Irland **5** die Schweiz **6** Österreich **7** Frankreich **8** England **9** Schottland **10** Wales.

Die Hauptstadt von Italien ist Rom

Gapped sentences about countries of Europe and their capitals.

Solution:

1 Italien+Rom **2** Schottland+Edinburg **3** Deutschland +Berlin **4** Frankreich+Paris **5** Schweiz+Bern.

Lernziel 2

Das Auto kommt aus ...

Students must work out which country the various cars come from.

Solution:

1 D = aus Deutschland **2** F = aus Frankreich
3 Dk = aus Dänemark **4** Lux = aus Luxemburg
5 A = aus Österreich **6** CH = aus der Schweiz.

Purzelwörter

Jumbled words to practise the spelling of towns and countries.

Solution:

Länder: **1** Luxemburg **2** Schweiz **3** Deutschland **4** Belgien **5** Wales **6** Dänemark **7** Frankreich.

Städte: **1** Hamburg **2** Wien **3** Linz **4** Zürich **5** Bern **6** Bonn **7** Berlin.

Zahlenrätsel

A puzzle based on the letters of the alphabet and countries.

Solution:

1 sechs **2** zwei **3** acht

Lernziel 3

Alphabeträtsel

A riddle based on letters of the alphabet in names of towns, countries, greetings, numbers, points of the compass, and aspects of grammar.

Solution:

Wie schreibt man das?

IT suggestion

Using word-processing software, students could try and produce a similar riddle for the name of a country, for others to guess.

Wo liegt Grasdorf?

A map showing the relative positions of a number of towns and villages to practise *in der Nähe von ...*

Solutions: (pairs of towns can be either way round)

Grasdorf liegt im Nordosten in der Nähe von Strandburg.
Marschdorf liegt im Nordwesten in der Nähe von Bergstadt.
Hügeldorf liegt im Westen in der Nähe von Seeburg.
Sandbach liegt im Osten in der Nähe von Flußstadt.
Steindorf liegt im Südwesten in der Nähe von Felsenstadt.
Waldburg liegt im Südosten in der Nähe von Hafenstadt.

Zum Lesen

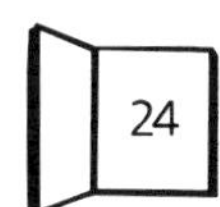

Auch wir sprechen Deutsch! *Reading*

This item comprises information about five people from German-speaking communities around the world. It is included for interest and information, but it could lead on to a project in which students investigate to what extent German is spoken throughout the world. There is a large German-speaking community in Prague and in Bozen (Bolzano), northern Italy. The Amish communities are widespread in North America, including Pennsylvania, Ohio, Indiana, Illinois, Iowa, Nebraska, Kansas and Ontario. They began migrating there from Europe in 1720. There are numerous German-speaking communities in Poland and Russia.

Grammar exercise 1, on copymaster 72, is based on the material in this chapter.

After completing work on this chapter, check whether any further reinforcement is appropriate from the video material, Activity Box cards and Assessment Support Pack tasks.

3 Meine Familie

Main teaching points

Lernziel 1: Talking about brothers and sisters

Grammar presented:
Accusative case (direct objects) indefinite article
Noun plurals

Vocabulary presented:
bald, *der Brief*, *der Bruder (Brüder)*, *der Dialog*, *das Einzelkind*, *die Familie*, *(keine) Geschwister*, *die Reihenfolge*, *die Schwester(n)*, *worum geht es hier?*

Lernziel 2: Introducing your family

Grammar presented:
sein + noun complements (*Das ist mein Bruder*)
Possessive adjectives (*mein/e*)
Genitive of proper nouns (*Jürgens Schwester*)

Vocabulary presented:
der Cousin, *die Cousine*, *die Eltern*, *die Fledermaus*, *die Großeltern*, *die Großmutter*, *der Großvater*, *ich lege dir ein Foto bei*, *Jürgens Familie*, *die Mutter*, *der Onkel*, *paßt*, *der Stammbaum*, *stellt ... vor*, *die Tante*, *der Vater*, *Vorsicht*

Grammar revised:
heißen (third person singular present tense)
passen zu + dative case

Lernziel 3: Talking about pets

Grammar presented:
Accusative case (direct objects) indefinite article

Vocabulary presented:
aufmachen, *die Bombe*, *Drogen*, *dabei*, *denken Sie auch an Ihre Katze*, *die Ferien*, *Flöhe*, *frißt*, *füll die Lücken aus*, *das Gedicht*, *ging*, *der Hamster*, *das Haustier*, *der Hund*, *der Hut*, *das Hündchen*, *hundert*, *der Igel*, *ich möchte so gerne*, *das Hotel*, *jede(s)*, *der Kanarienvogel*, *das Kaninchen*, *die Katze*, *das Kätzchen*, *der Koffer*, *die Leute*, *Mathematik*, *die Maus*, *nach*, *natürlich*, *nichts*, *der Papagei*, *das Pferd*, *die Ratte*, *der Satz*, *die Schildkröte*, *der Schimpanse*, *die Schlange*, *die Spinne*, *die Stabheuschrecke*, *der Text*, *das Tier*, *der Titel*, *vorlesen*, *der Wellensittich*, *der Witz*, *die Wüstenmaus*, *weiß*, *zu Gast*

Grammar revised:
haben (1st, 2nd and 3rd person singular present tense)
sein (3rd person singular present tense)
kein(e)

Before beginning work on this chapter, check where the video material, Activity Box cards and Assessment Support Pack tasks will be most appropriate.

Lernziel 1
Hast du Geschwister?

Wie heißen sie?

Listening
Speaking
Reading
Writing

Tell the students that you are going to play a recording and ask them to say what they think is being said, in addition to the speakers giving their names. Try to bring out the fact that new language relating to brothers and sisters is being introduced. Provide more help by bringing in photos (or other visuals) of yourself and members of your family. You could be creative and use cartoon versions or photos of celebrities who you claim are your relatives. You could also draw your own family tree and talk about it briefly. Then ask the students to look at the students' book and listen to the recording again, in order to work out the order in which people speak. Finally, ask them to work out from the text what each person actually says.

Teacher: *Hört gut zu. Worum geht es hier? Schlagt jetzt Seite 26 auf. Lest den Text, und hört gut zu.*
Beispiel: Wie heißt Nummer 1? Ute? Maria? Oder David? Schreibt die Namen in der richtigen Reihenfolge auf.

(After the students have completed the listening task:)
Was sagt David? Wie heißt das auf englisch?

Wie heißen sie?

1 — Ich heiße David. Ich habe einen Bruder und eine Schwester.

2 — Ich bin Ute. Ich habe zwei Schwestern.

3 — Mein Name ist Oliver. Ich habe drei Brüder und zwei Schwestern.

4 — Ich heiße Maria. Ich habe einen Bruder.

5 — Mein Name ist Raphael. Ich bin ein Einzelkind.

6 — Ich heiße Peter. Ich habe zwei Brüder und eine Schwester.

7 — Ich bin Emine. Ich habe einen Bruder und eine Schwester.

8 — Ich heiße Maren. Ich habe eine Schwester.

9 — Ich heiße Ahmed. Ich habe keine Geschwister.

10 — Ich bin Dorit. Ich habe einen Stiefbruder.

Solution:

1 David **2** Ute **3** Oliver **4** Maria **5** Raphael **6** Peter **7** Emine **8** Maren **9** Ahmed **10** Dorit

Hast du Geschwister?

Listening
Speaking

Draw stick figures of one boy and one girl. Write numbers next to them, e. g.

Following on from the previous activity, get the students to use the new language themselves. Ask the question *Hast du Geschwister?* Then point to a number and a stick figure (boy or girl) to elicit the reply *Ich habe zwei Schwestern* etc. Point out that *einen* is used for one brother, and *eine* for one sister. This is also presented in the ***Tip des Tages***, and dealt with more fully in *Lernziel 3*, when pets are being talked about.

Incorporate the terms for stepbrother (*Stiefbruder*) and stepsister (*Stiefschwester*). Make sure that the students can distinguish between *Bruder* and *Brüder* and between *Schwester* and *Schwestern*, and that they understand the terms *keine Geschwister* and *ein Einzelkind*. Reinforce these points on the board/OHP. Once they are confident, encourage the students to take over the teacher's role.

Wieviel Geschwister hast du?

Listening
Speaking
Reading
Writing

Further listening material on the theme of brothers and sisters. Write up the list of names alongside the two column headings as shown in the solution.

Ask the students to copy the grid and to listen to the recording. They should write down the number of brothers and sisters each person has.

Teacher: *Hier sind zehn Personen. Schreibt diese Tabelle in euer Heft und hört gut zu. Wieviel Geschwister haben sie?*

Do the first item as an example.

Wieviel Geschwister hast du?

1 — Ich heiße Andrea. Ich bin elf Jahre alt und wohne in Kassel. Ich habe einen Bruder, Michael, und zwei Schwestern, Regina und Carola.

2 — Ich heiße Jörg, und ich wohne in Köln. Ich habe eine Schwester. Sie heißt Birgit.

3 — Ich bin Sabine. Ich habe zwei Brüder: Paul — der ist sechzehn — und Hans — der ist dreizehn.

4 — Ich heiße Kurt. Ich komme aus Stuttgart. Ich habe einen Bruder und eine Stiefschwester.

5 — Mein Name ist Wolf. Ich bin fünfzehn Jahre alt, und ich wohne in Österreich. Ich habe keine Geschwister.

6 — Ich bin Katrin. Ich habe drei Brüder. Leider habe ich keine Schwester.

7 — Ja, mein Name ist Sven. Ich komme aus Lingen. Ich habe nur einen Stiefbruder. Der heißt Torsten.

8 — Ich heiße Kirsten. Ich bin elf Jahre alt. Ich habe zwei Schwestern, Trudi und Jutta. Ich wohne in Halle.

9 — Ich bin Paolo. Ich komme aus Südtirol in Norditalien. Ich habe vier Brüder.

10 — Ich heiße Sarinda. Ich bin zwölf Jahre alt. Ich habe drei Schwestern.

Solution:

	Brüder	Schwestern
Andrea	1	2
Jörg	0	1
Sabine	2	0
Kurt	1	1
Wolf	0	0
Katrin	3	0
Sven	1	0
Kirsten	0	2
Paolo	4	0
Sarinda	0	3

You could also follow up the activity with a more demanding SCHWARZ activity in which students must listen again and note other details about the speakers' ages and where they live. Students could also record the details of the ten interviewees on a barchart.

Familienumfrage

Listening
Speaking
Reading
Writing

Ask the students to interview five or six others about their own families using the same type of grid as above.

Teacher: *Macht jetzt fünf Interviews. Schreibt die Antworten auf.*
(Demonstrate with one student:) *Hast du Geschwister?*

Student: *Ja, (ich habe) einen Bruder.*

You might like to collate the class results and record the information on a barchart and/or in a database.

Ich habe eine Schwester

Listening
Speaking
Reading
Writing

A matching activity in which the students have to write the appropriate text from the options menu in empty speech bubbles. Complete the first one with the class.

Teacher: *Hier sind acht Jungen und Mädchen. Was sagen sie? Zum Beispiel, was sagt das Mädchen Nummer eins?*
(Point to the menu and say:) *Füll die Lücken aus — Ich habe eine ...*

Student: *Schwester.*

Teacher: *Ausgezeichnet. Jetzt seid ihr dran. Füllt die Lücken aus.*

Solution:

1 Schwester **2** Bruder **3** einen Bruder / eine Schwester **4** zwei Schwestern **5** zwei Brüder **6** eine Schwester / zwei Brüder **7** habe zwei Brüder / zwei Schwestern **8** Ich habe drei Schwestern

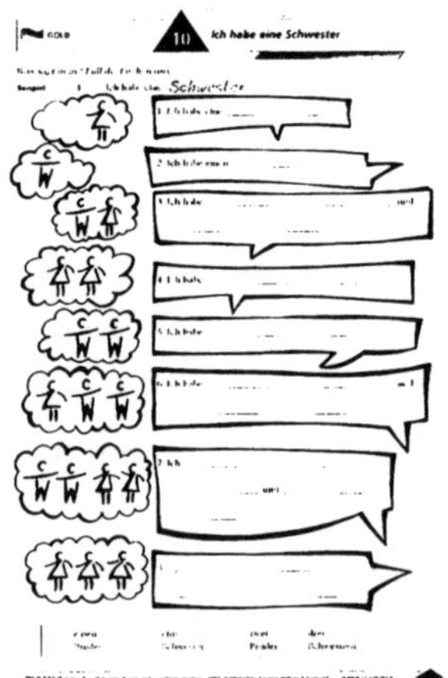

Partnerarbeit. Welche Familie ist das?

Listening
Speaking
Reading

A pairwork activity based on twelve different combinations of brothers and sisters in pictorial form. Partner A decides on a particular family. Partner B has to ask questions in order to deduce which family Partner A has chosen. All questions must be answered with only *Ja* or *Nein*. Perform a model dialogue to demonstrate the activity, making sure that the students can pronounce *Familie* correctly.

Teacher: *Hier sind zwölf Familien. Partner/in A wählt eine Familie — Nummer eins oder Nummer zwei oder Nummer drei usw. Partner B stellt Fragen. Zum Beispiel* (to a student): *wähl eine Familie, und ich stelle Fragen. Bist du fertig?*

Student: *Ja.*

Teacher: *Hast du Brüder?*

Student: *Ja.*

Teacher: *Hast du einen Bruder?*

Student: *Ja.*

Teacher: *Hast du Schwestern?*

Student: *Nein.*

Teacher: *Also ... du hast einen Bruder aber keine Schwestern. Das ist Familie eins.*

Student: *Richtig.*

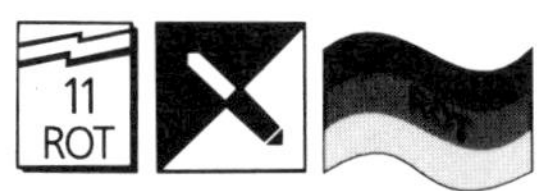

Und du? Wie heißt du?

Listening
Speaking
Reading

A groupwork activity providing further practice in exchanging personal details.
Cut up the completed role cards on the copymaster and give one to each student. Then distribute one sheet of blank forms to each student. They should now write the details they have been given on the card in the grid outlined in bold in the top left-hand corner. Then they must interview other students in the class until they have completed the details of the five other identities.
Write up on the board or OHP the names of the six towns and people together with the following four questions.

Wie heißt du? Wie alt bist du? Wo wohnst du? Hast du Geschwister?

Check the results of one or two students orally.

Teacher: *Ihr macht Interviews.* (Point to one of the completed forms:) *Das bist du.* (Point at parts of the copymaster:) *Du schreibst hier deinen Namen, dein Alter, usw.* (demonstrate). *Suche jetzt die fünf anderen Leute (Anne, Uschi, Paul, usw.) Mach Interviews und schreib alles auf.*

11 Und du? Wie heißt du?

Peter 15 Bonn 1 Bruder	Uschi 13 München 1 Bruder 2 Schwestern	Thomas 12 Kassel 2 Brüder

Anne 14 Hamburg 1 Schwester	Paul 16 Berlin keine	Trude 14 Frankfurt 1 Bruder 1 Schwester

Students may now attempt the *Lernziel 1* activities in the *Selbstbedienung* section on page 32 of the students' book. See pages 49–50 of this book for more details.

Mein Stammbaum

Listening
Speaking
Reading
Presentation

A humorous family tree. Draw a simple family tree to start with and introduce members of your family. Then ask the students to listen to Jürgen introducing the members of his family, all of whom are sitting on, climbing, or hanging from, the branches of the tree in the illustration. They are labelled according to their relationship to Jürgen. Their names all appear in the box at the bottom of the page. Refer the students also to the ***Tip des Tages*** for *er/sie heißt*, and for the written forms *mein Vater*, etc. The students must listen to Jürgen and match the names he mentions to the appropriate members of the family.

Teacher: *Seht euch meinen Stammbaum an. Das ist meine Familie = mein Onkel, meine Großmutter, meine Mutter. Wie heißt ‚Tante' auf englisch? Und ‚Großvater'?* (Referring to the students' book:) *Seht euch den*

Stammbaum an. Das ist Jürgens Familie. Hört gut zu. Wer ist Lutz? Jürgens Bruder oder Jürgens Vater? Hier unten sind die Namen.

(Play the cassette and complete the first one or two to demonstrate.)

Mein Stammbaum

— Das ist meine Familie. Mein Bruder Lutz ... meine Mutter Gisela ... mein Vater Paul ... meine Stiefschwester Nicole ... mein Onkel Bernd ... meine Tante Luise ... meine Großmutter Helga ... mein Großvater Kurt ... meine Cousine Sonja ... und mein Cousin Michael.

Wie sind die Namen? *Listening*

Check the students' answers using Jürgen's quiz questions, also on cassette. Tell the students Jürgen is going to test them on the names of his family. Pause the cassette after each member of the family is mentioned and give the students time to agree on the correct name. Provide multiple-choice alternatives each time if the students cannot remember.

Teacher: *Hört zu. Jürgen macht ein Quiz. Wie sind die Namen?*

Play the cassette and complete the first question.

Wie sind die Namen?

— Mein Bruder, wie heißt er? ...
Lutz. Mein Bruder heißt Lutz.

Und meine Mutter, wie heißt sie? ...
Gisela.

Wie heißt mein Vater? ...
Mein Vater heißt Paul.

Und meine Stiefschwester? ...
Sie heißt? ... Nicole.

Wie heißt mein Onkel? ...
Er heißt Bernd.

Wie heißt meine Tante? ...
Sie heißt Luise.

Und meine Großmutter? ...
Meine Großmutter heißt Helga.

Und mein Großvater heißt? ...
Kurt.

Wie heißt meine Cousine? ...
Meine Cousine heißt Sonja.

Und mein Cousin? ...
Er heißt Michael.

Follow this up by asking the students to practise pronunciation of the new vocabulary in a chain-game. Tell them they are all called Jürgen, and that they are going to introduce the members of their family, just as Jürgen did. The game can be a simple one in which the students take it in turns to introduce one member only of the family; or it can be made more demanding by playing it cumulatively, so that successive students must repeat all the details presented so far by the students before them and add one more to the list. Write up *er/sie heißt* to support the activity.

Teacher: *Kettenspiel. Ihr heißt alle Jürgen.* (Point to the book:) *Das ist eure Familie. Stellt sie vor. Zum Beispiel — ich fange an — das ist mein Bruder. Er heißt Lutz.* (Turn to the first student:) *Du sagst ‚Das ist meine Schwester. Sie heißt ...' usw.* (Or if playing cumulatively:) *Du sagst ‚Das ist mein Bruder. Er heißt Lutz. Das ist meine Schwester. Sie heißt ...'*

Partnerarbeit *Speaking Practice*

Finally, ask the students to complete the ***Partnerarbeit*** activity shown in the book. Ask students to take it in turns to be Jürgen and answer questions about the members of their family. If necessary, provide the student asking the questions with a list of the answers.

Teacher: *Jetzt Partnerarbeit.* (To one student:) *Du bist Jürgen. Ich stelle Fragen. Wie heißt deine Tante?*

Student: *(Sie heißt) ...*

Meine Familie *Listening Speaking Reading Writing*

As part of a homework task, the students can draw pictures or get photographs (perhaps cut out from magazines) to present their real or imaginary family. This could also become a class display project. Ask the students to label the illustrations, and perhaps to present them to the rest of the class. Use your own real or (preferably) imaginary family tree to illustrate.

Teacher: *Das ist meine Familie.* (Show your illustrations and present the members of your family.) *Jetzt seid ihr dran. Bringt Fotos oder Bilder aus Zeitschriften* (show one or two magazine cut-outs) *und stellt eure Familie vor.*

IT suggestion

Students could produce their own family trees using desktop-publishing software — or if this is too personal, they could instead produce the family tree of a well-known family such as the Royal family.

Junge oder Mädchen?

Listening
Speaking
Reading
Writing

Further practice of the alphabet and names, and consolidation of *er/sie heißt.*

Either write up, or spell out orally, the first few letters of a student's name (either from the class or from a list of German names on the board/OHP). The first student to recognise the name you are spelling calls out *Junge — (er heißt) Michael.*

You either say *Ja, richtig* or *Nein*, and continue until the correct answer is given. Once they are confident, students can play this game themselves in pairs or groups.

Teacher: *Junge oder Mädchen? Hört zu:* (or *Schaut auf die Tafel:*) *P – A – U ...*

Student: *Junge. Er heißt Paul.*

Teacher: *Nein. P – A – U – L –*

Student: *Mädchen. Sie heißt Paula.*

Teacher: *Prima ...*
(For pair/groupwork:) *Jetzt seid ihr dran. Partner-/Gruppenarbeit. Spielt weiter.*

Zwei Briefe

Listening
Speaking
Reading

A matching activity, based on two letters. The letters contain familiar language, except for the beginning and end and the reference to the birthday. The context should, however, enable the students to understand these unfamiliar phrases. The students must identify which photograph accompanies which letter. One of the three photographs serves only to distract.

Read through the letters with the class and ask them to read them back to you. Draw the students' attention to the capital D in *Du* and *Dein/Deine.* Also point out the convention of using an exclamation mark after the addressee's name, but mention that this is less common than it used to be.

Teacher: *Hört gut zu, und wiederholt. Seht euch die Fotos an: welches Foto paßt zu welchem Brief?*

Solution: *Brief 1 + Foto C, Brief 2 + Foto A*

Schreib einen Brief auf deutsch!

Listening
Speaking
Reading
Writing

Ask the students to write a similar letter about themselves, referring to the students' book versions where necessary. The copymaster version that follows provides extra support for a GOLD/ROT approach. Elicit from the students the difference between *lieber* and *liebe* in the two letters in the book.

Teacher: *Jetzt seid ihr dran. Schreibt einen Brief an einen Freund/eine Freundin in Deutschland (mit Hilfe von den Briefen im Buch). Vorsicht bei ‚lieber' oder ‚liebe'.* (Write both words up and ask:) *Schreibt man ‚lieber' für einen Jungen oder für ein Mädchen?*

Lieber oder Liebe?

Listening
Speaking
Reading
Writing

A more structured version of the previous activity. Ask the students to write their own letters, using the multiple-choice letter on the copymaster. Talk them through the choices, and start writing up your own version to demonstrate.

Teacher: *Jetzt schreibt ihr einen Brief. Seht euch den Arbeitsbogen an, und wählt. Zum Beispiel: Ich schreibe an einen Jungen. Darum schreibe ich: ‚Lieber Martin' ... Für ein Mädchen schreibt man?... richtig: ‚Liebe'.*

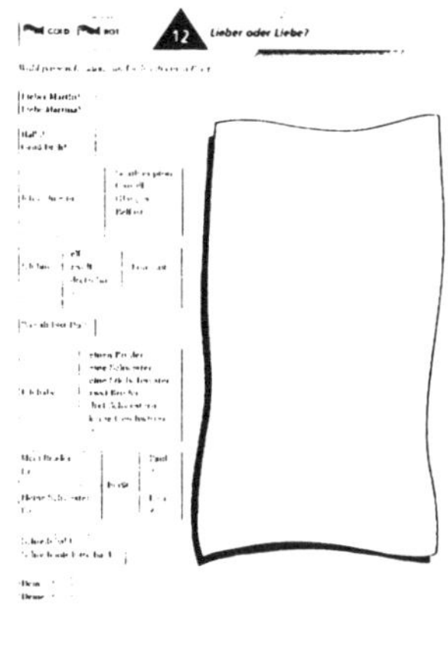

IT suggestion

For a more professional result, the letter could be produced using word-processing software.

Steffi

Reading

This cartoon is intended for general interest, not detailed exploitation.

Students may now attempt the activity for *Lernziel 2* in the *Selbstbedienung* section on page 33 of the students' book. See page 50 of this book for more details.

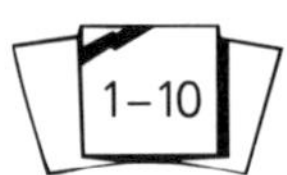

Presentation of pets/animals

Listening
Speaking

Introduce pets by showing the flashcards and saying what pets you have. Then ask the students if they have pets, using the flashcards again to support the activity.

Teacher: *Seht euch die Bildkarten an. Ich habe einen Hund und eine Katze*, etc.
(To one student:) *Und du? Hast du eine Katze? Ja oder nein?*

Student: *Ja.*

Teacher: *Hast du einen Hund?*

Play a variety of flashcard games (see Introduction pages 10–11) to consolidate pronunciation.

Hast du ein Haustier?

Listening
Speaking

Write five names on the board: Oliver, Martina, Maria, Mehmet and Sonja. Display and number the flashcards. Ask the students to listen to the recording to find out what pets each person has.

Teacher: *Hört gut zu. Hat Oliver einen Hund? Hat Sonja eine Katze? Schreibt die Namen und die passende/n Nummer/n auf. Zum Beispiel: Oliver* ... (and numbers according to those assigned to the flashcards).

Hast du ein Haustier?

— Hast du ein Haustier, Oliver?
— Ja, ich habe einen Hund und eine Katze.

— Martina, hast du ein Haustier?
— Ja, einen Wellensittich.

— Hast du ein Haustier, Maria?
— Ja, ein Pferd und eine Maus.

— Mehmet, hast du ein Haustier?
— Ja, ich habe ein Meerschweinchen und einen Hamster.

— Hast du ein Haustier, Sonja?
— Ja, einen Goldfisch und ein Kaninchen.

Solution:

According to the numbers you assign to the flashcards.

Tiere

Listening
Speaking
Reading
Writing

This copymaster can be used in a variety of ways: as reinforcement or as a possible homework activity. Used as an OHP master, it also provides an alternative way of presenting and practising the names of animals. If you cut it up into cards, the students can play various games such as pelmanism or bingo with them. Use the copymaster visual to introduce the word for gerbil (*Wüstenmaus*), if you have not already needed to do so.

Presentation of language (genders)

Listening
Speaking
Reading

Use the flashcards to revise the pets as above. Collate the answers under three gender columns on the board. Ask students: *Hast du einen Hund? ... eine Katze? ... ein Pferd?* etc. to cue the reply: *Ja/Nein*. Then practise *einen/eine/ein* in the above question in the following way:

Teacher: *Hast du einen Hund? Hast du ... Hund?* (Indicate the gap by tapping on the desk or silently mouthing the answer.) *Wie ist die Frage? Hast du ... ?*

Student: *Hast du einen Hund?*

Continue similarly with other masculine animals. When the students consistently produce *einen*, write *Hast du ... ?* on the board and *einen* above the column of masculine pets. Follow the same procedure for the other genders. Clear articulation of the articles is important, but be careful not to distort the natural flow of speech by undue emphasis. The final layout on the board should look like this:

Hast du ... ?

einen	*eine*	*ein*
Hund	Katze	Pferd
Hamster	Schildkröte	Meerschweinchen
Goldfisch	Maus	Kaninchen
Wellensittich	Wüstenmaus	

Ask the students to ask each other the question *Hast du ... ?* using the board for reference. Then gradually cover or wipe out the names of the animals from the columns and continue, obliging the students to work from memory.

Ich habe einen Hund

Listening
Speaking
Reading

Consolidation of pet animal names and of the use of the accusative indefinite article. Ask the students to look at the photographs and listen to the recording, and then to identify the photo that corresponds to each speaker.

Teacher: *Seht euch die Fotos an, und hört gut zu. Welches Foto paßt?*
(Complete the first one to demonstrate.)

Ich habe einen Hund

— Hallo! Ich heiße Christa. Ich habe einen Hund.
— Mein Name ist Renate. Ich habe eine Katze.
— Hallo! Ich bin David. Ich habe kein Haustier.
— Guten Tag! Ich bin Martin. Ich habe einen Wellensittich.
— Ich heiße Stefan. Ich habe eine Maus.
— Grüß dich! Ich bin Heike. Ich habe ein Kaninchen.

Solution:

Christa 3; Renate 2; David 1; Martin 6; Stefan 5; Heike 4

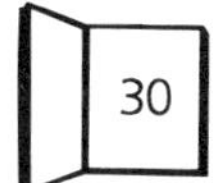

Klaus hat eine Maus

Listening
Speaking
Reading
Writing

A gap-filling activity, requiring the students to identify from drawings animals to rhyme with the names of their owners. Point out the word *hat*, which they meet here for the first time.

Teacher: *Seht euch die Tiere und die Leute an. Schreibt die Sätze, und füllt die Lücken aus. Zum Beispiel: Klaus hat eine ...*

Student: *Maus.*

Teacher: *Prima! Gerd hat ...*

Solution:

1 Klaus hat eine Maus.
2 Gerd hat ein Pferd.
3 Frau Bamster hat einen Hamster.
4 Herr Lund hat einen Hund.
5 Sabinchen hat zwölf Kaninchen.

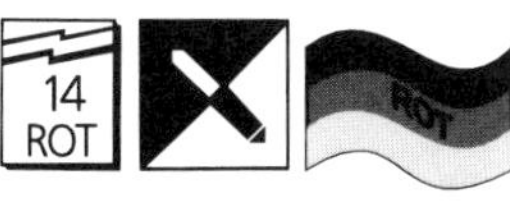

Lauter Tiere

Listening
Speaking
Reading
Writing

Ask the students to work out from the visuals and text what each person says about his/her pets. For a GOLD approach, use the numbers rather than the sentences for answers.

Teacher: *Seht euch die Bilder an. Was sagen die Jugendlichen? Zum Beispiel:* (talk the students through the example on the copymaster) *Was sagt Paul?*

Student: *‚Ich habe einen Hund und zwei Kaninchen.'*

Teacher: *Gut. Schreibt die Antworten so auf.* (Write up the number of the answer or the full sentence.)

Solution:

Paul=Ich habe einen Hund und zwei Kaninchen. (1)

Sven=Ich habe einen Hund und eine Katze. (2)

Oliver=Ich habe eine Katze und eine Maus. (3)

Anne=Ich habe eine Katze und eine Wüstenmaus. (4)

Heike=Ich habe ein Pferd und einen Hund. (5)

Ralf=Ich habe einen Hamster und eine Wüstenmaus. (6)

Gabi=Ich habe einen Wellensittich und eine Katze. (7)

Susi=Ich habe eine Katze und einen Goldfisch. (8)

Tierisch kompliziert

Reading
Writing

A riddle for the students to solve.

Solution: Hast du ein Haustier?

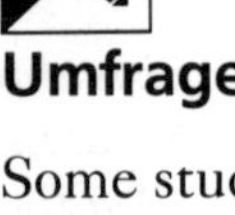

Umfrage

Listening
Speaking
Reading
Writing

Some students could carry out a class survey of pets and design a piechart to display the results. On the board/OHP, show how to collate the information in a grid, and how to transfer the results to a piechart.

Teacher: *Macht eine Umfrage über Haustiere. Stellt einander Fragen, und macht Notizen.*
(Write up a sample question and answer, such as:

— *Hast du ein Haustier?*

— *Ja, (ich habe) einen Hund ...*

and draw a simple grid for recording the information.)

Name	*Hund*	*Katze*	*Gold-fisch*	*Pferd*	
1.					
2.					
3.					
4.					
5.					
Total:					

IT suggestion

These results could be stored in a database. Students could also establish from the results which is the most popular pet in their class, compared with a class of similar-aged students in your partner school.

Partnerarbeit. Wie heißt der Hund?

Presentation
Listening
Speaking
Reading

Illustrations to cue further oral practice of animals and pets, and to present genders in the *der/die/das* form. The drawings in the students' book are in three columns according to gender. Ask the students to look at the animal pictures.

Teacher: *Schlagt die Bücher auf Seite 30 auf. Seht euch die Tiere an.*

Then present the lists in three sections:

Der Hund heißt Schnuffel.
Der Hamster heißt Max.
Der Wellensittich heißt Hansi.
Die Katze heißt Mitzi.
... etc.

Then ask students:

Teacher: *Wie heißt der Hund?*

Student: *Schnuffel.*

Teacher: *Richtig! Der Hund heißt Schnuffel.*

Divide the board/OHP into three columns. Write *Hund* (or display the flashcard) in the first column. Continue asking for the names of the other pets, and enter them in the appropriate columns. Then practise *der/die/das* in the same way as *einen/eine/ein.*

Repetition of the same procedure should emphasise the concept and link the forms. The final layout on the board/OHP should look something like this:

Wie heißt ... ?

der	*die*	*das*
Hund	Katze	Kaninchen
Hamster	Maus	Meerschweinchen
Wellensittich	Wüstenmaus	Pferd

To reinforce the students' understanding of gender, refer them to ***Auf einen Blick*** on page 35.

Ask students to ask their partners the questions *Wie heißt ... ?* using the board/OHP for reference. Later remove the names of the animals from the three columns and continue.

Teacher: *Jetzt seid ihr dran. Susan, du fragst ‚Wie heißt ... ?'*

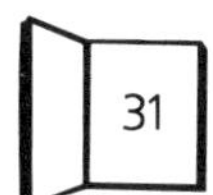

Tanjas Haustiere

Reading
Presentation
Writing

The extract from Tanja's letter to her British penfriend reinforces *mein/meine*, and introduces *er/sie/es*, giving students a more complete picture of genders. They should read Tanja's letter and then produce a similar piece of work presenting their own (real or imaginary) pets, using photos or visuals. The final result would make a good class display.

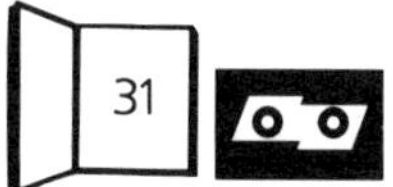

Hast du kein Haustier?

Listening
Reading

The concept of *kein* has already been briefly introduced in the phrase *keine Geschwister.* Ask the students to listen to the recording and read the cartoon dealing in a humorous way with a problem cat who keeps eating the other pets. Some students might like to act out the scene, but it is not intended for detailed exploitation.

Teacher: *Hört gut zu, lest den Text, und wiederholt.*

Hast du kein Haustier?

— Hast du eine Maus?
— Nein, ich habe keine Maus.

— Hast du keinen Wellensittich?
— Nein, ich habe keinen Wellensittich.

— Aber du hast einen Goldfisch?
— Nein, ich habe keinen Goldfisch.

— Und deine Katze?
— Nein, ich habe auch keine Katze mehr!

— Du hast also kein Haustier?
— Nein, ich habe kein Haustier.

Meine Familie und meine Haustiere

Speaking

For homework you could now ask the students to prepare a short description of their family and pets. They should learn it by heart and present it orally to the class.

Students may now attempt the *Lernziel 3* activities in the *Selbstbedienung* section on page 33 of the students' book. See page 50 of this book for more details.

sb Selbstbedienung

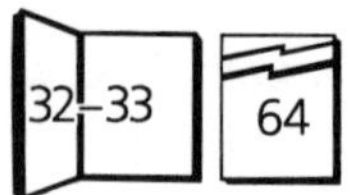

Lernziel 1

Und du?

A jumbled conversation for the students to re-write in a sensible order.

Possible solution:

— Hallo! Wie heißt du?

— Ich heiße Jens. Und du?

— Christa.

— Wo wohnst du?

— In Hamburg. Und du? Wo wohnst du?

— Ich wohne in Bremen.

— Wie alt bist du?

— Dreizehn. Und du?

— Vierzehn.

— Hast du Geschwister?

— Nein. Und du?

— Ich habe eine Schwester und einen Bruder.

Hallo!

A letter from which the students should identify the names of Uschi's brother and sister.

Solution:

Bruder = Bernd
Schwester = Jutta

Lernziel 2

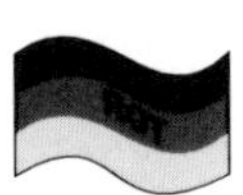

Graf Draculas Familie

The students have to read a number of statements by Count Dracula, and identify the members of his family from the 'photograph'.

Tell the students to look up the unknown animal names as preparation for *Lernziel 3*.

Solution:

1 Katze **2** Bruder **3** Großvater **4** Großmutter
5 Schwester **6** Hund **7** Fledermaus

Lernziel 3

Was ist das?

Partial drawings of animals with a jumbled menu of their names. The students must write the names in the correct order.

Solution:

Das ist ... **1** mein Hund **2** meine Katze
3 meine Maus **4** mein Pferd
5 meine Wüstenmaus **6** mein Wellensittich

Such die Tiere

A matching activity in which the students must read short texts from a magazine on pets and find the most suitable title or headline for each.

Solution:

1c 2b 3a 4d

Bildvokabeln

Ungewöhnliche Haustiere

Reading
Writing

The illustration is not intended for detailed exploitation, but provides the students with the opportunity to expand their vocabulary.

A version of the students' book drawing is provided on copymaster 16 for students to label and colour.

Wie viele Flöhe?

Listening
Speaking
Reading

A poem based on

As I was going to St Ives,
I met a man with seven wives ...

Read through the poem with the students, and refer them to a dictionary for new items of vocabulary. Talk them through the multiple-choice alternatives, and see how long it takes them to realise that the answer is *keine*. If necessary, stress the point that, as in the original riddle, the key word is *von*.

Teacher: *Lesen wir das Gedicht zusammen. Gruppenarbeit. Schaut im Wörterbuch nach. Zum Beispiel, wie heißt ‚Floh' auf englisch?*

Write up the unknown words and ask the students in their groups to find out what they mean. Finally, focus on the key question and provide multiple-choice answers. Ask the groups to decide for themselves, then tell them who was right and why.

Teacher: *Gruppenarbeit. Wie viele Flöhe gingen nach Holzkirchen?*

A fünfundzwanzigtausendsechshundert
B tausendsechshundert
C null/keine Flöhe
D zweihundertsechsundfünfzig?

Wie heißt ‚von' auf englisch?

Grammar exercises 2–6, on copymaster 72 and 73, are based on the material in this chapter.

After completing work on this chapter, check whether any further reinforcement is appropriate from the video material, Activity Box cards and Assessment Support Pack tasks.

4 Bei mir zu Hause

Main teaching points

Lernziel 1: Saying where your house or flat is

Grammar presented:
Prepositions (*in, an*)
First person plural present (*haben*)
Interrogatives
Adjectives (*groß, klein*)
Qualifiers (*ziemlich, sehr*)

Vocabulary presented:
andere, *bald*, *bei*, *das Dorf*, *du weißt*, *Einfamilienhaus*, *groß*, *das Haus*, *heute*, *ich habe gewählt*, *der Marktplatz*, *ihre Mutter*, *der Stadtrand*, *im Stadtzentrum*, *in der Nähe von*, *klein*, *Lieber Florian*, *mittelgroß*, *das Reihenhaus*, *schon*, *schreiben über* + acc, *sehr*, *die Stadtmitte*, *das Symbol*, *viele Grüße*, *der Wohnort*, *die Wohnung*, *wie geht's?*, *wo denn?*, *ziemlich*

Grammar revised: *in* + countries

Lernziel 2: Talking about the rooms of a house or flat

Grammar presented:
Prepositions (*in, von, mit*)
Intensifier (*zu*)
Infinitive constructions (*zu* + infinitive)
Dative case of possessive adjective (*meinem, meiner*)

Vocabulary presented:
das Badezimmer, *der Bungalow*, *beste*, *dreißig*, *Quadratmeter*, *das Eßzimmer*, *fließend Wasser*, *für*, *der Garten*, *das Hochhaus mit Seeblick*, *hell*, *der Immobilienmarkt*, *der Keller*, *die Küche*, *kalt*, *komm doch heraus!*, *kompakt*, *die Luxuswohnung*, *mit Balkon*, *modern*, *modernisierte Altbauwohnung*, *der Plan*, *das Schild*, *das Schlafzimmer*, *das Schloß*, *sag mal*, *die Toilette*, *das Traumhaus*, *viel besser*, *der Wohnwagen*, *das Wohnzimmer*, *zeichne*, *was für Zimmer hat es?*, *das Zimmer*, *zu (alt)*, *zu verkaufen*

Grammar revised: Interrogatives (*wie? wo?*)

Lernziel 3: Telephone numbers and addresses

Grammar presented:
Third person singular present tense (*tippen*)
Adjectival ending accusative case (masculine singular)
Indirect questions (*wie, wo*)

Vocabulary presented:
der Absender, *die Adresse(n)*, *die Badewanne*, *das Bett*, *der Computer*, *der Computerfan*, *die Computerliste*, *die Couch*, *das Dach*, *der Dachboden*, *die Dusche*, *durcheinanader*, *der Fernseher*, *der Freund(e)*, *finde heraus*, *die Garage*, *der Herd*, *hinten*, *der Kamin*, *der Kleiderschrank*, *die Lampe*, *nur*, *der Schrank*, *die Sekunde(n)*, *das Sofa*, *die Telefonnummer(n)*, *der Tippfehler*, *die Treppe*, *tippt*, *der Umschlag*, *der Vorhang*, *vergiß nicht ... zu*, *vorne*, *die Waschmaschine*, *wie bitte?*

Grammar revised:
Numerals 1–10
haben and *sein* (third person singular present tense)

Before beginning work on this chapter, check where the video material, Activity Box cards and Assessment Support Pack tasks will be most appropriate.

Ich wohne in ...

Presentation
Listening
Speaking

Tell the students where you live, including the surrounding areas.

Teacher: *Ich wohne in Eastbourne. Eastbourne ist eine Stadt in Südengland. Ich wohne in der Stadtmitte. Der Supermarkt Tesco ist auch in der Stadtmitte.* (For students living in large towns, teach:) *Ich wohne in einer Großstadt ... im Stadtviertel ...*

Draw a simple outline of the town on the board to illustrate the meaning of *Stadtmitte*. For example: *Ich wohne hier. Das ist mein Haus. Das ist die Stadtmitte.*

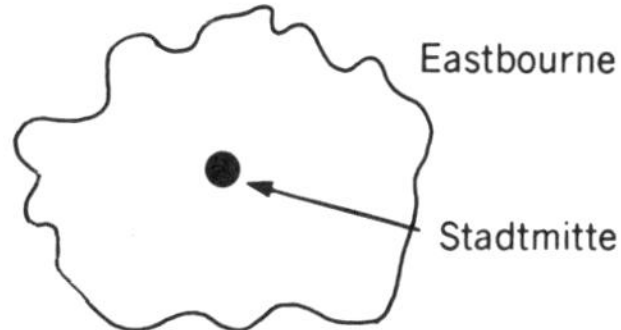

Herr/Frau (name of other teacher) *wohnt auch in Eastbourne, aber nicht in der Stadtmitte. Er/Sie hat ein Haus am Stadtrand, in Willingdon. Herr/Frau ... wohnt in Alfriston. Alfriston ist ein Dorf in der Nähe von Eastbourne.*

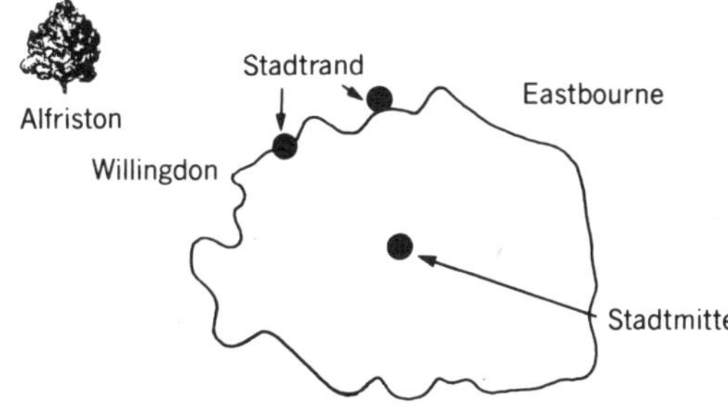

Practise the vocabulary just introduced by asking students about their own homes. Write up: *in der Stadtmitte, am Stadtrand* and *in der Nähe von*. If appropriate, use the symbols that feature in *Wo wohnen sie?* (copymaster 17) and *Wo denn?* (students' book page 37). Then question individual students.

Teacher: *Wo wohnst du?*

Student: *(Ich wohne) in Eastbourne, in der Stadtmitte.*

Teacher: *Und du?*

Student: *(Ich wohne) in Willingdon, am Stadtrand.*

Teacher: *Wohnst du auch in Willingdon?*

Student: *Nein. Ich wohne in Alfriston. Das ist ein Dorf in der Nähe von Eastbourne.*

Presentation of language (homes)

Listening
Speaking

Use the flashcards to introduce and practise *Wohnung, Reihenhaus, Doppelhaus, (Einfamilien)haus* and *Bungalow*. Allow students the opportunity to work out for themselves which of the displayed cards matches *Wohnung, Doppelhaus* etc. Blu-tack the flashcards on the board/OHP and number them. Ask the students to say the correct number when they hear each item.

Teacher: *Seht euch diese Bildkarten an. Das sind Häuser und eine Wohnung. Was paßt wozu? Zeigt auf die passenden Karten. Zum Beispiel: das ist ein Bungalow.*

(Student gives correct number.)

Teacher: *Richtig. Wiederholt ... Gut. Und das ist ein Doppelhaus/ein Einfamilienhaus/ein Reihenhaus.*

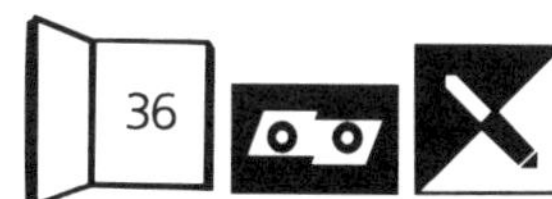

Ich wohne in einem Dorf

Listening
Speaking
Reading

Six teenagers talking about where they live. Ask students to listen to the recording and look at the photos in order to work out who is speaking.

Teacher: *Seht euch die Bilder an, und hört gut zu. Wer spricht? Schreibt die Namen in der richtigen Reihenfolge auf. Zum Beispiel ...* (complete the first example shown in the book).

Ich wohne in einem Dorf

1 — Wo wohnst du?
— Ich wohne in einem Dorf. Wir haben ein Haus. Es ist ziemlich groß.

2 — Hallo! Wo wohnst du?
— Ich wohne auch in einem Dorf, am Marktplatz. Wir haben ein Einfamilienhaus. Es ist sehr groß.

3 — Wo wohnst du?
— Ich wohne in der Stadtmitte. Wir haben eine Wohnung. Sie ist klein.

4 — Und du? Wo wohnst du?
— Ich wohne am Stadtrand. Wir haben eine Wohnung. Sie ist ziemlich klein.

5 — Und du?
— Ich wohne auch am Stadtrand. Wir haben einen Bungalow. Er ist sehr groß.

6 — Hallo! Wo wohnst du? Auch am Stadtrand?
— Nein. Ich wohne in der Stadtmitte. Wir haben ein Reihenhaus. Es ist mittelgroß.

Solution:

1 Jutta **2** Dorit **3** Bernd **4** Halil **5** Frauke **6** Sven

Once students have completed the first activity, draw their attention to the use of *wir haben*, as opposed to *ich habe*.

Teacher: *Jutta wohnt in einem Dorf. Sagt sie ‚Ich habe ein Haus'?*

Student: *Nein — ‚Wir haben ein Haus'.*

Teacher: *Ausgezeichnet. Was ist der Unterschied? ‚Ich habe' heißt ... ?*

Student: 'I have'.

Teacher: *Genau — und ‚Wir haben' ... ?* (Use a gesture to imply 'more than one'.)

Student: 'We have'.

Teacher: *Fantastisch. Was habt ihr: ein Haus/eine Wohnung/einen Bungalow?*
(Ask round the class:) *Was habt ihr? Wir ... ?*

Student: *Wir haben ein Reihenhaus.*

Teacher: *Prima! Und ihr? ...*

Now you can focus on the use of the adjectives *(sehr/ziemlich) groß, mittelgroß* and *klein*. Write them up on the board/OHP in the following chart:

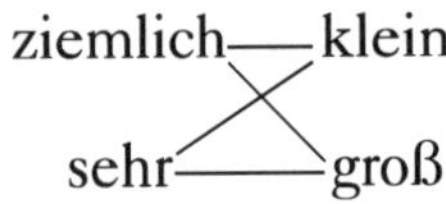

mittelgroß

Practise the pronunciation, both in chorus and individually. Once students are confident, ask them to describe their own homes in the same terms. Finally, see if the students can also remember the link between *der/ein* and *er*, *die/eine* and *sie*, and *das/ein* and *es*. Write up on the board/OHP:

der/ein → er
die/eine → sie
das/ein → es

Teacher: *Wie ist Juttas Haus? Sehr klein? Ziemlich klein? Ja, es ist ziemlich groß. Und Halils Wohnung?*

Student: *(Sie ist) ziemlich klein.*

Teacher: *Wie heißt ‚ziemlich'? ... Genau:* 'fairly'. *Und euer Haus oder euer Bungalow oder eure Wohnung?*
(To one student:) *Habt ihr ein Haus oder eine Wohnung oder einen Bungalow?*

Write up *Wie ist euer Bungalow?* etc, followed by *ein (der)*, *eine (die)* and *ein (das)*, in three distinct columns as shown below. After students have answered using *er*, *sie* or *es*, enter these pronouns on the third line — thus:

Wie ist euer Bungalow?	***Wie ist eure Wohnung?***	***Wie ist euer Haus?***
ein (der)	*eine (die)*	*ein (das)*
er	*sie*	*es*

Refer the students to ***Auf einen Blick*** on page 45 of the students' book, and to the practice exercise on copymaster 17.

> Students could follow up the whole activity by presenting their own details, either to the rest of the class, or on cassette as part of a class-to-class cassette link.

Teacher: *Jetzt seid ihr dran. Wie ist euer Haus?*

Wo wohnen sie?

Listening Speaking Reading Writing

Eight people describing where they live. Talk students through the symbols and make sure they understand what each stands for. Then ask them to listen to the recording and complete the grid by putting a cross in the appropriate columns.

Teacher: *Seht euch die Symbole an. Das ist ein Dorf, und das ...*
Hört gut zu. Was sagen sie? Macht Kreuze in die richtigen Spalten.
Zum Beispiel: (complete number 1).

Wo wohnen sie?

1 — Ich wohne in Gauting. Das ist ein Dorf in der Nähe von München. Wir haben ein Haus am Marktplatz. Es ist sehr groß.

2 — Ich wohne in Kassel. Wir haben ein Haus am Stadtrand. Es ist mittelgroß.

3 — Ich wohne in Braunau in Österreich. Wir haben eine Wohnung in der Stadtmitte. Sie ist mittelgroß.

4 — Ich wohne in Rostock. Wir haben eine Wohnung in der Stadtmitte. Sie ist ziemlich klein.

5 — Ich wohne in Krempe in Deutschland. Wir haben ein Reihenhaus am Stadtrand. Es ist ziemlich groß.

6 — Ich wohne in Worms. Wir haben eine Wohnung in der Stadtmitte. Sie ist sehr groß.

7 — Ich wohne in Zermatt in der Schweiz. Wir haben ein Haus am Marktplatz. Es ist ziemlich klein.

8 — Ich wohne in Lübeck. Wir haben eine Wohnung am Stadtrand. Sie ist ziemlich groß.

As a follow-up, the gap-filling exercise (SCHWARZ) provides further written consolidation of the vocabulary, if required.

Teacher: *Lest die Sätze und füllt die Lücken aus.*

1 Gauting: Wir haben ein Haus am Marktplatz. Es ist sehr groß.

2 Kassel: Wir haben ein Haus am Stadtrand. Es ist mittelgroß.

3 Braunau: Wir haben eine Wohnung in der Stadtmitte. Sie ist mittelgroß.

4 Rostock: Wir haben eine Wohnung in der Stadtmitte. Sie ist ziemlich klein.

5 Krempe : Wir haben ein Reihenhaus am Stadtrand. Es ist ziemlich groß.

6 Worms: Wir haben eine Wohnung in der Stadtmitte. Sie ist sehr groß.

7 Zermatt: Wir haben ein Haus am Marktplatz. Es ist ziemlich klein.

8 Lübeck: Wir haben eine Wohnung am Stadtrand. Sie ist ziemlich groß.

ROT 17 Wo wohnen sie?

Hör gut zu. Was sagen sie? Mach Kreuze in die richtigen Spalten.

	Dorf	Stadtrand	Stadtmitte	Marktplatz	Haus	Reihenhaus	Wohnung	groß	mittelgroß	klein
Beispiel 1	X			X	X			X		
2		X			X				X	
3			X				X		X	
4			X				X			X
5		X				X		X		
6			X				X	X		
7				X						X
8		X					X	X		

Füll jetzt die Lücken aus. SCHWARZ

1 Gauting: Wir haben ein Haus am Marktplatz. Es ist sehr groß.
2 Kassel: Wir haben ein Haus am Stadtrand. Es ist mittelgroß.
3 Braunau: Wir haben eine Wohnung in der Stadtmitte. Sie ist mittelgroß.
4 Rostock: Wir haben eine Wohnung in der Stadtmitte. Sie ist ziemlich klein.
5 Krempe: Wir haben ein Reihenhaus am Stadtrand. Es ist ziemlich groß.
6 Worms: Wir haben eine Wohnung in der Stadtmitte. Sie ist sehr groß
7 Zermatt: Wir haben ein Haus am Marktplatz. Es ist ziemlich klein
8 Lübeck: Wir haben eine Wohnung am Staatrand Sie ist ziemlich groß.

ZICKZACK neu 1 © Rogers, Briggs and Goodman-Stephens 1993 Published by Thomas Nelson & Sons Ltd ISBN 0 17 439787 9

Partnerarbeit. Wo denn?

Listening
Speaking
Reading

A game of logic. Ask the students to look at the map in the students' book. Remind them, if necessary, of the meanings of the symbols, which match those used in ***Wo wohnen sie?*** on copymaster 17. Revise *im Norden, im Süden, im Osten* and *im Westen* in the following way:

Teacher: *Wo ist Bonn?*

Student: *In Deutschland.*

Teacher: *Ja. Im Norden? Im Süden? Im Osten? Im Westen?*

Student: *Im Westen.*

Now ask the students to take it in turns to choose a 'home' shown on the map, and to get their partner to work out where they live, using the questions and symbols printed below the map. Ask them to note the number of questions they each ask.

Teacher: *So, jetzt Partnerarbeit. Wählt ein Dorf oder eine Stadt, Erdberg oder Hamburg oder Limerick usw. Das ist das Dorf (die Stadt), wo ihr wohnt. Dein/e Partner/in muß herausfinden, wo du wohnst. Ihr beantwortet alle Fragen mit ‚Ja' oder ‚Nein'. Wieviel Fragen stellt ihr? Zum Beispiel:*

Write up *Fragen* with the numbers 1 to 10. Call a student to the front and whisper: *Du wohnst in Bonn.* Now begin the guessing game in the following sequence:

Teacher: *Wohnst du in Österreich?*

Student: *Nein.*

Teacher (put a line through number 1 on the board/OHP): *Wohnst du in der Schweiz?*

Student: *Nein.*

Teacher (put a line through number 2, and so on for each guess/question): *Wohnst du in Deutschland?*

Student: *Ja.*

Teacher: *Wohnst du im Norden?*

Student: *Nein.*

Teacher: *Wohnst du im Süden?*

Student: *Nein.*

Teacher: *Wohnst du im Westen?*

Student: *Ja.*

Teacher: *Wohnst du in einem Dorf?*

Student: *Nein.*

Teacher: *Wohnst du in einem Reihenhaus?*

Student: *Nein.*

Teacher: *Du wohnst in einem Haus in Bonn!*
Student: *Ja.*
Teacher: *Wieviel Fragen sind das?*
Student: *Acht.*

Students may now attempt the *Lernziel 1* activities in the *Selbstbedienung* section on page 42 of the students' book. See page 60 of this book for more details.

Welches Zimmer ist das?

Presentation
Listening
Speaking

Use the copymaster and/or an OHP version to present the rooms of a house. If you use the OHP, you can reveal the rooms one by one initially; then, later on, you can play various guessing games by covering up (parts of) rooms and rotating the transparency before asking the students to work out which room is being partially revealed.

Teacher: *Seht euch den Arbeitsbogen an. Das ist ein Haus. Und dies hier sind die Zimmer. Wie heißt das auf englisch? ... Richtig:* 'rooms'.

Also, das ist der Keller/Dachboden, die Küche/Garage, das Wohnzimmer/Eßzimmer/Badezimmer/ Schlafzimmer.

Students could label and stick their own version of the copymaster in their exercise books.

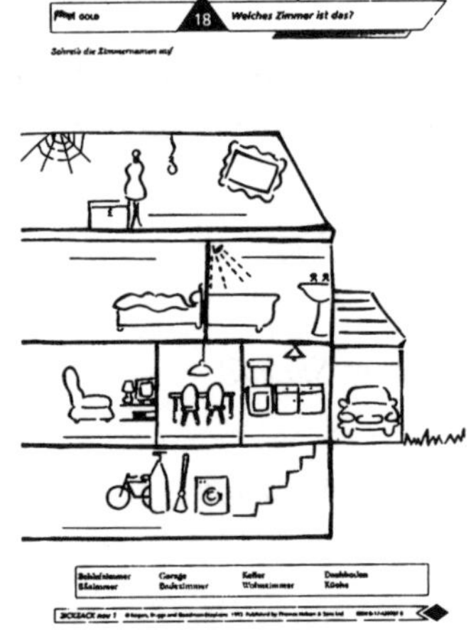

Das ist das Wohnzimmer

Listening
Speaking
Reading
Writing

A teenager showing a friend around her home. Ask the students to listen to the cassette and identify the order in which she presents the rooms. They could simply write the numbers of the photos on a first hearing, adding the room names the second time through.

Teacher: *Seht euch dieses Haus an, und hört gut zu. Wie ist die richtige Reihenfolge der Zimmer? Schreibt die Antworten auf. Zum Beispiel:* (complete the first one).

> **Das ist das Wohnzimmer**
>
> — Willst du das Haus sehen, Gabi? Komm mit, ich zeig' es dir! Das hier ist das Wohnzimmer. ... Das ist das Schlafzimmer von meiner Mutter und meinem Vater, also von meinen Eltern. ... Das ist das Badezimmer, ... und das ist mein Zimmer. ... Das hier ist das Zimmer von meinem Bruder, ... und das ist das Zimmer von meiner Schwester. ... Die Toilette ... und dann das Eßzimmer. ... Das ist die Küche, ... und das ist der Keller. Das war's.

Solution:

2 das Wohnzimmer **10** das Schlafzimmer von meinen Eltern **3** das Badezimmer **4** mein Zimmer
9 das Zimmer von meinem Bruder **8** das Zimmer von meiner Schwester **6** die Toilette **7** das Eßzimmer
1 die Küche **5** der Keller.

Consolidate the students' grasp of the new vocabulary by asking them to point quickly to the rooms you name, or to call out the number you have assigned to them on the board/OHP or on the copymaster.

Teacher: *Jetzt bin ich dran. Zeigt auf die Zimmer in meinem Haus. Wo ist die Küche?*

Hand the activity over to the students as soon as they are ready.

Partnerarbeit

Listening
Speaking
Reading

Ask the students first to draw a plan of their own home, or copy the version in the students' book, or copy one that you draw on the board/OHP — and then to decide which room is which. They can then play a guessing game with their partners, taking it in turns to say what they think the rooms are on their partner's plan. Use your own plan to demonstrate, and write up some cues for support. For example: *Ist das die Küche? Ist das dein Zimmer? Ist das das Schlafzimmer von deiner Schwester/deinen Eltern?*

Teacher: *Partnerarbeit. Wie ist euer Haus/eure Wohnung? Zeichnet einen Plan, und stellt einander Fragen. Zum Beispiel, das hier ist mein Plan. Beantwortet meine Fragen.* (Point to the model dialogue in the book, and then to a room. Ask one student:) *Was ist das?*

Student (pointing): *Die Toilette?*

Teacher: *Nein, das ist das Badezimmer*, etc.

Finally, tell them they can label the rooms, using ***Das ist das Wohnzimmer*** on page 38 of the students' book or the ***Tip des Tages*** on page 39.

IT suggestion

Students could also draw and label a plan of their own home using a graphics package.

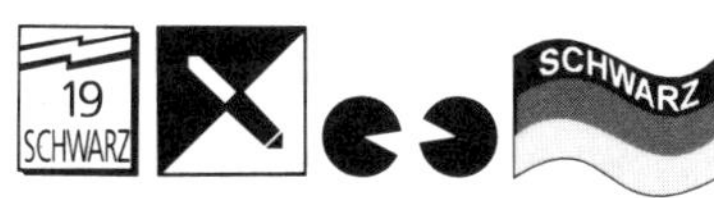

Was für Zimmer habt ihr?

Listening Speaking Reading

An information-gap activity in which students must exchange details of a number of different homes they have on their sheets. Cut the worksheet in half, and give part A to one partner and part B to the other. Ask them to work together in order to find out the different locations of the houses and flats, and the number and types of rooms in each one. Work through the first example with one pair, and write the answers on the board/OHP.

Teacher: *Jetzt Partnerarbeit.* (To Partner A:) *Stell die Frage Nummer 1.* (Point to question 1.)

Partner A: *Wo wohnst du?*

Partner B: *Ich wohne in Köln.*

Teacher (to A)**:** *Du schreibst hier:* (pointing to appropriate space on sheet) *B Köln.*

Repeat the formula for questions 2 to 5, if necessary, and then tell the students to continue in their pairs and to make a note of all the details. When the students have finished, collate the information on the board in words or in symbols. For example:

A Appen — Dorf — am Marktplatz — Reihenhaus — 2 Schlafzimmer, 1 Badezimmer, Küche, Wohnzimmer.

B Köln — Stadt — am Stadtrand — Wohnung — 3 Schlafzimmer, Badezimmer, Küche, Wohnzimmer, Eßzimmer.

C ...

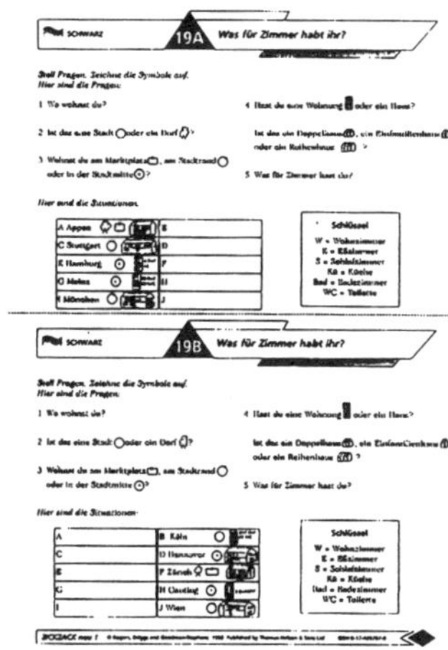

Krabbi

Listening Speaking Reading

A poem intended primarily for enjoyment and consolidation of some of the vocabulary relating to the rooms of a house. Play the cassette and ask the students to read the poem. Then find out how much they have understood by focusing on the adjectives following *zu*. Finally, as the poem is played through again, you could use mime and gesture to bring out the malevolent guile of the hermit crab.

Teacher: *Lest den Text und hört zu. ... was heißt ‚zu alt und zu kalt und zu groß'? Toll! ‚Zu' heißt* 'too'. *Was will diese Krabbe? Hört nochmal zu.*

Krabbi

— Morgen, Krabbi. Was ist los?
— Mein Haus ist zu alt und zu kalt und zu groß.
Dein Haus ist viel besser. Ich möchte so gern
Ein Reihenhaus haben, so klein und modern.
— Sag mal, was für Zimmer hat es, dein Haus?
Ich möchte sie sehen. Komm doch heraus!

Students might like to make their own recordings of the poem and a large illustration for display, to accompany it.

Zu verkaufen

Reading

A matching activity with a humorous slant on different types of accommodation. Ask the students to identify which 'For Sale' notice best fits which picture.

Teacher: *Seht euch die Bilder und die Schilder an. Welches Schild paßt zu welchem Bild?*

Solution: **1** B **2** C **3** D **4** A

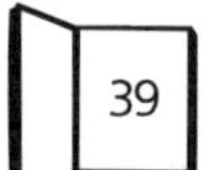

Mein Traumhaus

Listening Speaking Reading Writing

Two teenagers musing over their ideal home. Students can either choose one of the two and use his/her words to describe their own dream home, or they can make up their own description. Whichever they choose, there are plenty of possibilities for drawing (or using photographs, magazine cut-outs etc) and labelling.

Teacher: *Lest den Text. Zwei Teenager beschreiben ihr Traumhaus. Was ist euer Traumhaus? (Zeichnet es und) beschreibt es. Wieviel Zimmer? Wo? Sehr groß oder sehr klein?*

Some students may wish to describe the dream homes of other people (real or fictitious), animals or cartoon characters.

IT suggestion

The ideas for a *Traumhaus* could be word-processed and made into a display — or students could draw an impressionistic view of their ideal home (or cut out a picture of a perfect home) and label it.

Students may now attempt the *Lernziel 2* activities in the *Selbstbedienung section* on pages 42 and 43 of the students' book. See page 61 of this book for more details.

Meine Adresse

Listening Speaking Reading Writing

Revise the numbers 0–20 using a variety of games, such as counting around the class, counting in twos or threes, or providing the next number in a series (*zehn, elf* ...). Point out the use of *zwo* as an alternative to *zwei* for telephone numbers. Teach the numbers 21–100. Begin by introducing the tens (*zehn, zwanzig* etc.). Write various numbers on the board, and ask two students to come to the front of the class and point to each number you say. For further consolidation, you can use any of the numbers activities described on pages 9–10 of the Introduction.

Then ask the students to look at the address book on page 40 and to listen to the recording. Practise the question forms *Wo wohnt ... ? Wie ist die Telefonnummer?* and the replies. The digits may be given singly or in groups of two. For example, you can say 65577 as *sechs–fünf–fünf–sieben–sieben*, or as *sechs–fünfundfünfzig–siebenundsiebzig.*

Teacher: *Seht euch die Adressen und Telefonnummern an. Hört jetzt gut zu! Wer spricht?* (Do number 1 as an example.)

Meine Adresse

1 — Ich heiße Barbara Kulpe. Ich wohne in Halstenbek. Meine Adresse ist Papenmoorweg 29, und meine Telefonnummer ist 45917.

2 — Ich heiße Sigrid Blömeke. Ich wohne in Pinneberg. Meine Adresse ist Jappopweide 4, und meine Telefonnummer ist 65577.

3 — Ich heiße Maria Feyerabend. Ich wohne in Moorrege. Meine Adresse ist Klinkerstraße 88, und meine Telefonnummer ist 81273.

4 — Ich heiße Bernd Goerke. Ich wohne in Norderstedt. Meine Adresse ist Am Stadtpark 4, und meine Telefonnummer ist 27040.

5 — Ich heiße Elke Hauschildt. Ich wohne in Klein Nordende. Meine Adresse ist Am Redder 22. Meine Telefonnummer ist 94968.

6 — Ich heiße Hans-Heinrich Möller. Ich wohne in Uetersen. Meine Adresse ist Heidweg 32, und meine Telefonnummer ist 43214.

7 — Ich heiße Jürgen Meyer. Ich wohne in Itzehoe. Meine Adresse ist Geschwister-Scholl-Allee 96, und meine Telefonnummer ist 64446.

8 — Ich heiße Annalies Lakaw-Dörsel. Ich wohne in Quickborn. Meine Adresse ist Rotdornweg 39, und meine Telefonnummer ist 69231.

Solution:

1 Barbara **2** Sigrid **3** Maria **4** Bernd **5** Elke **6** Hans-Heinrich **7** Jürgen **8** Annalies

Follow this up by asking the students to work in pairs: partner A gives his/her own details and partner B notes them down.

This could also be extended into a communicative activity for the whole class: ask the students to note down the details of as many other students as possible within a given deadline.

IT suggestion

Names, addresses and phone numbers of classmates could be put together on a database.

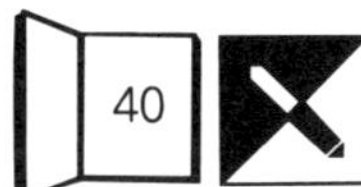

Wie sind die Adressen?

Listening
Speaking
Reading
Writing

Addressed envelopes showing also the reverse side, on which is written the sender's name and address (*Absender*, often abbreviated to *Abs.*). Ask the students to read the details and then to choose someone from the diary entries to address an envelope to. Write up on the board/OHP the surnames from the ***Meine Adresse*** tapescript. Make sure that the students realise they must put their own details under *Absender* on the 'reverse' of their envelope.

Teacher: *Seht euch die Umschläge vorne und hinten an — wie sind die Adressen? Barbara schreibt einen Brief an Elke. Wie heißt ‚Absender' hier? ... Richtig. Wählt jetzt eine Person, und schreibt die passende Adresse vorne auf den Umschlag. Hier sind die Familiennamen ...* (Write them up.) *Vergeßt nicht, hinten eure Adresse draufzuschreiben — ihr seid der Absender.*

If necessary, explain that by convention German addresses are written differently from English ones: the house number comes after the street name, not before; the town name is underlined and follows the postcode. Tell the students that each German town and village has its own numerical postcode. If you wish, you could practise the codes as follows:

Teacher: *Die Postleitzahl von Quickborn ist zwei–fünf–vier–fünf–eins. Wie heißt ‚Postleitzahl' auf englisch? Was ist die Postleitzahl von Moorrege?*

German postcodes were all changed in 1993 to include the five new *Länder.*

Partnerarbeit. Wer bin ich?

Listening
Speaking
Reading

A game to practise giving and understanding telephone numbers. Ask the students to choose to be one of the people in the address book and to write down the corresponding telephone number. They then take it in turns to exchange the information without pausing. When they have written out the details they have to 'race' to be the first to say who their partner is.

Teacher: *Wählt eine Telefonnummer und schreibt sie auf. Stellt und beantwortet die Frage und findet heraus, wer euer/eure Partner/in ist! Ihr habt nur 10 Sekunden.*

(Perform a model dialogue with a student:)

Teacher: *Wie ist deine Telefonnummer?*

Student: *Vier–fünf–neun–eins–sieben. Und deine Telefonnummer?*

Teacher: *Zwei–sieben–null–vier–null ...*

Teacher: *Du bist Barbara!*

Student: *Du bist Bernd!*

Computerliste

Listening
Speaking
Reading

Ask the students to look at the computer printout and listen to the tape to spot the three mistakes Elsa has made when typing the data in.

Teacher: *Lest den Text ‚Computerliste'. Hört gut zu! Was sind die drei Tippfehler von Elsa?*

Computerliste

1 **Elsa:** Schau mal, Anne. Stimmt das alles?
Anne: Nein. Anne schreibt man mit ‚E', nicht mit ‚A'.
Elsa: Du, Entschuldigung ... A–N–N–E. Anne. Ist sonst alles in Ordnung?
Anne: Ja, meine Telefonnummer stimmt.
Elsa: Danke, Anne.

2 **Elsa:** Ist hier alles richtig, Peter?
Peter: Warte mal ... Feldstraße 1, das stimmt. Und die Telefonnummer: vier–acht–acht–acht: ja, in Ordnung.

3 **Elsa:** Na, Klaus. Stimmt das alles?
Klaus: Moment mal ... Vorname Klaus, stimmt, ... Adresse ... ja, die Straße ist richtig, aber die Nummer ist falsch.
Elsa: Wie ist die Nummer denn?
Klaus: Ich wohne in der Poststraße 32.

4 **Elsa:** Du, Barbara. Ist das hier alles richtig?
Barbara: Moment. Ich schau' mir das mal an: Vorname, richtig ... Adresse, Telefonnummer, alles richtig. Ja, ich glaube, das stimmt!
Elsa: Toll!

5 **Elsa:** Ist das richtig, Monika?
Monika: Ja, ich glaube schon. Zum Sportplatz 7, ja.
Elsa: Und die Telefonnummer?
Monika: Ach nein, die ist falsch.
Elsa: Wie ist deine Telefonnummer?
Monika: Drei–drei–zwei–null–vier ... nicht eins.
Elsa: Klar. Drei–drei–zwei–null–vier.

Solution:
1 Anne **2** Poststraße 32 **3** 33204

IT suggestion

You could change some details on your database of class names and addresses, run off some copies, and get the students to point out the mistakes using phrases like *Das hier ist falsch*, *Das stimmt nicht*, *Allison schreibt man mit zwei l* etc.

Alter Mann

Listening
Speaking
Reading

Play the song to the class and ask the students to sing it line by line, either together or in groups. A final stage could be to let students perform it in their own style and make their own recording.

Alter Mann

In der Stadtmitte steht ein alter Mann,
Sechzig oder siebzig Jahre alt.
Keine Adresse, er steht, wo er kann,
Im Winter auf der Straße ist es kalt.

Und niemand weiß,
Wie der Alte heißt,
Das ist eine Frage, die niemand stellt.
Hat er Geschwister?
Hat er einen Freund?
Ist er ganz alleine auf der Welt?

In der Stadtmitte steht ein alter Mann,
Alte Schuhe und ein alter Hut.
Keine Adresse, er wohnt, wo er kann,
Doch im Sommer ist das Wetter gut.

Und niemand weiß,
Wie der Alte heißt,
Das ist eine Frage, die niemand stellt.
Hat er Geschwister?
Hat er einen Freund?
Ist er ganz alleine auf der Welt?

In der Stadtmitte steht ein alter Mann,
Er ist nicht mehr so aufrecht, wie er war.
Keine Adresse, er schläft, wo er kann,
Eines Tages ist er nicht mehr da.

Und niemand weiß,
Wie der Alte heißt,
Das ist eine Frage, die niemand stellt.
Hat er Geschwister?
Hat er einen Freund?
Ist er ganz alleine auf der Welt?

Students may now attempt the *Lernziel 3* activities in the *Selbstbedienung* section on pages 42 and 43 of the students' book. See page 61 of this book for more details.

Selbstbedienung

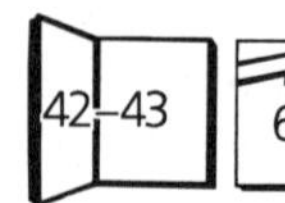

Lernziel 1

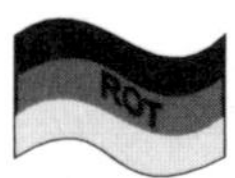

Meine Familie

A letter describing where Anne and the various members of her family live. Students must match the information to symbols.

Solution: **1** Anne und ihre Mutter **2** Annes Großeltern **3** Sonja **4** Annes Vater **5** Ulrike

Lernziel 2

Welches Zimmer ist das?

Photographs of rooms in a house/flat at unusual angles.

Solution: **1** die Küche **2** das Schlafzimmer **3** das Wohnzimmer **4** das Badezimmer **5** das Eßzimmer **6** der Keller.

Der Immobilienmarkt

A matching exercise based on house and flat advertisements.

Solution: **A** 8 **B** 3 **C** 2 **D** 4 **E** 5 **F** 1

Lernziel 3

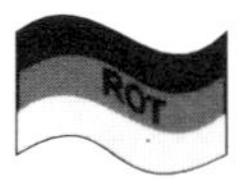

Wie bitte?

Questions and answers jumbled.

Solution:

Wie ist deine Telefonnummer? Sieben–null–acht–drei–fünf.
Wie heißt du? Martina Feyerabend.
Wohnst du am Stadtrand? Nein — in der Stadtmitte.
Wie alt bist du? Siebzehn.
Wo wohnst du? In einem Dorf, am Marktplatz.
Was ist das? Mein Zimmer.
Wie ist deine Adresse? Leipziger Straße 19.
Wohnst du in einem Reihenhaus? Nein, wir haben eine Wohnung.
Wie ist dein Haus? Ziemlich klein.

Students then think of questions and answers of their own.

Komm zu uns!

Five questions relating to two letters which contain some unknown vocabulary. Students are then invited to write a similar letter about their own home.

Solution: **1** Werner **2** Bettina **3** Bettina **4** Groß und alt **5** Groß **6** Auf der Couch **7** Auf der Couch.

Bildvokabeln

Im Haus

Reading
Writing

The illustration is not intended for detailed exploitation, but provides students with the opportunity to expand their vocabulary. A version of the drawing in the students' book is provided on copymaster 20 for students to label and colour.

> Grammar exercise 7, on copymaster 73, is based on the material in this chapter.

> After completing work on this chapter, check whether any further reinforcement is appropriate from the video material, Activity Box cards and Assessment Support Pack tasks.

5 Mein Alltag

Main teaching points

Lernziel 1: Asking and telling the time

Grammar presented:
Interrogatives
Prepositions (*um, vor, nach, in*)

Vocabulary presented:
halb drei
Mittag
Mitternacht
Moskau
minus
Neu Delhi
plus
Rio de Janeiro
San Franzisko
eine Stunde
später
Tokio
ein Uhr
die Uhrzeiten
Viertel nach
viereinhalb Stunden
vor drei
die Weltkarte
wie spät ist es?
wieviel Uhr ist es?

Grammar revised: Numbers 1–30

Lernziel 2: Talking about daily routines

Grammar presented:
Separable verbs (*aufstehen, fernsehen*)
Reflexive verb (*sich waschen*)
Time expressions (*nachmittags, abends*)

Vocabulary presented:
der Alltag
anders
beginnt
beschreibt
ins Bett
damit
Hausaufgaben
ich esse
ich fange
ich frühstücke
ins Haus
nach Hause
der Katzenalltag
nachmittags
natürlich
ich schlafe
die Schule ist ...
aus
ich stehe ... auf
die Tagesroutine
ich treffe mich ...
mit Freunden
um sechs Uhr
der Unterricht
ich vergesse
ich verlasse
vervollständige
ich wache auf
ich wasche mich
ins Wohnzimmer

Grammar revised: First and third person singular present tense

Lernziel 3: Talking about dates and festivals, including birthdays

Grammar presented:
Ordinal numbers
Months of the year
Imperatives (singular)

Vocabulary presented:
der Anfang
April
die Auferstehung
August
am zehnten Januar
anonym
austreiben
der Beginn
das Bildkalender
böse Geister
bunt
chinesisch
christlich
das Datum (Daten)
Dezember
Diwali
dauert
das Ende
eigen
der/die erste
der Fastmonat
Februar
fehlt
feiern
der Feiertag
der Feierzug
das Ferienspiel
das Fest
die Geburt Christi
der Geburtstag
gefärbtes Ei
größte
Hanukka
der Heilige Geist
heilig
hinduistisch
die Jahreswende
Juli
Juni
jüdisch
das Kalender
die Kerze
das Lichtfest
der Liebhaber
Mai
März
die Menora
malen
mohammedanisch
müde
das Neujahr
nichts Besonderes
November
Oktober
das Osterei
das Osterfest
der Osterhase
Ostern
der Papst
eine Party
der Pfingsten
Ramadan
das Straßen-theaterstück
Sylvester
schicken
um ... zu
der Valentinstag
Weihnachten
das Weihnachts-geschenk
das Weihnachtslied
ich weiß
zündet ... an
der/die zweite

Before beginning work on this chapter, check where the video material, Activity Box cards and Assessment Support Pack tasks will be most appropriate.

Die Uhrzeit

Listening
Speaking
Reading
Presentation

Make an OHP transparency or an enlarged cardboard version of copymaster 21. Cut out the hands of the clock and fix them with a split-pin. This can be used throughout the course for presentation and revision of the times. Initially teach the hours only, and play a number of games to practise and consolidate both question *and* answer:

1 Guessing game: conceal the clock face and ask the students to guess the time. Encourage students to take over your role as soon as they are confident.

Teacher: *Wie spät ist es?*

Student: *Es ist ein Uhr/zwei Uhr*, etc.

Teacher: *Ja, es ist ein Uhr.*

2 Mime: act out daily routine activities (such as getting dressed) and ask the students to say what time they would do them.

3 Sequences: Ask the students to add an hour to each time shown on the clock face.

Teacher: *Wie spät ist es in einer Stunde?* (Demonstrate.)

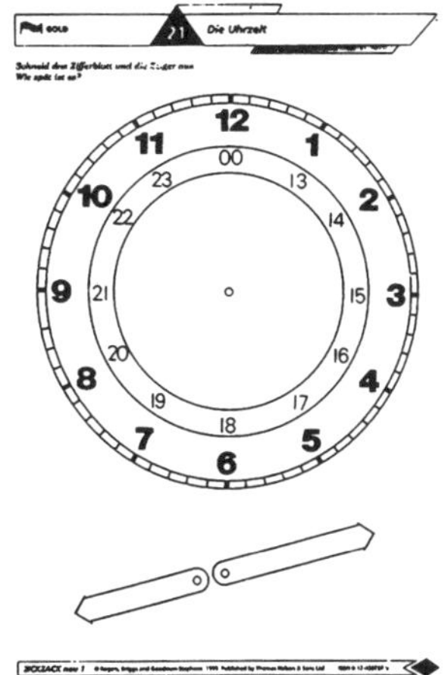

Es ist ein Uhr

Listening
Speaking
Reading

Now ask the students to look at the large clock in the students' book and talk them through the times on the hour again, including *Mittag* and *Mitternacht*. Point out also the alternative question form *Wieviel Uhr ist es?*

Teacher: *Seht euch die große Uhr an, hört gut zu und wiederholt. Wie spät ist es? Es ist ein/zwei/drei Uhr*, etc.

Then play the recording; students must identify what time (which hour) it is in each case.

Es ist ein Uhr

1 — Wie spät ist es?
— Es ist ein Uhr.
— Danke.

2 — Wie spät ist es, bitte?
— Es ist fünf Uhr.

3 — Wieviel Uhr ist es?
— Es ist neun Uhr.

4 — Wie spät ist es, bitte?
— Es ist Mittag.
— Danke.

5 — Wieviel Uhr ist es, bitte?
— Es ist drei Uhr.
— Vielen Dank.

6 — Wieviel Uhr ist es?
— Es ist Mitternacht.

Solution:

1 1.00 **2** 5.00 **3** 9.00 **4** 12.00 noon **5** 3.00 **6** 12.00 midnight

Partnerarbeit. Zeig auf die Uhr

Listening
Speaking
Reading

Use the clocks arranged in sequence around the hour to teach all other times.
Stress the use of *nach* for times past the hour until you are halfway to the next hour — at which point explain the expression *halb drei* etc. Thereafter emphasise the use of *vor* for times leading up to the next hour. Point

out also the usage *Viertel nach/vor eins*, and contrast this with *ein Uhr*.

Teacher: *Seht euch die Uhren an. Wie spät ist es? Oder: wieviel Uhr ist es?*
(Point to five past two:) *Ist es zwei Uhr? Nein — wieviel Minuten nach zwei?*

Student: *Fünf.*

Teacher: *Prima. Fünf nach zwei. Und jetzt ... wieviel Uhr ist es? Zehn nach ... ?*
(For half past:) *Guckt mal. Es ist nicht mehr ‚nach zwei', es ist bald drei Uhr ... es ist halb drei. Dann zwanzig vor drei ...*

Once students are confident you can ask them to work in pairs, playing various games to consolidate, such as *Zeig auf die Uhr*, in which one nominates a time and the other points to it, and *Ich denke mir eine Uhrzeit aus*, in which one chooses a time and the other guesses it.

Zeitdomino

Listening
Speaking
Reading

A domino-matching activity to consolidate the times just introduced. The *Anfang* and *Ende* dominos should both be played first, and the others filled in from either end.

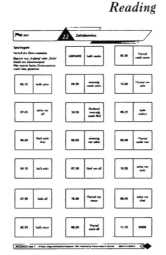

Teacher: *Partner-/Gruppenarbeit. Seht euch die Dominosteine an. Wie ist die richtige Reihenfolge? Ihr fangt mit ‚Anfang' an und endet mit ‚Ende'.* (Demonstrate on board/OHP.)

Entschuldigung. Wieviel Uhr ist es?

Listening
Speaking
Reading

A number of times for the students to identify from the digital timepieces in the students' book. Play the cassette, and ask the students to note the times in order or to write down the corresponding letters.

Teacher: *Seht euch die Uhren an und schreibt die passenden Buchstaben/die Uhrzeiten. Zum Beispiel:* (complete number 1).

Entschuldigung. Wieviel Uhr ist es?

1 — Entschuldigung. Wieviel Uhr ist es, bitte?
— Es ist ... halb zehn.
— Vielen Dank.
— Bitte.

2 — He, Birgit, wieviel Uhr ist es?
— Es ist ... neun Uhr.
— Neun Uhr schon?

3 — Entschuldigen Sie, bitte.
— Ja?
— Wie spät ist es?
— Drei Uhr.
— Drei Uhr? Danke schön.
— Bitte.

4 — Wann kommt Martin morgen an?
— Um Viertel nach zwölf. Kommst du mit?
— Viertel nach zwölf? Ja gut, dann komm' ich.

5 — Wieviel Uhr ist es?
— Zwanzig nach neun.

6 — Wie spät ist es, Katrin?
— Fünf nach acht.
— Fünf nach acht schon! Ich bin hungrig.

7 — Wann ist Musikbox, Ralf?
— Um Viertel vor sieben.
— Ach ja, natürlich.

8 — Komm, Werner. Es ist schon sieben Uhr.
— Ja, Mutti.
— Also komm schon! Du mußt in die Schule.

Solution:

1 G (9.30) **2** C (9.00) **3** E (3.00) **4** B (12.15)
5 H (9.20) **6** A (8.05) **7** F (6.45) **8** D (7.00)

Partnerarbeit. Zehn Minuten später

Listening
Speaking
Reading

A follow-up activity based on ***Entschuldigung. Wieviel Uhr ist es?*** Tell the students they must take it in turns to nominate one of the times shown on the page and ask their partner what time it will be in ten minutes. Perform a model dialogue to illustrate, and write up the answers.

Teacher: *Partnerarbeit. Wählt eine Uhrzeit hier:* (point to the times) ... *und stellt einander die Frage: ‚Wie spät ist es in zehn Minuten?' Zum Beispiel:* (follow the example given in the students' book).

Was zeigt deine Uhr?

Listening
Speaking
Reading

Over a number of lessons, consolidate the students' grasp of the times by asking them occasionally what the time really is. You could introduce the variant *Was zeigt deine Uhr?* and write it up for reference purposes.

Teacher: *Du Helen. Wie spät ist es? Was zeigt deine Uhr?*

Student: *Fünf nach zehn.*

Teacher: *Danke.*

Partnerarbeit. Wie spät ist es in New York?

Listening
Speaking
Reading
Writing

Using the information given about time zones, the students have to work out what time it is in various parts of the world when it is a particular time in Germany. Depending upon the class, this can be done as a spoken or a written activity — or both. Times are intentionally given in the 12-hour format at this stage.

Teacher: *Seht euch die Weltkarte an. In Bonn ist es zwölf Uhr. Aber in London ist es minus eine Stunde, also es ist elf Uhr. Wie spät ist es in Moskau?*

Student: *Drei Uhr.*

Teacher: *Ja, prima.*

Follow this up by asking the students to continue in pairs, either using the model dialogue and the time given (i.e. 12 o'clock in Germany) or, once they are confident, choosing a new 'starting time' for Germany.

Solution (for times from 12 o'clock in Germany):
San Franzisko = drei Uhr, New York =sechs Uhr, Rio de Janeiro = acht Uhr, London = elf Uhr, Moskau = drei Uhr, Neu Delhi = halb fünf, Tokio = halb acht, Adelaide = halb neun, Wellington = elf Uhr.

Wann beginnt der Film?

Listening
Speaking

A more demanding activity containing times embedded in a variety of unfamiliar contexts and providing practice in scanning for detail. Ask students to listen to the conversations and write down the time that is mentioned in each. The activity can be made more straightforward, if you provide a menu on the board/OHP of the times mentioned. You may also decide it is not necessary to use all of the examples on the cassette.

Teacher: *Hört gut zu. Schreibt die Uhrzeiten auf. Zum Beispiel:* (complete number 1).

Wann beginnt der Film?

1 — He, Else, wann beginnt der Film?
— Zehn nach sieben.
— Oh, dann müssen wir aber jetzt gehen.

2 — Wann haben wir heute Deutsch?
— Um Viertel vor neun. Nach der Pause. Wieso?
— Meine Schulaufgaben sind noch nicht ganz fertig.

3 — Tag, Anja! Heute kommt deine Brieffreundin, nicht?
— Ja, sie kommt um halb vier an.
— Hoffentlich ist sie nett!
— Naja, hoffen wir.

4 — Pst! Dieter. Wie spät ist es?
— Fünf vor elf.
— Na, Dieter, was ist?
— Nichts, Herr Fuhrmann.

5 — Christine, gehen wir heute zusammen nach Hause?
— Nee, heute ist die Schule für mich um Viertel nach zwölf aus.
— Oh, OK. Dann morgen, vielleicht?

6 — Komm doch! Es ist fünfundzwanzig nach sechs. Wir kommen zu spät an.
— Ach, was. Wir haben noch Zeit. Ich trinke noch eine Tasse Kaffee.

7 — Brr! Mir ist kalt.
— Mir auch. Wann kommt der Bus?
— Um zwölf Minuten vor neun.
— Noch sechs Minuten, also! Mensch! Es ist aber kalt!

8 (*Zeitansage*)
— Beim nächsten Ton ist es acht Uhr, zehn Minuten und zwanzig Sekunden.

9 — Oh, ich bin müde. Ich glaub', ich gehe ins Bett.
— Aber es ist doch noch früh!
— Ich weiß. Aber morgen steh' ich um halb sechs auf.
— Naja. Also, schlaf gut.
— Ja, danke. Gute Nacht.

10 — Was machen wir morgen?
— Ähm ... morgen früh gehen wir in die Schule, nicht?

— Ach ja, natürlich. Auch samstags ist bei euch Schule.
— Aber nur bis zwanzig nach elf. Dann ist Mittagessen.

Solution:

1 7.10 **2** 8.45 **3** 3.30 **4** 10.55 **5** 12.15 **6** 6.25 **7** 8.48 **8** 8.10 and 20 seconds **9** 5.30 **10** 11.20

Students may now attempt the *Lernziel 1* activities in the *Selbstbedienung* section on page 52 of the students' book. See pages 71–72 of this book for more details.

Martina beschreibt ihren Alltag

Listening
Speaking
Reading
Presentation

Presentation of the language needed to describe daily routines. Begin by describing your own daily routine, using mime where appropriate.

Teacher: *Meine Tagesroutine. Ich stehe um sieben Uhr auf. Ich wasche mich um. ...*

Make sure the students have the opportunity to repeat the statements after you on a number of occasions. Then ask them to look at the pictures and text in the students' book and to listen to the cassette. They should identify at what time Martina does each activity.

Teacher: *Seht euch die Fotos an und hört gut zu. Nummer eins. Martina sagt: ‚Ich stehe auf!' Um wieviel Uhr?*

Martina beschreibt ihren Alltag

1 — Ich stehe um sechs Uhr auf.
2 — Ich wasche mich um Viertel nach sechs.
3 — Ich frühstücke um halb sieben.
4 — Ich verlasse das Haus um zehn nach sieben.
5 — Der Unterricht beginnt um halb acht.
6 — Die Schule ist um ein Uhr aus.
7 — Ich esse mein Mittagessen um Viertel vor zwei.
8 — Ich mache meine Hausaufgaben nachmittags von drei Uhr bis halb fünf.
9 — Ich treffe mich um fünf Uhr mit Freunden.
10 — Ich sehe um sieben Uhr fern.
11 — Ich esse mein Abendbrot um acht Uhr.
12 — Ich gehe um halb zehn ins Bett.

Solution:

1 6.00 **2** 6.15 **3** 6.30 **4** 7.10 **5** 7.30 **6** 1.00 **7** 1.45 **8** 3.00–4.30 **9** 5.00 **10** 7.00 **11** 8.00 **12** 9.30

Copymaster 23 can then be used in a variety of ways. Begin by using the visuals at the top of the sheet, cut up, to reinforce the language just taught. Make statements, and ask the students to pick the corresponding visuals:

Teacher: *Hört gut zu. Seht euch die Bilder an. ‚Ich frühstücke.' Welches Bild ist das?*
(Students show correct picture.) *Richtig.*

Then hand the activity over to the students. Working in pairs, they should use the visuals from the top half of the copymaster and match them to the sentences from the bottom half (also cut up), assembling the whole sequence in the correct order. Some students could then be asked to read out the whole sequence. Finally, for written consolidation, the visuals could be stuck into exercise books and labelled.

Teacher: *Partnerarbeit. Seht euch die Bilder und Texte an. Was paßt wozu?*

Presentation of language (word order)

Listening
Speaking
Reading

Write up familiar sentences into which you have incorporated expressions of time. This introduces the notion that the verb retains second position in the main clause. Ask the students to practise with you, incorporating time elements into the sentences. Number the elements, as shown below.

Teacher (write up and repeat):

Ich	*frühstücke*	*um sieben Uhr.*	
1	2	3	
Ich	*verlasse*	*das Haus*	*um Viertel nach sieben.*
1	2	3	4

Show what happens when you move the time element to the start of the sentence:

Um sieben Uhr	*frühstücke*	*ich.*
1	2	3

See if the students can deduce the rule after a few examples. Refer them to ***Auf einen Blick*** on page 55 and to the ***Grammatik: Überblick*** for further clarification. The following activity emphasises the rule and provides further practice.

Das Verb bleibt sitzen

Listening
Speaking
Reading
Writing

A grammar-focused activity to emphasise the point that the main verb in German sentences retains its position of second idea. Students could colour the verb cards in order to highlight the fact that the verb remains 'sitting' in the second position. There are enough items to make nine sentences.

Teacher: *Schneidet den Arbeitsbogen aus, und bildet Sätze. Zum Beispiel: ‚Ich frühstücke um sieben Uhr zwanzig', oder ‚Um sieben Uhr zwanzig frühstücke ich'. Paßt auf! Das Verb bleibt sitzen!*

SCHWARZ 24 *Das Verb bleibt sitzen*

Ich	Ich	ich	ich	
aus	Die Schule	um halb eins	Dann	
stehe	esse	wasche	frühstücke	ist
sehe	mache	beginnt	um zwanzig vor acht	
meine Hausaufgaben	mich	fern	auf	
Um zwanzig nach sieben	ich	Um acht Uhr		
nachmittags	Um zehn nach sieben	Der Unterricht		
Um sieben Uhr	aus dem Haus	um halb zehn		
Ich	ich	gehe	um ein Uhr	

Und du?

Speaking
Writing

Once students are confident in their use of inversion, refer them back to ***Martina beschreibt ihren Alltag*** and ask them to produce spoken and/or written statements about their own daily routines. Perform one or two model dialogues to illustrate, and write them up as necessary.

Teacher: *Und eure Routine? Was macht ihr normalerweise? Zum Beispiel ...*

Katzenalltag

Listening
Speaking
Reading

A poem about the routine of a cat. Ask the students to read the poem and then to try to reproduce their own version using the clocks alongside to include times. This use of times will oblige them to invert the verb and subject on occasions. Provide examples to illustrate, and/or ask questions which require the use of inversion.

Teacher: *Lest das Gedicht. Es geht um den Alltag von einer Katze.*

(For the version including times:) *Wann steht die Katze auf? Um wieviel Uhr? Was sagt sie? ‚Um ... stehe ich auf. Dann wasche ich mich um ... Uhr.' Wie geht das Gedicht weiter? Partnerarbeit. Schreibt das Gedicht anders.*

Brainstorm with the whole class, and write up students' suggestions. Accept both inverted and non-inverted forms, and be flexible over time/place word order.

IT suggestion

Students could produce their own poems using word-processing software, and these could be wall-mounted for display.

Students may now attempt the *Lernziel 2* activities in the *Selbstbedienung* section on pages 52–53 of the students' book. See page 72 of this book for more details.

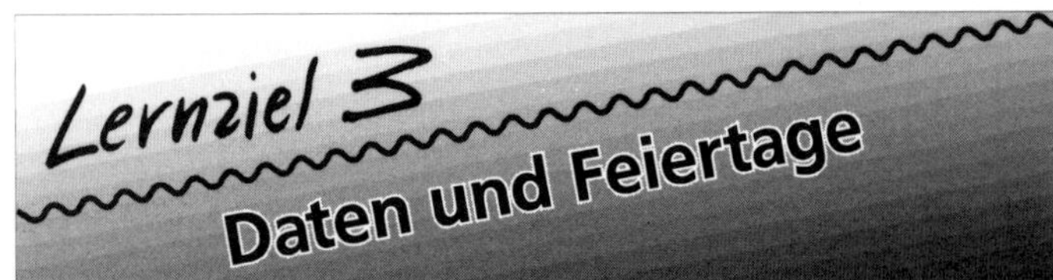

Presentation of language (days of the week)

Listening
Speaking

If you have not already done so, present the days of the week. Practise saying which day it is each time a class has a German lesson. The students could also write the day of the week alongside the date on their written work.

Teacher: *Welcher Tag ist heute? Montag? Dienstag? ... Wann habt ihr Deutsch? Am Mittwoch? Am Donnerstag?* etc.

Presentation of language (months of the year)

Listening
Speaking
Reading

Present the months of the year in groups of three, using both choral and individual repetition. Consolidate with a number of games and activities such as:

1 Von Januar bis Dezember

Rank-ordering of students according to their month of birth. Ask them to form a line beginning with *Januar* and ending with *Dezember*. They can simply say to each other their own month and rank themselves, or you could give them the model dialogue on the board/OHP, thus:

A: *Wann hast du Geburtstag?*

B: *Im Januar/Februar/März ...*

This activity can be repeated with the full birth dates once the students have learned to use ordinals.

2 Welcher Monat ist das?

Begin to spell out months and ask students to 'race' to be the first to say which it is. They can then continue in pairs or groups.

Teacher: *Hört zu (und hebt die Hand): Welcher Monat ist das? J–U– ...*

3 Ich denke mir einen Monat aus

Students take it in turns to choose a month and see how many guesses their partner needs to get it right. Demonstrate the activity first.

Teacher: *Ich denke mir einen Monat aus. Ich schreibe den Monat auf einen Zettel.* (Demonstrate.) *Was habe ich geschrieben? Juli? August?* etc.

4 Nicht alle zusammen!

A test of students' concentration. Ask them to form a circle of four or five and to try to name the months of the year in order from *Januar* to *Dezember*, one person speaking at a time. No specific order of speaking is prescribed. The task must be achieved without anyone speaking at the same time as anyone else. Any student can speak at any time, provided only one voice is ever heard saying the one correct month.

Teacher: *Gruppenarbeit. Ihr sagt Januar–Februar–März bis Dezember. Aber Vorsicht. Ihr sprecht nicht alle zusammen!* (Ask one group to try and do this. Start them off with *Januar*, then allow them to continue, but stop them as soon as two speak together.)

5 Wann hast du Geburtstag?

Now present and practise the question form *Wann hast du Geburtstag?* linked with the simple reply *im* + the month.

Teacher: *Wann hast du Geburtstag? Im Oktober? Im November? Im Juli?*

Continue this as a chain game round the class. As a follow-up, conduct a brief class survey, recording the results on the board/OHP.

Teacher: *Wer hat im Januar Geburtstag? Hebt die Hand.* (Write up *im Januar* and the number of students with their birthday in that month, etc.)

Presentation of language (ordinal numbers)

Listening
Speaking
Reading

Introduce ordinal numbers by talking about your own (real or fictitious!) birthday. Ask the students to guess the month first. Then tell them the date. Write up cardinal and ordinal numbers as follows, and ask the students to deduce the pattern, i.e. when *-sten* and *-ten* are used.

eins	*am ersten*
zwei	*am zweiten*
drei	*am dritten*
vier	*am vierten*
fünf	*am fünften*
sechs	*am sechsten*
sieben	*am siebten*
acht	*am achten*
...	...

...	...
neunzehn	*am neunzehnten*
zwanzig	*am zwanzigsten*
einundzwanzig	*am einundzwanzigsten*
dreißig	*am dreißigsten*

Teacher: *Wann habe ich Geburtstag? Im Januar? Nein ... ja, im Oktober. Aber wann im Oktober? Am ersten?* (Point to the numbers.) *Nein. Am zweiten? Nein. Am dritten auch nicht. Wann denn? ...*

Und ihr? Wann habt ihr Geburtstag? Am zehnten Juni? Am dritten März? Am einunddreißigsten Dezember? Wann schreibt man ‚-ten' und wann schreibt man ‚-sten'?

Ask a number of students when their birthday is. Then, in groups of four or five, ask them to continue in preparation for the following activity.

Teacher: *Gruppenarbeit. Stellt einander die Frage ‚Wann hast du Geburtstag?'.*

Wann hast du Geburtstag?

Listening
Speaking
Reading
Writing

A survey of birthdates in a class of German students. Tell the students they are going to hear ten young Germans saying when their birthdays are. Write the ten names on the board and ask the students to copy them down. Ask them to write the date of each person's birthday next to the name, using the same conventions as in the previous activity, including the shorthand numerical version if required.

Teacher: *Hört zu. Das ist eine Umfrage in der 7ten Klasse in der Realschule in Rellingen. Wie antworten diese zehn Teenager? Schreibt die Geburtstagsdaten auf.*
(Write up the ten names and complete the first one with the class.)

Wann hast du Geburtstag?

Sonja: Ich heiße Sonja. Ich habe am 3. August Geburtstag.

Bernd: Ich heiße Bernd. Ich habe am 11. Juli Geburtstag. Wann hast du Geburtstag, Murat?

Murat: Am 16. Mai.

Sabine: Mein Name ist Sabine. Ich habe am 30. September Geburtstag.

Miriam: Ich heiße Miriam, und ich habe am 7. April Geburtstag. Gerd, wann hast du Geburtstag?

Gerd: Am 24. September.

Jutta: Ich heiße Jutta. Ich habe am 17. Juni Geburtstag. Wann hast du Geburtstag, Kai?

Kai: Am 21. Januar.

Asla: Ich heiße Asla. Ich bin 14, und ich habe am 15. November Geburtstag. Wie heißt du?

Uwe: Uwe.

Asla: Und wann hast du Geburtstag?

Uwe: Am 29. Februar.

Asla: Also, einmal in vier Jahren!

Uwe: Ja.

Solution:
Sonja — am 3. August; Bernd — am 11. Juli; Murat — am 16. Mai; Sabine — am 30. September; Miriam — am 7. April; Gerd — am 24. September; Jutta — am 17. Juni; Kai — am 21. Januar; Asla — am 15. November; Uwe — am 29. Februar.

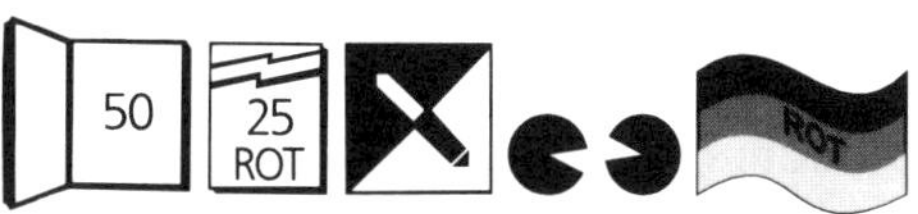

Partnerarbeit. Geburtstagsumfrage

Listening
Speaking
Writing
Reading

Follow up the previous activity by referring the students to the barchart on page 50 of the students' book, showing the birthdates by month of the members of class 7 in the Realschule in Rellingen.

Teacher: *Seht euch jetzt die Resultate der Umfrage in der Klasse 7 an. Wieviel Schüler haben im Januar Geburtstag? Und im Februar? Jetzt seid ihr dran.* (Hand over the activity as pairwork.)

Then ask the students to ask others in the class when their birthdays are, and to write in their names on the calendar on copymaster 25. Collate the results in barchart form on the board/OHP. Some students might like to produce a poster-sized version of the chart for display. The information could also be stored in a database.

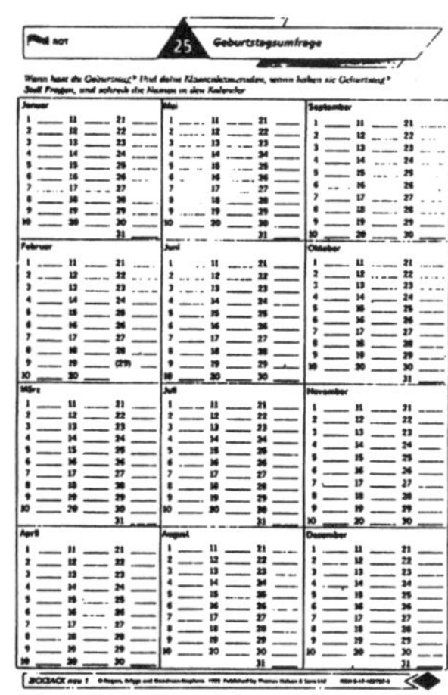

Teacher: *Stellt einander die Frage ‚Wann hast du Geburtstag?' Schreibt die Antworten so auf:* (point to the calendar). *In welchem Monat sind die meisten Geburtstage?*

IT suggestion

Having first assembled the information on a database (see above), students could then reproduce the results in graph format using a graphing package.

Wann ist es?

Listening
Speaking
Reading
Writing

Further dialogues in which dates are embedded. You may not feel it necessary to use all of them. Ask the students to say or write down the date mentioned each time. If they are writing their answers, explain the letter-writing convention of using the cardinal number plus a full stop, and ask them to do the same. Alternatively, the students can simply note both parts of the dates in numerical shorthand while listening to the cassette, e.g. 3.6. The dates could then be written in full afterwards.

Teacher: *Hört zu. Das sind Daten. Aber was für Daten? Zum Beispiel:* (complete the first one or two with the class). *Nummer eins: am 3. Juni/3.6* (write this up).

Wann ist es?

1 — Du, wann ist das Konzert in Köln?
— Am dritten Juni, nicht?
— Ja, ich glaube, das stimmt. Am dritten.

2 — Guck' mal, Alex. Am zwanzigsten November spielt Mönchengladbach in Hannover.
— Ja? Da möchte ich hin!

3 — Sag mal, wann ist Ostern dieses Jahr?
— Moment mal, ich schau' nach. Ostern ist ... am elften April.

4 — Welches Sternzeichen ist Andreas?
— Skorpion, glaub' ich.
— Nee, das kann's nicht sein. Skorpion beginnt am vierundzwanzigsten Oktober.

5 — Wann fährst du nach England?
— Wir fahren am einunddreißigsten März ab. In fünf Wochen.

6 — Hast du gehört? Am ersten Februar macht eine neue Disco in der Stadt auf.
— Ja? Wie heißt sie?
— Top Ten.

7 — Oh, schau' mal. Der neue Film von Werner Herzog.
— Wann kommt der?
— Am siebzehnten August im Metropolis-Kino. Toll, nicht?

8 — Esther, vergiß nicht, du mußt am vierzehnten Januar wieder ins Krankenhaus.
— Ja, ich weiß. Ach, dieser blöde Arm!

9 — Also, ihr lest bis zum Ende des Kapitels, und dann am zweiten Juli (also nächsten Donnerstag) schreiben wir eine Klassenarbeit. OK? Alles klar?
— Ja.

10 — Du, wann ist denn Jörgs Party?
— Am dreiundzwanzigsten, glaub' ich.
— September?
— Ja, klar.
— Ist das ein Sonnabend?
— Ich glaube schon.

Solution:

1 am 3. Juni **2** am 20. November **3** am 11. April
4 am 24. Oktober **5** am 31. März **6** am 1. Februar
7 am 17. August **8** am 14. Januar **9** am 2. Juli
10 am 23. September

Ein Geburtstag in der Familie

Listening
Speaking
Reading

Further practice listening to birth dates. This time the students hear a family of five saying when their birthdays are. They must list the dates alongside the names, then work out whose is the first birthday in the calendar year, whose is the second, and so on.

Teacher: *Hört zu. Das ist die Familie Bromma: Herr und Frau Bromma und ihre Kinder: Maria, Lutz und Steffi. Wann haben sie Geburtstag? Und wer ist der oder die erste im Jahr?*

Ein Geburtstag in der Familie

— Frau Bromma, wann haben Sie Geburtstag?
— Am neunundzwanzigsten Juli.
— Und Sie, Herr Bromma?
— Ich habe auch im Juli Geburtstag, aber am Anfang — am siebten.
— Steffi, wann hast du Geburtstag?
— Am dritten Mai.
— Und du, Lutz?

— Ich habe am zweiten März Geburtstag.
— Hast du auch im März Geburtstag, Maria?
— Nein, ich habe im Mai Geburtstag — wie meine Schwester.
— Wann denn?
— Am zwölften.

Solution (in calendar order): Lutz: am 2. März; Steffi: am 3. Mai; Maria: am 12. Mai; Herr Bromma: am 7. Juli; Frau Bromma: am 29. Juli.

Wann sind die Feiertage?

Listening Speaking Reading

Introduce the idea of celebrations by referring to *feiern* in terms of birthdays. Then ask the students to complete the reading activity on page 51 of the students' book. They simply have to read the information on annual festivals and significant dates, and — using the vocabulary at the end of the book — find out or work out which dates match which festivals.

Teacher: *Ich habe am ... Geburtstag. Für mich ist das ein Feiertag. Wie heißt ‚Feiertag' auf englisch? Hier sind noch ein paar Feiertage ... aber das ist alles durcheinander. Wann ist zum Beispiel Ostern? Und Sylvester? Schlagt im Wörterbuch nach, und findet die passenden Daten oder Monate heraus.*

Solution:

Valentinstag = am 14. Februar; Sylvester = am 31. Dezember; Weihnachten = am 25. Dezember; Ostern = Ende März/Anfang April; das chinesische Neujahr = Ende Januar/Anfang Februar; Neujahr = am 1. Januar; Hanukka (Jewish Festival of Light) = im Dezember; Diwali (Hindu festival from *dipavali* — row of lights) = Ende Oktober; Ramadan (Muslim festival) = Ende Februar/Anfang März; Pfingsten = im Mai.

Students could follow up the activity by producing their own poster versions, perhaps including their own significant calendar dates.

IT suggestion

Students might like to make a chart of all the special festivals they know, with dates, in German, and reproduce it on word-processing or desktop-publishing software. You will need to supply the German for unknown festivals or encourage the use of dictionaries.

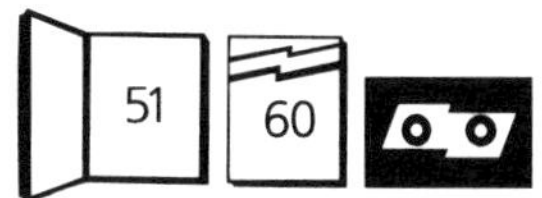

Steh auf!

Listening Speaking Reading

Play the song (to the tune of *London's Burning*) to the class, and ask the students to sing it line by line, either together or in groups. It can also be sung as a round. A final stage could be to let students perform it in their own style and make their own recording.

Steh auf!

Guten Morgen! Guten Morgen!
Steh auf! Steh auf!
Noch nicht! Noch nicht!
Ich bin müde! Ich bin müde!

Halb sieben! Halb sieben!
Mach schnell! Mach schnell!
Ach nein! Ach nein!
Ich bin müde! Ich bin müde!

Und die Schule? Und die Schule?
Halb acht! Halb acht!
Ich weiß! Ich weiß!
Ich bin müde! Ich bin müde!

Acht Uhr zwanzig! Acht Uhr zwanzig!
Zu spät! Zu spät!
Gut' Nacht! Gut' Nacht!
Ich bin müde! Ich bin müde!

Students may now attempt the *Lernziel 3* activities in the *Selbstbedienung* section on page 53 of the students' book. See page 72 of this book for more details.

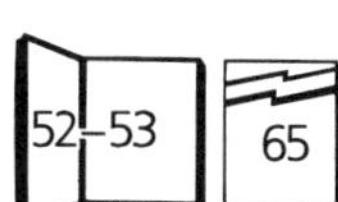

Lernziel 1

Wieviel Uhr ist es?

A series of times on digital clocks for students to copy out from the menu.

Solution:

1 Es ist fünfundzwanzig nach elf.
2 Es ist Viertel nach acht.
3 Es ist halb sieben.
4 Es ist zwanzig vor zehn.
5 Es ist Viertel vor neun.
6 Es ist Mittag.

Wo sind sie?

An activity on times based on the time zones shown on the world map on page 47 of the students' book.

Solution:

1 New York **2** Moskau **3** Rio de Janeiro **4** London
5 Tokio **6** San Franzisko

Lernziel 2

Füll die Lücken aus

Drawings showing someone's daily routine. Students must copy and complete the sentences.

Solution:

1 Ich stehe um 7 Uhr auf.
2 Dann frühstücke ich um halb acht.
3 Ich verlasse das Haus um zehn nach acht.
4 Die Schule ist um Viertel vor vier aus.
5 Um Viertel nach sieben sehe ich fern.
6 Ich gehe um halb elf ins Bett.

Evi Bamms Tagesroutine

Students must write sentences to describe the daily routine of rock star Evi Bamm.

Solution:

1 Sie steht um elf Uhr morgens auf.
2 Um Viertel vor zwölf frühstückt sie.
3 Um halb vier geht sie in die Stadt.
4 Um zehn Uhr arbeitet sie.
5 Um Mitternacht geht sie in die Disco.
6 Sie geht um halb drei ins Bett.

Lernziel 3

Wann denn?

Students must 'translate' the details of dates and times on posters into everyday spoken/written language.

Solution:

1 Evi Bamm — am Sonntag, dem vierzehnten November um acht Uhr abends.
2 Ede Funk auf Tournee — am Freitag, dem dreizehnten Februar um Viertel vor acht abends.
3 ROCK-JAZZ-CHANSON — am Samstag, dem dreißigsten März um neun Uhr abends.

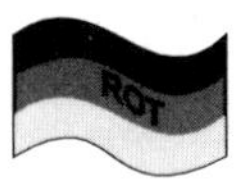

Was fehlt?

Gapped texts in simple arithmetical sequences. Students must work out the missing numbers.

Solution:

1 neunten, dreiundzwanzigsten **2** vierundzwanzigsten, einunddreißigsten **3** zwölften, sechsundzwanzigsten

Zum Lesen

Was machst du an deinem Geburtstag?

Speaking
Reading

Six teenagers talking about what they do on their birthday. It is not intended that all the vocabulary and structures should become active at this stage. The focus of this activity is on some cultural aspects and dictionary skills. Ask the students to read the statements and look at the drawings.

Teacher: *Seht euch die Bilder und Texte an. Schlagt die unbekannten Worte in der Wörterliste nach.* (Suggest some words that they might look up if required.) *Was machen diese Teenager an ihrem Geburtstag? Wer gibt eine Party? Und wer macht nichts Besonderes? Wie heißt das auf englisch?*

54

Und du?

Listening
Speaking
Reading

As a follow-up to the above activity, the students can identify which statement most clearly matches what they do on their birthday.

Teacher: *Und ihr? Was macht ihr? Stellt einander die Frage: ‚Was machst du an deinem Geburtstag?'.*

Grammar exercises 8–10, on copymasters 73 and 74, are based on the material covered in this chapter.

After completing work on this chapter, check whether any further reinforcement is appropriate from the video material, Activity Box cards and Assessment Support Pack tasks.

6 Wie schmeckt's?

Main teaching points

Lernziel 1: Talking about breakfast

Grammar presented: First, second and third person singular and third person plural present tense

Vocabulary presented:

der Apfelsaft	*Cornflakes*	*der Honig*	*lange*	*der Onkel*	*das Wasser*
der Athlet	*das Foto*	*ißt*	*liegt*	*die Scheibe*	
das Bett	*das Frühstück*	*der Joghurt*	*die Margarine*	*der Schinken*	
das Brot	*die Frühstücks-*	*der Kaffee*	*die Marmelade*	*die Statistik*	
die Butter	*palette*	*der Kakao*	*jede Menge*	*schmeckt's?*	
bei	*gar nichts*	*der Käse*	*die Milch*	*das Toast*	

Grammar revised: Third person singular and plural present tense

Lernziel 2: Talking about lunch and evening meal

Grammar presented: *gern*

Vocabulary presented:

das Abendessen	*die Frikadelle*	*der Knoblauch*	*der Paprika*	*die Pizzeria*	*die Wurst*
Bratkartoffel	*der Gulasch*	*das Mittagessen*	*die Pepperoni*	*Pommes frites*	*Zutaten*
bestellt	*gern*	*die Nudel*	*der Pilz*	*der Saft*	
Cola	*das Hähnchen*	*die Olive*	*das Pizza*	*die Salami*	

Grammar revised: Interrogatives

Lernziel 3: Talking about healthy eating

Grammar presented:
Infinitive constructions — *man sollte*

Vocabulary presented:

der Apfel	*der Fisch*	*die Kalorie*	*das Obst*	*die Schüssel*	*das Thema*
alles	*die Flasche*	*die Karotte*	*öfter*	*der Servierlöffel*	*der Tisch*
die Banane	*das Fleisch*	*der Käseteller*	*das Päckchen*	*das Steak*	*die Tischdecke*
der Becher	*frisch*	*der Keks*	*der Pfeffer*	*das Stück*	*die Tomatensuppe*
das Bier	*die Gabel*	*die Konfitüre*	*das Picknick*	*die Suppe*	*die Untertasse*
Bonbons	*das Gemüse*	*der Kuchen*	*die Portion*	*Süßigkeiten*	*unglücklich*
die Bratwurst	*das Getränk*	*der Löffel*	*pro Tag*	*schlecht*	*viel*
das Brett	*das Gummibärchen*	*lieber*	*der Salat*	*solange es schmeckt*	*der Wein*
Chips	*gebratener Fisch*	*die Mahlzeit*	*das Salz*	*solche Sachen*	*weniger*
die Erbse	*gegrillter Fisch*	*die Mayonnaise*	*Salzkartoffeln*	*sprechen über*	*der Zucker*
das Essen	*gesund*	*das Menü*	*die Schale*	*die Tasse*	*zwischen*
einfach	*der Hamburger*	*das Messer*	*die Schokolade*	*der Tee*	*zwischendurch*
das Fett	*ich tu's*	*die Nuß*	*der Schokoriegel*	*der Teller*	

Before beginning work on this chapter, check where the video material, Activity Box cards and Assessment Support Pack tasks will be most appropriate.

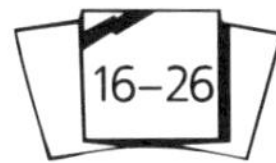

Presentation of language (breakfast food and drink)

Listening
Speaking

Using the flashcards, present the items of breakfast food and drink in groups of three or four. Make sure the students have the opportunity to repeat the words chorally and individually, and use some of the suggested games for consolidation (see Introduction, pages 8–9, 10–11).

Listening
Speaking
Reading

Was ißt man zum Frühstück?

This copymaster can be used in a variety of ways: as reinforcement or as a possible homework activity, especially for students with learning difficulties; as an OHP master providing an alternative way of presenting and practising breakfast items; or cut up into cards to play various word games.

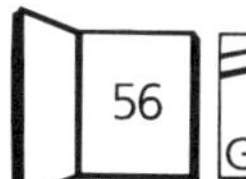

Das Frühstück bei der Familie Braun

Listening
Speaking
Reading

Dialogue based on a family at breakfast in Germany. Refer the students to the photos on page 56, and ask them to name the items of food and drink they can see. Tell them they are going to hear each member of the family saying what he or she is going to have for breakfast. Students can give their answers orally after each person has spoken, or if you prefer they can write their answers, using the information in ***Tip des Tages***. For a GOLD approach, use copymaster 26 and ask the students to write each person's name next to the items which he/she has for breakfast.

Teacher: *Seht euch die Fotos an. Das ist die Familie Braun. Sie frühstücken. Was gibt's zum Frühstück bei Brauns? Cornflakes, Müsli, Toast ... usw. Und was gibt's zu trinken? Tee, Milch ...*

Was ißt Renate? Und was trinkt sie?

GOLD: *Hört gut zu und schreibt die Namen in die richtigen Spalten auf. Zum Beispiel:* (complete the first example).

Das Frühstück bei der Familie Braun

— Guten Morgen, Renate. Was willst du zum Frühstück?
— Eine Scheibe Brot mit Honig ... und gib mir bitte die Milch.
— Ja, gerne. Bitte.
— Was ißt du denn, Papa?
— Müsli, Toast und Margarine. Gib mir bitte die Teekanne.
— Na, Mutti. Was nimmst du?
— Brot mit Käse.
— Und zu trinken?
— Kaffee natürlich!
— Morgen!
— Mach schnell, Peter. Es ist schon Viertel nach sieben.
— Ja, ich weiß.
— Was nimmst du?
— Hmmm ... Cornflakes.
— Und zu trinken? Tee oder Kaffee?
— Eine Tasse Kakao.

Solution:

	ißt	trinkt
Renate	Brot mit Honig	Milch
Herr Braun	Müsli, Toast mit Margarine	Tee
Frau Braun	Brot mit Käse	Kaffee
Peter	Cornflakes	Kakao

Die Frühstückspalette

Listening
Speaking
Reading
Writing

Seven young people saying when they have breakfast and what they eat and drink. Play the first dialogue and see how much the students understand. Recap on the basic questions *Was ißt du zum Frühstück?* and *Und was trinkst du?* Then refer the students to the text in their books. Play the dialogues again and then ask students to note what each person has. Mention could be made that tea in Germany tends to be served without milk unless otherwise specified. Write up two columns thus:

	ißt	trinkt
Silvia		
Bernd		
... etc		

Take the students through the first example.

Teacher: *Hört gut zu! Seht euch die Frühstückspalette an. Wer ißt was zum Frühstück? Zum Beispiel ... schreibt die Antworten so auf.*

Die Frühstückspalette

1 — Wie heißt du?
— Ich heiße Silvia.
— Wann ißt du dein Frühstück?
— Um sieben.
— Was ißt du zum Frühstück?
— Cornflakes mit Milch.
— Und was trinkst du?
— Kaffee mit Milch.

2 — Wie heißt du?
— Ich heiße Bernd.
— Wann ißt du dein Frühstück?
— Um Viertel nach sieben.
— Und was ißt du?
— Brot mit Marmelade.
— Und was trinkst du?
— Ein Glas Milch.

3 — Wie heißt du?
— Ich heiße Oliver.
— Um wieviel Uhr frühstückst du?
— Um halb acht.
— Was ißt du zum Frühstück?
— Ein Brötchen mit Nutella.
— Was trinkst du?
— Eine Tasse Tee.

4 — Guten Tag. Wie heißt du?
— Emine.
— Wann frühstückst du?
— Meistens um Viertel nach sieben.
— Was ißt du zum Frühstück?
— Eine halbe Scheibe Brot mit Honig.
— Und was trinkst du?
— Normalerweise eine Tasse Kakao.

5 — Wie heißt du?
— Michael.
— Um wieviel Uhr ißt du dein Frühstück?
— Um halb sieben.
— Was ißt du zum Frühstück?
— Toast mit Butter darauf und ein Ei.
— Und was trinkst du?
— Orangensaft.

6 — Wie heißt du?
— Ich heiße Udo.
— Um wieviel Uhr frühstückst du?
— Normalerweise um Viertel vor acht.
— Was ißt du zum Frühstück?
— Schwarzbrot, Käse und Wurst.
— Und was trinkst du?
— Kakao oder Milch.

7 — Wie heißt du?
— Ich heiße Petra.
— Wann frühstückst du?
— Um halb acht.
— Was ißt du zum Frühstück?
— Gar nichts.
— Was trinkst du?
— Eine Tasse Tee mit Milch.

Solution:

	ißt	trinkt
Silvia	**d** Cornflakes mit Milch	**f** Kaffee mit Milch
Bernd	**a** Brot mit Marmelade	**b** Milch
Oliver	**k** ein Brötchen mit Nutella	**g** Tee
Emine	**j** eine halbe Scheibe Brot mit Honig	**i** Kakao
Michael	**h** Toast mit Butter und ein Ei	**e** Orangensaft
Udo	**c** Schwarzbrot, Käse und Wurst	**i/b** Kakao oder Milch
Petra	gar nichts	**g** Tee mit Milch

As a SCHWARZ extension you could suggest that some students listen out for *when* the people have their breakfast as well as what they eat and drink.

Partnerarbeit

Speaking
Listening

Follow up ***Die Frühstückspalette*** using the pairwork activity suggested by the model dialogue in the students' book. Ask the students to take it in turns to choose something to eat and drink from the breakfasts illustrated, and to answer all their partner's questions by saying yes or no.

Teacher: *Partnerarbeit. Wählt ein Frühstück —also etwas zu essen und etwas zu trinken — und beantwortet alle Fragen mit ‚ja' oder ‚nein'. Zum Beispiel:* (perform a model dialogue with a student).

Eine Umfrage in einer Schule in Deutschland

Listening
Speaking
Reading

Tell the students that the two piecharts are the result of a survey of the breakfast habits of a German class. It might be interesting to point out that the students in class 6 would be about 12 years old. Read through the information with the students, and then ask them to complete the gapped sentences under the heading of *Statistik*.

Teacher: *Seht euch die Resultate einer Umfrage an. Diese Schüler aus Hamburg sind in der sechsten Klasse — das heißt, sie sind ungefähr 12 Jahre alt. Was essen sie und was trinken sie zum Frühstück? Vervollständigt die Sätze unter ‚Statistik'.*

Solution:

1 **a** 6 **b** 13 **c** 1 **d** 1 **e** 4

2 **a** Marmelade **b** ein gekochtes Ei **c** Margarine **d** Butter/Brötchen **e** Honig/Käse/Wurst/Quark

3 **a** Sieben Schüler trinken Kakao **b** Sechs Schüler trinken Milch **c** Sieben Schüler trinken Saft **d** Drei Schüler trinken Kaffee **e** Drei Schüler trinken Tee

Partnerarbeit. Zum Frühstück

Listening
Speaking
Reading
Writing

An information-gap activity based on a survey of breakfast habits of students in a school in Gütersloh. Divide the class into pairs, cut the worksheets up and give one half to each partner. Practise the structures first until the procedures are absolutely clear. Selected students could report back to the whole class, if desired.

Teacher (for the food chart): *Partnerarbeit. Ihr habt Informationen über Schüler und Schülerinnen in Gütersloh in Norddeutschland: was sie zum Frühstück essen. Aber jeder Partner hat Lücken:* (point to the gaps on the worksheets). *Zum Beispiel, Partner(in) A weiß nicht, wieviel Schüler Nutella essen.* (To a student with Partner B sheet:) *Wieviel Schüler essen Nutella?*

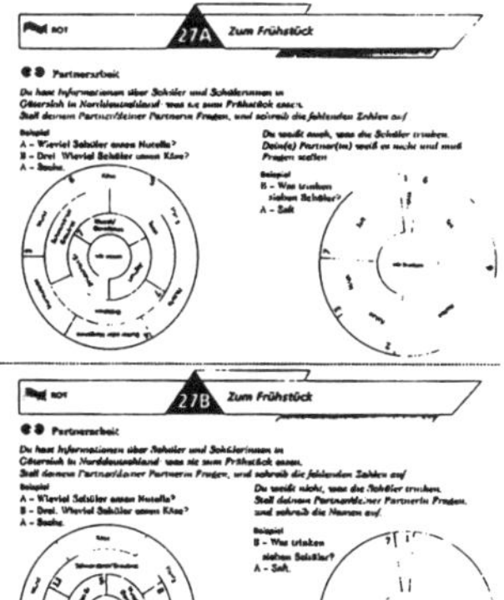

Student: *Drei.*

Teacher: *Danke. Ich schreibe ‚3' hier auf den Arbeitsbogen. Jetzt seid ihr dran. Stellt und beantwortet Fragen.*

Teacher (for the drinks chart): *Partner(in) A weiß, was die Schüler trinken. Partner(in) B muß es herausfinden. B stellt die Frage: ‚Was essen sieben Schüler?'* etc.

The students could follow up these activities by conducting their own class survey. Collate the findings on the board/OHP and ask the students to decide on the best means of recording the data. Possibilities include storing it in a database and/or producing barcharts or piecharts.

Teacher: *Jetzt seid ihr dran. Macht eine Umfrage in der Klasse. Was für Fragen stellt man?* (Collating results:) *Wieviel Schüler essen/trinken ... ? Was ist am populärsten als Frühstück?*

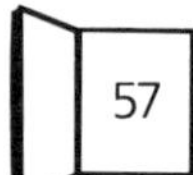

Frühstücksgedicht

Listening
Speaking
Reading
Writing

An amusing view in verse of the breakfast habits of a fictitious family. Students could recite and learn the poem by heart.

IT suggestion

Some students may be able to produce alternative versions on a word processor.

Frühstücksposter

Reading
Writing

As a final activity, provide the students with some German magazines and ask them to look for pictures, especially adverts, showing food and drink. A selection of these would make an attractive collage for classroom display, or for a project on German breakfast foods. You could also suggest that students collect labels from German produce either available in British supermarkets or brought back from trips to Germany.

Teacher: *Macht jetzt eine Frühstücks-Collage. Was ißt und trinkt man in Deutschland?*

Students may now attempt the *Lernziel 1* activities in the *Selbstbedienung* section on page 62 of the students' book. See page 82 of this book for more details.

Was ißt du gern zum Mittagessen?

Listening
Speaking
Reading

Tell the students that they are going to hear a recording of three teenagers talking about what they like eating and drinking for lunch. Write up the names of Sonja, Dorit and Dieter. Ask the students to listen carefully with their books closed, and to identify as many items as they can. The drinks should be well known, and some students will recognise *Nudeln* and *Pommes frites*. Encourage students to look up new words, such as *Frikadellen* and *Gulasch*, in the glossary. Consolidate by showing the students flashcards 27–38 after they have heard the cassette. They should then find it easy enough to match the speakers to the photos of the three meals mentioned.

Teacher: *Ihr hört jetzt ein Interview mit drei Teenagern: Sonja, Dorit und Dieter. Was essen sie gern? Was trinken sie gern? Welches Foto paßt?*

Was ißt du gern zum Mittagessen?

1 — Sonja, was ißt du gern zum Mittagessen?
— Gulasch mit Nudeln.
— Und was trinkst du gern?
— Milch oder Limonade.

2 — Und du, Dorit?
— Hähnchen mit Pommes frites.
— Und was trinkst du gern?
— Cola oder Saft.

3 — Dieter, was ißt du gern zum Mittagessen?
— Frikadellen mit Bratkartoffeln.
— Und was trinkst du?
— Nichts.

Partnerarbeit. Und du?

Reading
Listening
Speaking

Follow up the previous activity by first asking the students to read out the parts of the interviewer and interviewees. They could then begin to introduce variants when talking about some of the meals they like to have for lunch. Write up the details on a menu to enable students to see the possible combinations of the dishes mentioned in the interviews. You could also add some of the items that students have learned from the flashcards.

Teacher: *Jetzt Partnerarbeit. Spielt die Rollen vom Interviewer und von Sonja, Dorit oder Dieter. Könnt ihr auch andere Gerichte vorschlagen? Zum Beispiel: Hähnchen mit Nudeln, Frikadellen mit Pommes frites, Rindfleisch mit Bratkartoffeln und Tomaten.*

Some students could write out the names of their favourite dishes (and perhaps their ingredients) for display, using the glossary and/or dictionaries as appropriate.

Kantine Wochenplan

Reading

The students should look at the week's canteen menu and answer the questions. Explain to them the use of *Wann gibt es ... ?*

Solution:

1 am Mittwoch und am Freitag **2** am Donnerstag **3** am Montag und am Donnerstag **4** am Donnerstag **5** am Freitag

IT suggestion

As a follow-up, students might like to create a weekly menu for their school canteen and reproduce it using word-processing and desktop-publishing software. This could either be an ideal menu, or a German translation of the real menu obtained from the school kitchens!

Das Abendessen. Ein Interview mit der Klasse 6c

Listening
Speaking
Reading

The results — in the form of a barchart — of a further survey on eating habits amongst students in class 6c. Ask the students to study the barchart and see how much information they can draw from it.

Teacher: *Seht euch die Resultate des Interviews mit der 6ten Klasse an. Was für Informationen gibt es über die Schüler? Was essen und trinken sie am liebsten?*

Partnerarbeit

The follow-up pairwork activity provides a more structured approach to working out the information. Ask the students to take it in turns to ask and answer the questions listed. Bring out the point that most German families have their cooked meal at lunchtime and a cold snack in the evenings by asking the students:

Teacher: *Wann ißt man warm in Deutschland? (zum Frühstück? zum Mittagessen? zum Abendessen?) Ißt man abends kalt oder warm?*

Partnerarbeit. Stellt einander Fragen. Zum Beispiel: Wieviel Schüler in der Klasse essen Brot und Butter? Richtig — sechsundzwanzig. Jetzt seid ihr dran.

Once again, the students could conduct their own survey in class and choose how to record the results.

In der Pizzeria

Listening
Speaking
Reading
Writing

A problem-solving activity. Introduce *gern/ nicht gern* with foods, using simple examples and symbols (smiling/frowning faces, ticks and crosses, etc). Ask the students to work in groups, and give them a time limit in which to look up new vocabulary. Then ask them to use all the available clues to work out which pizza each person orders. The text on cassette is also reproduced in the students' book so that the students can have as much time as they need to solve the problem. Pause the cassette before the final order is made, to allow the students time to work out the answers. Students can also perform the dialogue themselves afterwards, perhaps with variants, to challenge their partners to work out which pizza they would choose.

Teacher: *Mmm, Pizza. Ich esse gern Pizza* (mime) ... *aber Pizza mit Oliven? Nein, ich esse nicht gern Oliven.* (Write up both *gern* and *nicht gern* + symbols ☺ ☹.) *Wie heißt auf englisch ‚Ich esse/trinke gern/nicht gern'?*

Gruppenarbeit. Lest den Text. Schlagt die unbekannten Wörter in der Wörterliste nach. Ihr habt zwei Minuten. Hört zu (und lest den Text wieder). Die Familie Bromma geht zur Pizzeria. Was bestellen sie?

In der Pizzeria

— Na, Jutta. Was für eine Pizza willst du?

— Ich esse nicht gern Salami, Pilze oder Peperoni, also ... Warte mal ...

— Sabine?

— Ich esse auch nicht gern Salami, aber ich esse sehr gern Pilze und Paprika ...

— Und du, Liesl?

— Ja. Ich esse gern Oliven und Knoblauch, also ... Tja, was bestellst du?

— Ich? Warte mal ... Ich esse gern Schinken und Pilze ...

— So, sind Sie so weit?

> — Ja, wir möchten: für Jutta, Pizza ‚Margherita'; für Sabine, Pizza ‚Spezial'; und auch für dich, Liesl, Pizza ‚Spezial'; und für mich Pizza ‚Schinken'.
>
> (PAUSE)
>
> — Wie schmeckt's?
>
> — Gut, danke!

Solution:

Jutta bestellt Pizza ‚Margherita' (oder ‚Meeresfrüchte').

Sabine bestellt Pizza ‚Spezial' (oder ‚Schinken' oder ‚Pilze').

Frau Bromma bestellt Pizza ‚Spezial'.

Herr Bromma bestellt Pizza ‚Schinken'.

ROT 28 Interviews

Füll die Lücken unter ‚Ich' aus.
Dann mach ein Interview mit deinem Partner/deiner Partnerin.

ICH	MEIN(E) PARTNER(IN)
Ich esse mein Mittagessen um ______	Wann ißt du dein Mittagessen? ______
Ich esse gern ______	Was ißt du gern? ______
Ich trinke gern ______	Was trinkst du gern? ______
Ich esse mein Abendessen um ______	Wann ißt du dein Abendessen? ______
Ich esse gern ______	Was ißt du gern? ______
Ich trinke gern ______	Was trinkst du gern? ______

Kreuzworträtsel

1 E	ß	2 Z	I	M	M	3 E	R
S		U				I	
S		C		4 F		N	
E		5 K	A	L	T	K	
6 N	I	E		E		7 A	M
		8 R	E	I	S	U	
	9 P			S		F	
10 B	R	Ö	T	C	H	E	N
	O			H		N	

→

1 Zu Mittag esse ich im ___
5 Zu Mittag essen wir warm, aber zu Abend essen wir ___.
6 Chips esse ich nicht gern – ich esse sie ___.
7 Sie sitzen ___ Tisch und trinken Kaffee.
8 Mit Gulasch ißt man normalerweise ___
10 Zum Frühstück esse ich gern ___ mit Honig oder Nutella darauf.

↓

1 Wir ___ dreimal am Tag.
2 Trinkst du Kaffee mit Milch und ___?
3 Ich muß ___ gehen – ich brauche Brot und Käse für morgen.
4 Frikadellen? Ist da ___ drin?
9 Einmal ___ Woche gehen wir zu McDonald's.

ZICKZACK neu 1

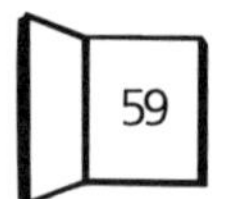

Und du?

Speaking

As a follow-up activity, you could ask the students to devise their own pizza recipes. They could then draw their pizza and label it for display.

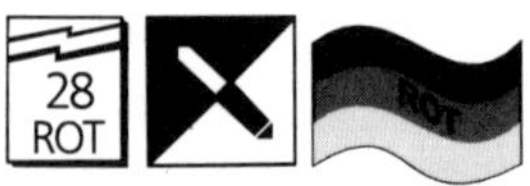

Interviews/Kreuzworträtsel

Listening
Speaking
Reading
Writing

Two activities to round off this *Lernziel.* The first is an information-gap activity in which students write in their own details and then exchange them. The second is a crossword, drawing together some of the associated vocabulary. Ask each student to complete the first part of the chart under *Ich.* Then they can interview each other, noting the answers in the gaps on the worksheet. After the interviews, students can compare charts.

Teacher: *Füllt die Lücken unter ‚Ich' aus. Dann macht ein Interview mit eurem Partner/eurer Partnerin.*

Teacher (after completion): *Vergleicht jetzt die Antworten. Was eßt ihr beiden gern?*
(To one pair:) *Was ißt du gern? Und du? Dasselbe also? Und was trinkt ihr?*

If necessary, the crossword puzzle can also be completed by students in pairs.

IT suggestion

Using a word processor, set up a 'pro-forma' selection of common cooking methods, which students could cut and paste to compile their own simple recipe. Methods could include:

x und x zusammenschlagen
x schmelzen lassen
x schälen
x dazugeben
x daraufgießen
x für 4 Minuten kochen lassen
x im Backofen kochen
x auf beiden Seiten braten
x in einer Bratpfanne kochen

English translations will also be needed!

Students may now attempt the *Lernziel 2* activities in the *Selbstbedienung* section on pages 62–63 of the students' book. See page 83 of this book for more details.

Was heißt ‚gesund essen'?

Listening
Speaking
Reading

Comments from seven teenagers on healthy eating. Ask the students to match the speakers to the visuals, and then to compare the speakers' views with their own. First present the fruit and vegetable vocabulary using a variety of flashcard activities. Then talk the students through the texts one by one, pausing to support their comprehension of new vocabulary by using drawings, photos and/or real items. Mime and gesture can also be used for terms such as *Fett.*

For the expressions of opinion, as opposed to personal knowledge of what healthy eating really is, encourage the students to work out or look up the meaning of expressions such as: *Solange es dir schmeckt, zwischendurch* and *Ich tu's einfach nicht!*

Teacher: *Hört zu. Seht euch die Bilder an. Diese Teenager sprechen über das Thema ‚gesund essen'. Was paßt zu wem? Was sagt Uli? Welches Bild ist das? Wie heißt auf englisch ‚Solange es dir schmeckt'?*

Was heißt ‚gesund essen'?

— Was heißt ‚gesund essen'? Uli?

— Viel Obst und Gemüse essen, aber nicht zuviel Fett.

— Thomas, was meinst du?

— Nicht zuviel essen — man sollte öfter weniger essen und viel Wasser trinken.

— Und du, Katrin. Was ist deine Meinung?

— Man sollte jede Menge Salat essen, und nicht zuviel Fleisch.

— Andreas?

— Solange es dir schmeckt, ist alles gesund. Dieses Gerede vom gesunden Essen ist doch Quatsch. Ich esse alles!

— Martina, was meinst du?

— Es ist schlecht, zwischen den Mahlzeiten zu essen, aber ich esse gerne zwischendurch Schokoriegel, Chips, Kekse und solche Sachen.

— Beate?

— Ich weiß, was gesundes Essen ist: frisches Obst, Salat, kein Fleisch usw., aber ich tu's einfach nicht! Wer tut das schon?!

— Was ist deine Meinung, Torsten?

— Es ist ungesund, zuviel Zucker zu essen, wie zum Beispiel Schokolade, Süßigkeiten, Kekse und Kuchen.

— Vielen Dank.

Solution:

Uli — e; Thomas — g; Katrin — d; Andreas — f; Martina — c; Beate — b; Torsten — a

Follow up with the most interesting part of the activity: the students' own opinions about healthy eating. Ask some of them what they eat, then ask them how healthy they think it is. Refer them to the comments in the students' book. When you feel they are ready, ask them to question each other about their eating habits and their attitudes to food. Write up key questions, such as *‚Was ißt du zum Frühstück/Mittagessen/Abendessen?'* or *‚Ist das gesund?'*

Teacher: *Was heißt ‚gesund essen'? Was eßt ihr meistens? Ist das gesund?* (For the communicative activity:) *Stellt einander die Fragen: ‚Was ißt du ... ?'*

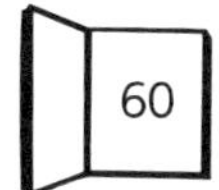

Und du?

Writing

The students could conclude this section by drawing and describing their own ideal healthy meal.

Kalorientabelle

Listening
Speaking
Reading
Writing

The calorie counter ranges over much of the food and drink vocabulary introduced so far. Practise the numbers 1–1000 before asking students to tackle the following activities both orally and in writing.

1 Wieviel Kalorien sind das?

Using the chart and the illustrations, the students should work out how many calories are contained in the illustrated meals and snacks.

Teacher: *Seht euch die Bilder und den Kalorienzähler an. Wieviel Kalorien sind in diesem Frühstück? Und im Mittagessen/Abendessen? Wieviel Kalorien macht das insgesamt?*

2 Wieviel Kalorien nimmst du zu dir?

The students should write down details of their own daily calorie intake by listing the food and drink they have and using the chart to work out how many calories each item has.

Teacher: *Was eßt ihr an einem typischen Tag? Schreibt eine Liste. Wieviel Kalorien sind das?*

3 Schmeckt gut und ist gesund!

The students can now work out a daily or weekly menu with a limit of 1200 calories per day.

Teacher: *Ihr macht jetzt ein Menü mit nicht mehr als 1200 Kalorien pro Tag. Schreibt eine Liste — mit den Kalorien darauf!*

IT suggestion

Any of these ideas will come out best if produced on word-processing software.

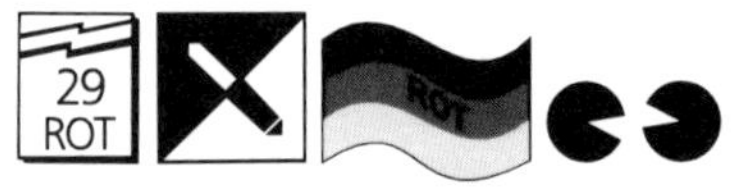

Partnerarbeit. Ißt du gern Süßes?

Listening
Speaking
Reading
Writing

A communicative pairwork activity with an emphasis on healthy eating. First ask the students to look up the vocabulary *sehr oft, oft, manchmal, selten* and *nie* in the wordlist at the back of the students' book. Practise the pronunciation.

Then ask the students to take it in turns to question each other about the items of food and drink listed on the copymaster. By following the guidelines provided, they can quickly work out how many 'penalty points' they notch up as a result of their eating habits. The comments in the *Resultat* section at the foot of the copymaster tell them how healthy, or otherwise, their eating and drinking habits are. Demonstrate by telling the students your own eating and drinking habits (preferably in a model dialogue with another student). Mark your scores on the board/OHP.

Teacher: *Partnerarbeit. Eßt und trinkt ihr gesund? Stellt einander Fragen und zahlt die Punkte. Zum Beispiel: ich esse dreimal am Tag Kuchen. Das ist sehr oft. Schaut mal auf die Tabelle:* (point to *sehr oft, oft* etc. in the list). *Also, jetzt mache ich hier ein Kreuz:* (point to the *sehr oft* box on the chart).

Continue similarly with other items to illustrate *oft, manchmal, selten, nie.*

Teacher: *Macht Kreuze in die richtigen Spalten. Wieviel Punkte sind das? ... Wie ist das Resultat?* (Point to copymaster.) *Wie gerne eßt ihr Süßes?*

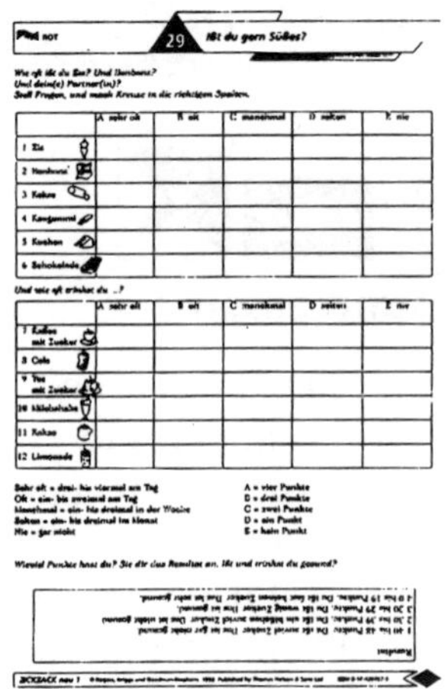

29 Ißt du gern Süßes?

	A sehr oft	B oft	C manchmal	D selten	E nie
1 Eis					
2 [illegible]					
3 Kekse					
4 [illegible]					
5 Kuchen					
6 Schokolade					

	A sehr oft	B oft	C manchmal	D selten	E nie
7 Kaffee mit Zucker					
8 Cola					
9 Tee mit Zucker					
10 Milchshake					
11 Kakao					
12 Limonade					

A = vier Punkte
B = drei Punkte
C = zwei Punkte
D = ein Punkt
E = kein Punkt

Students may now attempt the *Lernziel 3* activities in the *Selbstbedienung* section on page 63 of the students' book. See page 83 of this book for more details.

Selbstbedienung

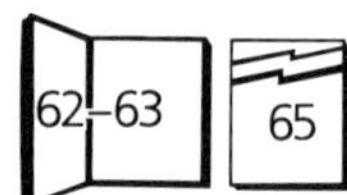

Lernziel 1

Frühstückskarte

Students must read the short menu of three set breakfasts and match it to the photographs.

Solution:

Gedeck 1 = B Gedeck 2 = C Gedeck 3 = A

Müsli, oder ... ?

Jumbled items of food and drink for breakfast.

Solution:

a Müsli **b** Toast **c** Honig **d** Marmelade **e** Kakao **f** Wurst **g** Orangensaft

Lernziel 2

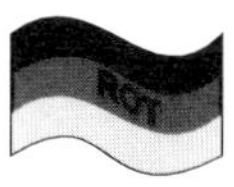

Namengedicht

A gapped poem on foods. Students have the names and visuals to help them work out from the rhyme scheme what the missing items of food are.

Solution:

Apfelsine, Tomate, Nutella, Margarine, Honig, (Pommes) frites, Paprika

Briefe aus Spanien, Frankreich und Italien

Students are asked to read what Gabi, Dorit and Peter say about their holiday food and decide whether the statements that follow are true or false.

Solution:

1 falsch **2** richtig **3** richtig **4** falsch **5** richtig **6** richtig

Lernziel 3

Picknickzeit!

Students plan a picnic for four people, then calculate how many calories will be contained in their choice.

Ein Poster für gesundes Essen

A poster project for display work.

Bildvokabeln

Zu Tisch!

Reading
Writing

Further items of vocabulary related to food and drink, including place settings. The copymaster version provides students with the opportunity to label the drawing.

Grammar exercises 11 and 12, on copymaster 74, are based on the material covered in this chapter.

After completing work on this chapter, check whether any further reinforcement is appropriate from the video material, Activity Box cards and Assessment Support Pack tasks.

7 Schule

Main teaching points

Lernziel 1: Talking about school subjects

Grammar presented: Interrogative adjective

Vocabulary presented:

die Ausrede	*Chemie*	*Französisch*	*Latein*	*Religion*	*Technologie*
anderthalb Stunden	*Deutsch*	*Geschichte*	*lernst*	*Schulaufgaben*	*was hast du heute auf?*
die Biologie	*das geht*	*hart*	*Mathe(matik)*	*die Schule*	*welches Fach?*
die Brille	*Englisch*	*Kunst*	*Physik*	*Spanisch*	
	Erdkunde	*kaputt*	*der Prozent*	*Sport*	

Grammar revised:

Interrogatives

Times

Lernziel 2: Talking about favourite subjects

Grammar presented:

Possessive adjectives

gefallen + dative

Adjectives

Vocabulary presented:

die Bemerkung	*gefällt*	*negativ*	*die Note*	*stinklangweilig*
ganz	*das Lieblingsfach*	*neutral*	*positiv*	

Grammar revised:

Adjectives

Interrogatives

Lernziel 3: Talking about the school day

Grammar presented: Negatives (*kein, (noch) nicht*)

Vocabulary presented:

der Bildschirm	*Großbritannien*	*die Maus*	*die Sportstunde*	*das Trampolin*
die Diskette	*der Handball*	*meistens*	*der Stundenplan*	*Tschüs!*
das Diskettenlaufwerk	*der Hochsprung*	*noch nicht*	*samstags*	*telefonierst mit*
der Drucker	*der Hundertmeterlauf*	*der Schultag*	*die Tastatur*	*der Weitsprung*
der Federball	*der Informatikraum*	*die Schuluniform*	*(du) telefonierst mit*	*zu Ende*
fällt aus	*der Laptop*	*die Speerwurf*	*der Tennisschläger*	*zu Mittag*

Grammar revised: Prepositions (*an, in* + dative)

Before beginning work on this chapter, check where the video material, Activity Box cards and Assessment Support Pack tasks will be most appropriate.

Lernziel 1 Schulfächer und Schulaufgaben

Welches Fach ist das?

Listening
Speaking
Reading

Use the illustrations in the students' book or on copymaster 31 to introduce school subjects in groups of three or four. Make sure the students have ample opportunity to repeat the new vocabulary both chorally and individually before asking them to play some of the language games suggested below and on pages 8–12 of the Introduction.

Some students might like to produce A4- or A3-sized versions of the illustrations for display and reference purposes. The copymaster version could also be used for enlargements, or copied to make individual worksheets for use in a number of ways. Students could stick the sheets in their exercise books and label them with the full German names for the subjects. Alternatively, cut the sheets up into individual cards to play various games in groups or in pairs, for example:

1 School subject bingo

The students each select five subject-cards and place them on their desks. You call out each subject in random order, and whoever has that subject turns the corresponding card over. The game continues until one student has turned over all his/her five subjects and is declared the winner. A student could then take over as caller.

2 Pairwork

The set of cards is placed between two students. They take it in turns to show a card and ask: *Was lernst du in der Schule?* If the partner answers correctly, (s)he keeps the card. The partner with the most cards at the end wins.

3 Guessing game

Student A chooses a card but doesn't show it. Student B must ask *Lernst du Mathematik?* etc. and try to guess A's card using the fewest questions.

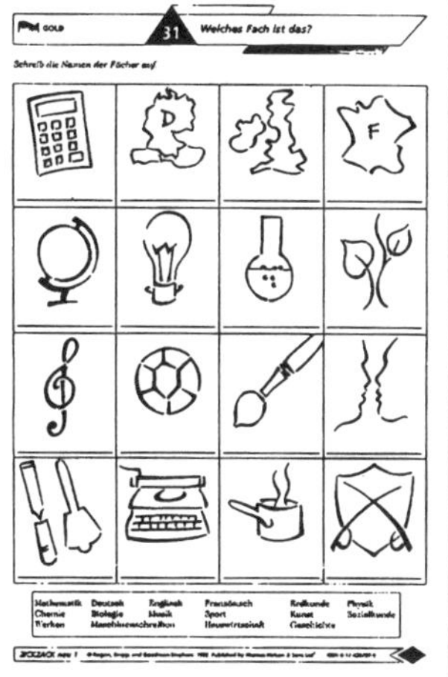

Then move on to the recording, which is a series of sound effects and some broken dialogue to cue school subjects. Ask students to say which lesson or subject is in progress each time.

Teacher: *Hört gut zu. Welches Fach ist das?* (Complete the first one with the class.)

Welches Fach ist das?

1 — (SPORTS NOISES)

2 — Travaillez à deux.
— Quelle est ta matière préférée?
— J'aime les mathématiques.

3 — Good morning everybody.
— Good morning.

4 — (MUSICAL INSTRUMENTS)

5 — Wieviel ist das — hundert durch fünf Komma drei?

6 — In welchem Jahr hat die französische Revolution begonnen?
— Siebzehnhundertneunundachtzig.

Solution:

1 Sport **2** Französisch **3** Englisch **4** Musik **5** Mathe **6** Geschichte

Welche Fächer hast du heute?

Listening
Speaking
Reading
Writing

Straightforward listening practice. Ask the students to listen to the cassette and say or write the subjects mentioned each time.

For a GOLD approach, you could use a cut-up version of copymaster 31 and ask the students to put the subjects named each time in the correct order. They can then feed back their answers orally.

For a ROT approach, ask them to copy the subjects from their book and write the number of the recorded item next to all the subjects mentioned in that item. Again they can give oral feedback.

For a SCHWARZ approach, ask them to listen and write down without support the names of the subjects mentioned.

Teacher: *Hört zu. Welche Fächer sind das?*

GOLD: *Wie ist die richtige Reihenfolge?* (Demonstrate with the cut-up visuals.)

ROT: *Schreibt die Fächer ab und schreibt die Nummern auf, so ...*

SCHWARZ: *Schreibt die Fächer auf.*

Welche Fächer hast du heute?

1 — Was hast du heute?
— Englisch und Mathe.

2 — Was hast du heute?
— Englisch, Kunst und Französisch.

3 — Was hast du heute?
— Erdkunde und Zeichnen.

4 — Was hast du heute?
— Deutsch, Biologie und Sport. Und du?
— Sozialkunde, Physik, Erdkunde und Religion.

5 — Was hast du heute?
— Chemie, Physik, Französisch, Religion und Geschichte.

Solution:

1 Englisch und Mathe **2** Englisch, Kunst und Französisch **3** Erdkunde und Zeichnen **4** Deutsch, Biologie und Sport, + Sozialkunde, Physik, Erdkunde und Religion **5** Chemie, Physik, Französisch, Religion und Geschichte

Purzelwörter

Listening
Speaking
Reading
Writing

In addition to being a game, this should help draw students' attention to the spelling of the subjects.

Teacher: *Seht euch diese Wörter an. Welche Fächer sind das?*

Solution:

a Physik **b** Englisch **c** Geschichte **d** Erdkunde **e** Französisch **f** Mathematik **g** Deutsch **h** Biologie

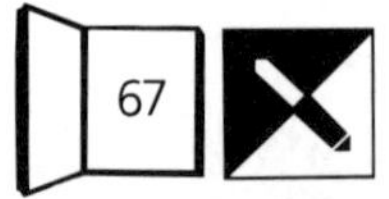

Schulaufgaben

Listening
Speaking
Reading
Writing

The results of a survey amongst German students about homework. The students' answers provide statistical information about when and for how long they do their homework. Ask the students to read the texts and look at the statistics.

Teacher: *Seht euch die Statistik an. Was sind ‚Schulaufgaben'? Richtig:* 'homework'. *Hier sind die Resultate von einer Umfrage über Schulaufgaben. Wann machen die Schüler das? Und für wie lange? Zum Beispiel* ... (Point to the first illustration and read out the text:) *also nach dem Abendessen und zwischen zwei und vier Uhr. Wie heißt ‚zwischen'? Gut.*

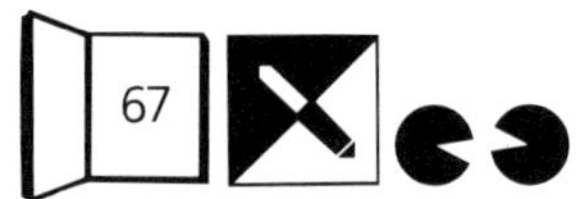

Partnerarbeit

Speaking
Reading
Listening

The pairwork activity requires them to practise percentages. Complete one or two examples and write up the information for the students to refer to. Emphasise the use of *zwischen* in your examples.

Teacher: *Jetzt Partnerarbeit. Stellt einander Fragen über die Statistik.*

Und du?

Speaking
Listening
Writing

Follow up by asking the students to do their own survey in groups. The results for the class could be collated in the same way as the German survey.

Teacher: *Jetzt seid ihr dran. Gruppenarbeit. Macht eine Umfrage. Hier sind die Fragen:* (point to the questions and practise them). *Schreibt die Resultate für eure Gruppe auf.*

IT suggestion

The results of the surveys could be stored on a database and reproduced in various forms.

Interviews über Schulaufgaben

Listening
Speaking
Reading
Writing

Recorded interviews with German teenagers about their homework. Ask the students to listen for *when* and *how long* the teenagers do their homework, and to enter the results on a chart. Write up the names of the teenagers and draw two further columns, as in the solution.

Teacher: *Hört gut zu. Deutsche Teenager sprechen über ihre Schulaufgaben. Wann machen sie die Aufgaben? Nach dem Essen? Um 6 Uhr? Um 9 Uhr? Schreibt die Antwort auf deutsch hier unter ‚Wann' auf. Und wie lange? Eine Stunde? Zwei Stunden?*

Interviews über Schulaufgaben

1 — Wann machst du deine Schulaufgaben, Asaf?
— Normalerweise gleich nach dem Mittagessen um halb drei. Ich arbeite dann bis halb vier.
— Du arbeitest also meistens eine Stunde?
— Ja, das stimmt. Eine Stunde.

2 — Bettina, wann machst du deine Schulaufgaben?
— Ich mache meine Schulaufgaben erst abends, so gegen zwanzig Uhr. Ich arbeite dann vielleicht 45 Minuten.

3 — Jens, wann machst du deine Schulaufgaben?
— Am Nachmittag normalerweise. Nicht gleich nach der Schule — so gegen drei Uhr. Ich arbeite dann bis fünf; so zwei Stunden arbeite ich in der Regel für die Schule.

4 — Sabine, wann machst du deine Schulaufgaben?
— Meistens spät am Abend. Ich habe keine Lust, gleich nach der Schule wieder zu arbeiten. Ich mache meine Schulaufgaben so um neun Uhr abends. Ich arbeite dann 40 Minuten, dann gehe ich ins Bett.

5 — Wann machst du deine Schulaufgaben, Sascha?
— Ich arbeite anderthalb Stunden nach dem Mittagessen, also von zwei bis halb vier.

6 — Maren, wann machst du deine Schulaufgaben?
— Ich mache sie gleich nach dem Mittagessen. Ich arbeite von zwei bis drei — eine gute Stunde.

7 — Wann machst du deine Schulaufgaben, Martin?
— Meistens am Abend — von sechs bis halb acht.
— Arbeitest du immer anderthalb Stunden?
— Ja, ich glaube schon.

8 — Claudia, wann machst du deine Schulaufgaben?
— Normalerweise abends. Dann bin ich nicht so müde. So um sieben Uhr.
— Wie lange arbeitest du für die Schule?
— 40 Minuten in der Regel.

Solution:

	Name	Wann?	Wie lange?
1	Asaf	nach dem Mittagessen/2.30	eine Stunde
2	Bettina	abends/20.00	45 Minuten
3	Jens	am Nachmittag/3.00	2 Stunden
4	Sabine	abends/9.00	40 Minuten
5	Sascha	nach dem Mittagessen/2.00	anderthalb Stunden
6	Maren	nach dem Mittagessen/2.00	eine Stunde
7	Martin	am Abend/6.00	anderthalb Stunden
8	Claudia	am Abend/7.00	40 Minuten

Eine gute Ausrede

Listening
Speaking
Reading
Writing

A cartoon in which a student explains how he manages to avoid doing his homework. Ask the students to read the text and listen to the cassette. See if they can work out the meaning of the word *Ausrede.* Although the students have not yet met leisure activities, the three activities mentioned are cognates or near-cognates and should not cause any difficulties. Students can produce their own variants by changing the subjects and the times they give for their leisure activities. You could also teach them a few other excuses (including translations of some of their ideas). Write them up and ask the students to work in pairs.

Teacher: *Lest den Text und hört gut zu. Wie heißt ‚Ausrede' auf englisch? Schlagt das im Wörterbuch nach. Jetzt seid ihr dran. Macht Dialoge. Ihr könnt die Fächer und die Uhrzeiten ändern. Hier sind noch ein paar Ausreden: ‚Ich war krank', ‚Mein Hund ist gestorben', ‚Jemand hat meine Bücher gestohlen' usw.*

Eine gute Ausrede

— Was hast du heute auf?

— Mathe, Physik, Deutsch und Latein.

— Mann oh Mann! Das ist hart!

— Ach, das geht. Ich gehe um 2 Uhr schwimmen, und dann um vier spiele ich Tennis. Und nach dem Abendessen gehe ich in die Disco.

— Und deine Schulaufgaben?

— Ich mache sie nicht. Ich habe eine gute Ausrede: meine Brille ist kaputt.

— Aber deine Brille ist doch OK!

— Ja, aber hier, meine andere Brille ist kaputt!

IT suggestion

Some students may wish to participate in the 'best excuse of the week' competition (*die beste Ausrede der Woche*). If so, encourage them to use the dictionary/ glossary and provide the necessary support. The results could be collated using word-processing software, and assembled for publication in the school magazine.

Students may now attempt the *Lernziel 1* activities in the *Selbstbedienung* section on page 72 of the students' book. See page 94 of this book for more details.

Deutsch ist mein Lieblingsfach

Listening
Speaking
Reading

Six dialogues in which students answer questions about their favourite subjects and the subjects they like least of all. Ask the students to copy the grid shown in the solution. Teach them the terms *Lieblingsfach* and *gefällt mir gar nicht*, using ticks and crosses, or.smiling and sad faces, or hearts etc. Ask a few students to say which are their favourite and least favourite subjects.

Teacher: *Biologie ist ein Fach. Mathe ist auch ein Fach, und Englisch und Deutsch usw. Wie heißt ‚Fach' auf englisch? Deutsch ist sehr gut. Deutsch ist mein Lieblingsfach. Wie heißt das auf englisch: Lieblingsfach?* (Draw a happy face ☺.) *Französisch ist nicht mein Lieblingsfach. Französisch gefällt mir gar nicht.* (Draw a sad face ☹.) *Wie heißt das auf englisch: ‚gefällt mir gar nicht'?*

(To a student:) *Und dir? Gefällt dir Französisch? Nein? Also, wie gefällt dir Französisch?* (Whisper *gar nicht.*) *Was ist dein Lieblingsfach?*

Teacher (for the grid activity): *Seht euch die Tabelle an. ‚Lieblingsfach' — das ist ein Fach. ‚Lieblingsfächer' — das sind zwei oder drei oder vier Fächer. Na, wie heißt ‚oder' auf englisch?*

Student: 'Or'.

Teacher: *Klar. Hört gut zu:* (complete the first example with the class).

Deutsch ist mein Lieblingsfach

1 — Wie heißt du?
— Susanne.
— Was ist dein Lieblingsfach, Susanne?
— Englisch.
— Und welches Fach gefällt dir gar nicht?
— Geschichte.
— Hast du heute Geschichte?
— Ja, leider.

2 — Wie heißt du?
— Ich heiße Yusuf.
— Was ist dein Lieblingsfach?
— Physik.
— Und welches Fach gefällt dir gar nicht?
— Kunst.
— Hast du heute Kunst?
— Nein. Kunst haben wir nur montags — Gott sei Dank!

3 — Wie heißt du?
— Ich heiße Sabine.
— Was ist dein Lieblingsfach?
— Sport ... oder Deutsch.
— Und welches Fach hast du nicht so gerne?
— Mathe!
— Mathe gefällt dir gar nicht?
— Nein, gar nicht.

4 — Wie heißt du?
— Markus.
— Was ist dein Lieblingsfach in der Schule?
— Tja, ich mag gern Erdkunde. Erdkunde ist mein Lieblingsfach.
— Und was gefällt dir gar nicht?
— Geschichte.

5 — Mein Name ist Katrin. Mein Lieblingsfach ist Biologie.
— Welches Fach gefällt dir gar nicht?
— Ooch ... Hauswirtschaft mag ich nicht so gern.

6 — Wie heißt du?
— Maria.

— Dein Lieblingsfach?
— Mathe.
— Und welches Fach gefällt dir gar nicht?
— Chemie.
— Hast du heute Chemie?
— Ja, nächste Stunde!

Solution:

	Name	Lieblingsfach/ Lieblingsfächer	gefällt mir gar nicht
1	Susanne	Englisch	Geschichte
2	Yusuf	Physik	Kunst
3	Sabine	Sport/Deutsch	Mathe
4	Markus	Erdkunde	Geschichte
5	Katrin	Biologie	Hauswirtschaft
6	Maria	Mathe	Chemie

Partnerarbeit. Was ist dein Lieblingsfach?

Reading
Speaking
Listening

A model dialogue dealing with favourite subjects. Refer students to the text, then ask one or two of them to take part as one of the people in the dialogue, and perform the dialogue with them. Then ask all the students to work in pairs and produce their own dialogues.

Teacher: *Hört gut zu und lest den Text. Es geht um Lieblingsfächer ...*
(To a student:) *Machen wir jetzt den Dialog? Ich bin Partner(in) A und du bist Partner(in) B.*

Teacher: *Was ist dein Lieblingsfach?*

Student: *Englisch. Und dein Lieblingsfach?*

Teacher: *Mathe. Welches Fach gefällt dir gar nicht?*

Student: *Französisch. Und dir?*

Teacher: *Physik.*
(To all the students:) *Jetzt seid ihr dran. Partnerarbeit. Macht Dialoge.*

Next get the students to interview each other in groups of four or five. The class results could be recorded in the form of a barchart on the board/OHP.

Teacher: *Jetzt Gruppenarbeit in Vierer- oder Fünfergruppen. Stellt einander die Fragen und schreibt die Resultate auf.*

IT suggestion

A whole-class survey could be carried out to find out the most and least popular subjects, and the results could be stored in a database or reproduced using a graphing package.

Wie gefällt dir Deutsch?

Listening
Speaking
Reading

An extension of likes and dislikes. Draw a 'meter' on the board with the following expressions:

Es gefällt mir gar nicht	Es gefällt mir nicht sehr	Es geht	Es gefällt mir gut	Es ist mein Lieblingsfach

Talk students through the range of answers shown on the meter, and ask them to question each other about various school subjects. Once again the results could be written up, and a list of subjects in rank order of popularity could be produced for display.

Teacher: *Jetzt Partnerarbeit. Stellt die Frage* (point to text): *‚Wie gefällt dir Geschichte?' oder ‚Wie gefällt dir Mathe?' usw. Hier sind die Antworten* (point to text again): *Es gefällt mir gar nicht ...* etc.

Schuldomino

Listening
Speaking
Reading

A domino game providing reading practice in language dealing with favourite subjects and subjects that students don't particularly like. The *Anfang* and *Ende* dominos should be laid first, and the others filled in from either end. Alternatively, students could first match *Anfang* and *Ende*, then match all the other dominos to form a circle.

Teacher: *Gruppenarbeit. Macht ein Dominospiel. Wer gewinnt? Ihr fangt mit ‚Anfang'* (show the domino) *oder ‚Ende'* (show this domino) *an.*

Solution:

See copymaster reduction on next page.

GOLD 32 Schuldomino

Spielregeln
Verteil die Dominosteine.
Beginn mit ‚Anfang' oder ‚Ende'. Mach ein Dominospiel.
Wer zuerst keine Dominosteine mehr hat, gewinnt.

ANFANG | Mein Lieblingsfach ist Deutsch

D | Mein Lieblingsfach ist Französisch

F | Deutsch gefällt mir gar nicht.

D | Mein Lieblingsfach ist Erdkunde.

Mein Lieblingsfach ist Sport.

Geschichte gefällt mir gar nicht.

Mathe gefällt mir gar nicht.

Mein Lieblingsfach ist Geschichte.

Sport gefällt mir gar nicht.

Physik gefällt mir gar nicht.

Erdkunde gefällt mir gar nicht.

Französisch gefällt mir gar nicht

F | Mein Lieblingsfach ist Physik.

Musik gefällt mir gar nicht.

Mein Lieblingsfach ist Kunst.

Mein Lieblingsfach ist Musik.

Mein Lieblingsfach ist Mathe.

ENDE

ZICKZACK neu 1

Hast du heute dein Lieblingsfach?

Listening
Speaking
Reading

Four teenagers talk about their favourite and least favourite school subjects. Ask the students to look at the thought bubbles which contain illustrations of the lessons they have today. They should read the statements made by each of the teenagers, and work out which of them is lucky enough to have their favourite subject today. They should then copy and fill in the table.

Teacher: *Seht euch die Bilder an. Das sind Helene, Jörg, Britta und Dirk. Das sind ihre Fächer für heute:* (point to the thought bubbles). *Helene hat Biologie und ... ?*

Student: *Erdkunde, Mathe und Englisch.*

Teacher: *Prima. Aber hat sie heute ihr Lieblingsfach? Lest den Text. Ja oder nein?*

Student: *Ja.*

Teacher: *Gut. Und Jörg? Hat er sein Lieblingsfach heute? Macht weiter.*

Now ask students to work out the opposite — namely to identify those students who have their least favourite subject today.

Teacher: *Helene sagt: ‚Französisch gefällt mir gar nicht.' Hat sie heute Französisch?*

Student: *Nein.*

Teacher: *Richtig. Und die anderen?*

Solution:

Lieblingsfach heute: Helene, Jörg, Dirk
gefällt mir gar nicht: Britta, Dirk

Sag mal

Listening
Speaking
Reading
Writing

A number of students exchanging views on school subjects. Ask students to listen to the cassette and identify the speakers in the correct order. Then ask them to classify the statements in positive, neutral or negative terms. Make sure they grasp the significance of the words *langweilig, stinklangweilig* and *toll.*

Teacher: *Hört gut zu. Diese Schüler besprechen ihre Schulfächer. Wer spricht? Wie ist die richtige Reihenfolge?* (For classification of comments:) *Ist das positiv? Neutral? Oder negativ? Was ist langweilig?* (YAWN) ... *Ja. Und stinklangweilig? Und toll?* (THUMBS UP, SMILING). *Gut. Macht drei Spalten* (write up the headings):

positiv	neutral	negativ

Teacher: *Zum Beispiel:* (complete one or two examples).

Sag mal

— Erdkunde? Super!
— Kunst gefällt mir gut.
— Geschichte ist ganz interessant.
— Religion gefällt mir gar nicht.
— Mathe? Ach, das geht.
— Französisch ist stinklangweilig!
— Musik finde ich toll!

Solution:

c – d – b – e – f – a – g

Umfrage

Speaking
Listening

Finally, students can conduct their own survey around the class.

Teacher: *Jetzt seid ihr dran. Stellt einander Fragen.* (Demonstrate with a student:) *Wie findest du Deutsch?*

Student: *Stinklangweilig.*

Teacher: *Und wie findest du Mathe?*

Student: *Das geht.*

Eine schlechte Note

Listening
Speaking
Reading
Writing

Tell the students they are going to hear a conversation between Karin and her father. Play the whole conversation once, then ask them to say what they think it was about (i.e. Karin's bad grades). Now explain the German marking system from 1 to 6. Write up the information thus:

1	sehr gut
2	gut
3	das geht
4	das geht
5	nicht gut
6	nicht gut

Write up the subjects in the order in which they are mentioned: *Mathe, Musik, Physik, Latein, Geschichte, Sport, Deutsch.* Play the recording a second time, asking the students to listen for the marks and write them down. Check their comprehension by first asking them the grade and then asking whether or not it's a good grade.

Teacher: *Hört zu. Das sind Karin und ihr Vater. Worum geht es hier? ... Ja gut — um Fächer und Noten. In Deutschland ist das System so:* (write up the marks as above and explain them). *Hier sind Karins Fächer. Schreibt sie ab. Hört nochmal zu. Welche Noten hat sie für Mathe, Musik usw?* (Complete the first one or two.) *Eine Fünf in Mathe — ist das gut?*

Eine schlechte Note

Vater: So, Karin. Schon wieder eine Fünf in Mathe!

Karin: In Musik hab' ich eine Eins gekriegt!

Vater: In Musik schon. Aber in Mathe, eine Fünf.

Karin: Ich kann nichts dafür — Mathe ist stinklangweilig!

Vater: Ach was! Ich verstehe das nicht. Du hast doch einen guten Lehrer.

Karin: Herr Kohler? Der ist so langweilig!

Vater: Und deine Physiklehrerin, Frau ... Wie heißt sie? ... Frau Weiß: ist die auch langweilig?

Karin: Och, die geht.

Vater: Und was hast du in Physik? Eine Vier!

Karin: Man kann nicht in allen Fächern gut sein.

Vater: In allen? In allen, sagst du! Eine Vier in Latein, eine Vier in Geschichte.

Karin: Aber Vati!

Vater: Eine Fünf in Sport! Das ist doch unmöglich!

Karin: Ich habe eine Drei in Deutsch.

Vater: Oh, wunderbar! Eine Drei in Deutsch. Karin, diese Noten sind nicht gut genug. Also jetzt gehst du auf dein Zimmer und lernst. Kapiert?

Karin: Ja, Vati.

Vater: Und spiel nicht Gitarre!

Karin: Nein!

Solution:

Mathe 5 Musik 1 Physik 4 Latein 4 Geschichte 4 Sport 5 Deutsch 3

Steffi

Reading

Another Steffi cartoon — for fun and interest.

Students may now attempt the *Lernziel 2* activity in the *Selbstbedienung* section on page 72 of the students' book. See page 94 of this book for more details.

Kirstens Stundenplan

Listening
Speaking
Reading
Writing

Introduce school timetables by referring to the timetable in the students' book. Bring out the fact that the word *Stunde* is used for both 'hour' and 'lesson'. Then you can introduce the expressions *in der ersten/zweiten/dritten Stunde* etc. Practise this new form by asking students what subjects they have in the first/second/third lessons on particular days.

Teacher: *Seht euch Kirstens Stundenplan an. Was heißt ‚Stundenplan' auf englisch? ... Prima. Und Stunde? ... Toll! Stunde heißt auch* 'hour' *— also sechzig Minuten. Was hat Kirsten am Montag in der ersten Stunde, um acht Uhr? ... Gut. Und in der zweiten Stunde? ... Und ihr?* (To one student:) *Was hast du am Montag in der ersten Stunde? Englisch oder?*

Student: *Mathe.*

Teacher: *Und in der zweiten?*

Reinforce the students' understanding of *in der* + ordinal numbers by drawing a blank copy of Kirsten's timetable on the board/OHP (days and times only). Point to a particular day and lesson, and ask the students to refer to the book and help you fill in the subjects. (Keep your own book closed in order to make this activity more communicative.)

Teacher: *Was hat Kirsten am Montag in der ersten Stunde?*

Student: *Biologie.*

Continue until the timetable is complete. Then, without looking at the board, question the class:

Teacher: *Hat Kirsten Englisch am Montag?*

Student: *Ja.*

Teacher: *Wann? In der ersten/zweiten Stunde?*

Student: *In der fünften Stunde.*

Teacher (to the whole class): *Stimmt das?*

As a variant you could play a memory game using the timetable. Progressively wipe out/cover up information on the timetable on the board/OHP, and ask the students what subjects are missing and when.

Teacher: *Seht euch den Stundenplan an. Was fehlt am Montag?*

Student: *Mathe.*

Teacher: *Gut. Wann? In welcher Stunde ist Mathe?*

Student: *In der zweiten.*

As soon as the students are confident, hand the activity over to them to perform in pairs. (Here are some other subjects that students may wish to know the German for: child care — *Kinderpflege*; economics — *Wirtschaftslehre*; Latin — *Latein*; RE — *Religion*; technical drawing — *technisches Zeichnen*.)

Richtig oder falsch?

Listening
Speaking
Reading
Writing

A 'true or false?' activity based on the timetable in the students' book.

Teacher: *Seht euch jetzt* ,**Richtig oder falsch?**' *an. Stimmt das?* (Complete the first one with the class.)

Solution:

1 richtig **2** richtig **3** falsch **4** falsch **5** richtig **6** richtig **7** falsch **8** richtig

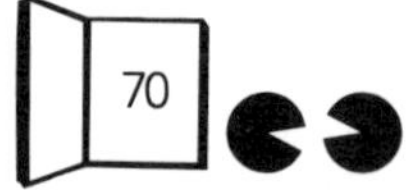

Partnerarbeit. Welcher Tag?

Listening
Speaking
Reading

A pairwork activity based on Kirsten's timetable. Ask the students to take it in turns to choose a day, and to answer their partner's questions with only *ja* or *nein*. Perform the model dialogue in the book.

Teacher: *Partnerarbeit. Welcher Tag ist das? Seht euch Kirstens Stundenplan an. Das ist jetzt euer Stundenplan. Wählt einen Tag. Dein(e) Partner(in) muß Fragen stellen, um herauszufinden, welcher Tag das ist. Zum Beispiel: ...*

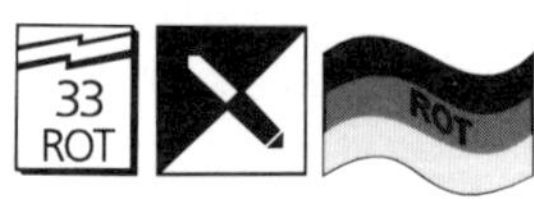

Kreuzworträtsel

Reading
Writing

A crossword providing practice in school subjects and ordinals, based on ***Kirstens Stundenplan***.

Solution:

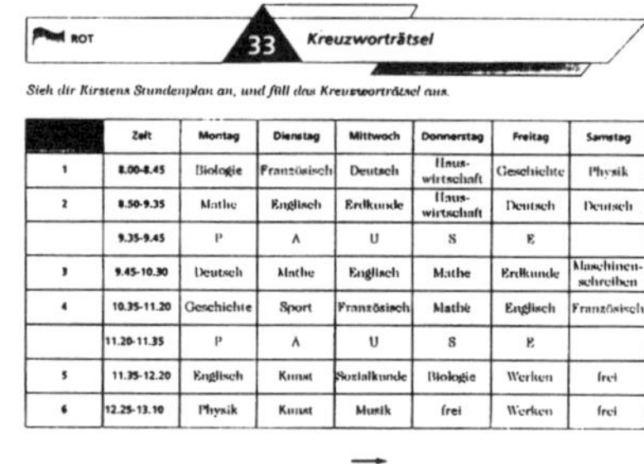

ROT 33 **Kreuzworträtsel**

Sieh dir Kirstens Stundenplan an, und füll das Kreuzworträtsel aus.

	Zeit	Montag	Dienstag	Mittwoch	Donnerstag	Freitag	Samstag
1	8.00-8.45	Biologie	Französisch	Deutsch	Hauswirtschaft	Geschichte	Physik
2	8.50-9.35	Mathe	Englisch	Erdkunde	Hauswirtschaft	Deutsch	Deutsch
	9.35-9.45	P	A	U	S	E	
3	9.45-10.30	Deutsch	Mathe	Englisch	Mathe	Erdkunde	Maschinenschreiben
4	10.35-11.20	Geschichte	Sport	Französisch	Mathe	Englisch	Französisch
	11.20-11.35	P	A	U	S	E	
5	11.35-12.20	Englisch	Kunst	Sozialkunde	Biologie	Werken	frei
6	12.25-13.10	Physik	Kunst	Musik	frei	Werken	frei

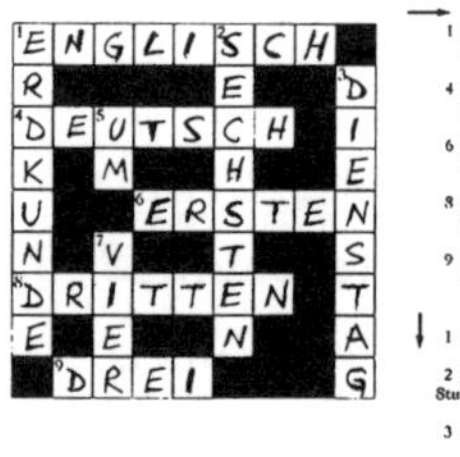

→

1 Am Montag in der fünften Stunde hat Kirsten ____

4 Am Samstag in der zweiten Stunde hat sie ____

6 Am Freitag in der ____ Stunde hat sie Geschichte.

8 Am Donnerstag hat sie Mathematik in der ____ Stunde

9 Kirsten hat ____ Stunden Französisch in der Woche.

↓

1 Kirsten hat mittwochs und freitags ____.

2 Montags hat sie Physik in der ____ Stunde.

3 Sie hat Kunst am ____.

5 Die erste Pause ist ____ halb zehn.

7 Samstags hat Kirsten nur ____ Stunden.

ZICKZACK neu 1 © Rogers, Briggs and Goodman-Stephens 1993 Published by Thomas Nelson & Sons Ltd ISBN 0-17-439787-9 36

Stundenplan-Lotto. Mein Stundenplan

Listening
Writing

Further practice in the names of school subjects. Ask the students to fill in the timetables along the lines of Kirsten's with the subjects in any order they like. This could be set as part of a homework in preparation for the following lesson. You could then play a bingo game, calling out subject names instead of numbers and asking the students to cross the subjects off their timetables. (If they do this lightly in pencil, the marks can be rubbed out and the game played again without their having to write out the timetable several times.) The first student to cross off a full day's lessons is the winner.

Teacher: *Hier ist ein Stundenplan. Hier sind die Fächer. Schreibt die Fächer auf den Stundenplan auf — zum Beispiel, vier Deutschstunden:* (write up four German lessons at random on your version).

Teacher (when the students have filled in their subjects): *Jetzt spielen wir Lotto! Hört zu und kreuzt die Fächer an. Ihr gewinnt, wenn ein Tag voll ist. Zum Beispiel:* (demonstrate). *Montag Deutsch, Dienstag Mathe, Mittwoch Deutsch, Donnerstag Geschichte ... usw.*

The second part of the copymaster can be used for students to write out their own timetable in German.

Partnerarbeit. Die Klasse 7c

Listening
Speaking
Reading

A communicative pairwork activity based on a class timetable. Cut the worksheets into two, and give one timetable A and one timetable B to each pair. Tell them that they each have part of Class 7c's timetable. They must work in pairs, questioning each other until they have both completed the full timetable on their sheets.

Teacher: *Partnerarbeit. Stellt einander Fragen und schreibt die Fächer in den Stundenplan. Zum Beispiel:*

Partner A: *‚Was hast du am Montag in der ersten Stunde?'*

Partner B: *‚Englisch. Was hast du am Dienstag in der ersten Stunde?'*

Partner A: *‚Physik.'*

Die erste Stunde fällt aus!

Listening
Speaking
Reading

A communicative numbers game based on the *Telefonkette* system sometimes set up in Germany to alert students to the fact that a member of staff is unavailable at the start of the day. The school (here, the teacher) phones the first person on the list to say that there is no first lesson; that person then phones the next person listed, and so on. Ask students to do the same thing in class.

Give each student a pair of numbers. Out of each pair, **a** is the number of the incoming call and **b** is the number of the next person on the list. There are only enough numbers given for 15 players, so a class of 30 could be split in half, with each group playing at either end of the room; alternatively the students could work in pairs, with Partner A responding to the incoming call and Partner B dialling the outgoing call.

If the game is played with more than 15 numbers, simply invent more numbers to fill in the gap, e.g. for 17 students:

15a 72201 **15b** (new number) **16a** (new number) **16b** (new number) **17a** (new number) **17b** 207625 (old **15b**)

Conversely, if fewer than 15 numbers are needed, cut out the last few pairs from the solution, e.g. for 11 pairs:

5a 26924 (omit **5b**, **12**, **13**, **14**, **15a**) **5b** 207625 (old **15b**)

Teacher: *Seht euch die Telefonnummern an.*
(To a student:) *Die erste Nummer **a*** (point to the appropriate number in the students' book) *ist deine Nummer zu Hause. Die Nummer **b** mußt du wählen* (mime dialling).

Start the game by ringing the first student.

Teacher (DIALS): *Zwei–null–sieben–sechs–zwei–fünf.*

Student 1: *Hallo.*

Teacher: *Du, die erste Stunde fällt aus.*

Student 1: *Oh, danke. Tschüs!* (DIALS) *Sechs–drei–eins–acht.*

Student 2: *Hallo ...*

Solution: Correct running order: 1–11–4–9–6–2–10–8–3–7–5–12–14–13–15–1.

If/when number 15 is completed and number 1 is dialled, intervene and say: *Ja, wir wissen schon Bescheid!*

Großbritannien oder Deutschland?

Listening
Speaking
Reading
Writing

The students have to read the list of statements and deduce whether each one was said by a British or a German pupil. In some cases it could be either. Students will have to use logic and the glossary to work out some of the answers.

Teacher: *Lest die Sätze. Wer spricht? Ein(e) Schüler(in) aus Deutschland oder aus Großbritannien?*

Solution:

1 D/GB **2** GB **3** D **4** D **5** GB **6** D **7** D **8** D **9** D **10** GB

> Students may now attempt the *Lernziel 3* activities in the *Selbstbedienung* section on page 73 of the students' book. See pages 94–95 of this book for more details.

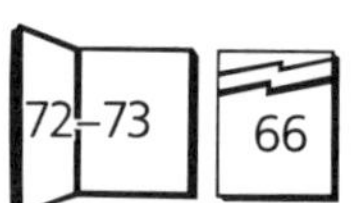

Lernziel 1

Was haben sie auf?

A series of visual clues to school subjects.

Solution:

1 Englisch **2** Erdkunde **3** Französisch **4** Mathe **5** Musik **6** Deutsch **7** Kunst

Kochen? Köstlich!

Alliterative links between school subjects and adjectives to describe them. Students are asked to identify matching pairs, check meanings where necessary, and if possible produce some of their own ideas.

Solution:

any pair of noun + adjective beginning with the same letter.

Lernziel 2

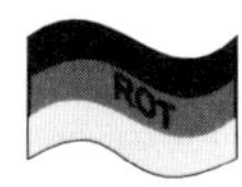

Lieblingsfächer oder?

A spaghetti diagram in which students must work out the favourite and least favourite school subjects of five teenagers.

Solution:

Name	☺	☹
Jutta	Biologie	Englisch
Bernd	Deutsch	Geschichte
Anne	Englisch	Mathe
Anke	Mathe	Biologie
Sven	Geschichte	Deutsch

Lernziel 3

Fragen und Antworten

A question and answer matching exercise. Some attention to detail is required, e.g. the plural *Lieblingsfächer* — students not noticing this may think the answer to this is *Englisch.*

Solution:

1 c **2** e **3** a **4** g **5** d **6** b **7** f

Hauptschule, Realschule ... ?

Eight statements by teenagers about their school subjects. By matching the statements to the four school timetables shown, students must deduce which type of school is referred to each time.

Solution:

1 Gymnasium **2** Hauptschule **3** Gesamtschule
4 Gesamtschule **5** Realschule **6** Gymnasium
7 Hauptschule **8** Realschule

Bildvokabeln

In der Schule *Reading Writing*

Specialist areas in a school. The copymaster version gives students the opportunity to label the drawings.

Grammar exercise 13, on copymaster 75, is based on the material covered in this chapter.

After completing work on this chapter, check whether any further reinforcement is appropriate from the video material, Activity Box cards and Assessment Support Pack tasks.

8 Meine Freizeit

Main teaching points

Lernziel 1: Talking about sport and pastimes

Grammar presented: First and second person singular present tense

Vocabulary presented:

Basketball
der Computer
der Computerpartner
die Computerpartnerin
einer
die Freizeit
der Fußball
das Hobby
der Hund
Informationen
das Klavier
spazieren
Tennis
wird

Lernziel 2: Talking about television

Grammar presented:
Modal verb first and second person singular present tense
Adjectives

Vocabulary presented:

ab 7 Jahren
dienstags
donnerstags
doof
das Fernsehen
die Fernsehsendung
der Film
das Fitnessprogramm
der Fußballer
freitags
insgesamt
die Komödie
der Mensch
die Musiksendung
mittwochs
montags
Nachrichten
die Natursendung
das Schauspiel
die Serie
das Spielshow
die Sportsendung
der Superglotzer
samstags
schon gut
sonntags
das Talkshow
der Trickfilm
ungefähr
die Werbung

Grammar revised: Adjectives

Lernziel 3: Saying what you most like doing

Grammar presented:
Superlative adverb
Inversion of subject and main verb

Vocabulary presented:

am liebsten
die Blockflöte
das Bummeln
Chansons
egal
es tut mir leid
die Flöte
frei
furchtbar
die Geige
die Gitarre
guckt ... fern
ich möchte
ich übe
Jazz
die Jugendlichen
das Keyboard
die Klarinette
klassische Musik
das Lesen
die Lieblingsmusik
nett
niemals
das Musikinstrument
das Orchester
die Popmusik
die Rockgruppe
der Saxophon
das Schlagzeug
die Statistik
selten
die Tanzmusik
die Trompete
wenn ich kann

Before beginning work on this chapter, check where the video material, Activity Box cards and Assessment Support Pack tasks will be most appropriate.

Was machst du in deiner Freizeit?

Listening Speaking Reading

Use the flashcards first to introduce the new leisure activities in groups of three or four. Then play some of the flashcard games.

Teacher: *Seht euch die Bildkarten an. Das sind Hobbys und Sportarten. Hört gut zu und wiederholt. Was machst du in deiner Freizeit? ... Ich spiele Tennis, ich lese, ich höre Musik ...*

Interviews nach der Schule

Listening Speaking Reading

A number of short interviews in which teenagers say what they do in their spare time. Ask the students to match what they hear to the lettered visuals and texts in the students' book.

Teacher: *Hier sind Interviews mit Teenagern. Was machen sie in ihrer Freizeit? Wählt die passenden Bilder.* (Play the first interview.) *Ist das Bild A oder B oder ... ?*

Interviews nach der Schule

1 — Was machst du nach der Schule?
— Ich spiele Tennis.

2 — Und du, was machst du nach der Schule?
— Ich spiele Klavier.

3 — Was machst du nach der Schule, Alima?
— Ich lese.

4 — Und du, Markus, was machst du nach der Schule?
— Ich spiele Fußball.

5 — Was machst du nach der Schule?
— Ich höre Musik.

6 — Katrin, was machst du nach der Schule?
— Ich gehe schwimmen.

7 — Was machst du nach der Schule?
— Ich gehe mit dem Hund spazieren.

8 — Was machst du nach der Schule, Ahmed?
— Ich gehe in die Disco.

9 — Was machst du nach der Schule?
— Ich spiele Basketball.

10 — Was machst du nachmittags nach der Schule?
— Ich sehe fern.

11 — Und du, was machst du nach der Schule?
— Ich reite.

12 — Was machst du nach der Schule?
— Ich sortiere meine Briefmarken.

13 — Also, Josef, was machst du nach der Schule?
— Ich treffe mich mit meinen Freunden.

14 — Und du, was machst du nach der Schule?
— Ich fahre mit dem Rad.

15 — Was machst du nach der Schule?
— Ich spiele mit dem Computer.

16 — Und du, Malik, was machst du nach der Schule?
— Ich bummle in der Stadt.

Solution:

1 D 2 F 3 I 4 N 5 C 6 O 7 G 8 Q 9 B 10 E 11 M 12 K 13 H 14 L 15 A 16 J

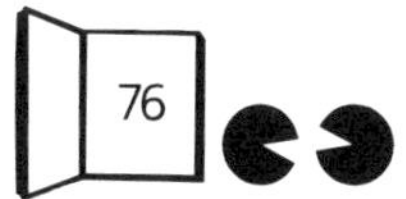

Partnerarbeit

Listening Speaking

The students work in pairs. Each partner chooses a picture which enables the other partner to describe what he or she does as a leisure activity.

Teacher: *Macht jetzt Dialoge. Zum Beispiel — ich bin Partner(in) A — was machst du in deiner Freiheit? Bild **a**?*

Student: *Ich spiele mit dem Computer ...*

Freizeitaktivitäten

Listening Speaking Reading

Make worksheets from copymaster 37 for the students to cut up and use in a number of activities:

1 Lotto

Ask the students to choose any six of the drawings and place them in a row. Read out at random the names of activities, and see who is the first one to turn over all six of their drawings.

2 Pelmanism

Ask the students to play this game in pairs or in groups of three or four. They place the drawings, and the separate texts that describe them, face down on the table. They then take it in turns to turn up a drawing and a text. If the two match, the student wins the set. The overall winner is the one with the most sets.

3. Was paßt wozu?

Students could stick (a selection of) the drawings in their exercise books, and then label them either in their own hand or by using the jumbled texts on the copymaster.

Was machen sie nach der Schule?

Listening
Speaking
Reading
Writing

A number of longer dialogues containing some redundant language. Ask the students to note — in groups, if you wish — the activities mentioned by each person.

Teacher: *Hört zu: Gruppenarbeit. Was sagen diese Teenager über ihre Freizeit? Schreibt alle Aktivitäten in der richtigen Reihenfolge auf. Hier sind die Namen:* (write the names).

Was machen sie nach der Schule?

1 — Was machst du nach der Schule, Peter?
— Ich esse zuerst, dann mache ich meine Schulaufgaben. Ich gehe zweimal in der Woche zum Basketball. Manchmal fahre ich mit dem Rad in die Stadt. Und ich treffe mich auch oft mit meinen Freunden.

2 — Was machst du nach der Schule, Christiane?
— Nach dem Mittagessen mache ich meine Hausaufgaben, dann spiele ich oft Tennis. Manchmal gehe ich in der Stadt bummeln. Im Sommer gehe ich oft schwimmen. Abends sehe ich fern oder höre Musik.

3 — Was machst du nach der Schule, Christoph?
— Nach dem Essen muß ich als allererstes meine Schulaufgaben machen. Zweimal in der Woche reite ich auf meinem Pony. Und dann gehe ich auch jeden Tag mit meinem Hund spazieren.

4 — Was machst du nach der Schule, Sabine?
— Nachmittags mache ich meine Schulaufgaben. Oft kommen meine Freundinnen zu mir, und wir trinken Tee und hören Musik. Manchmal gehe ich schwimmen oder Squash spielen.

Solution:

Peter: Schulaufgaben, Basketball, Rad, Freunde

Christiane: Hausaufgaben, Tennis, Bummeln, Schwimmen, Fernsehen, Musik

Christoph: Schulaufgaben, Reiten, mit dem Hund spazieren

Sabine: Schulaufgaben, Freundinnen, Tee trinken, Musik, Schwimmen, Squash

Eine Freizeitumfrage

Listening
Speaking
Reading
Writing

A class survey of spare-time activities. Ask the students to work in groups and take it in turns to interview each other about what they do in their spare time.

Teacher: *Macht eine Umfrage über Freizeitaktivitäten. Stellt einander die Frage ‚Was machst du in deiner Freizeit?‘*

The results could be displayed as barcharts or piecharts.

IT suggestion

The results could also be stored in a database.

Wer ist das?

Listening
Speaking
Reading
Writing

A guessing game for groups or the whole class. Ask each student to write down five things (s)he does in his/her spare time. You collect the sheets (or one student in each group can do so) and read them out in random order. The others must guess who the person is.

Teacher: *Gruppenarbeit. Schreibt fünf Aktivitäten auf, die ihr in der Freizeit macht. Zum Beispiel:* (write up five activities). *Das sind meine Aktivitäten.* (After they have finished writing:) *Jetzt sammle ich alle Papiere ein, vermische sie und wähle eins ... so. Hört zu. Wer ist das?* (Read out:) *Ich spiele Tennis ...*

Computerpartner

Listening
Speaking
Reading
Writing

A computer matching game. Ask the students to look at the photos of German teenagers, and tell them that they are going to be matched to one of them by means of a computer.

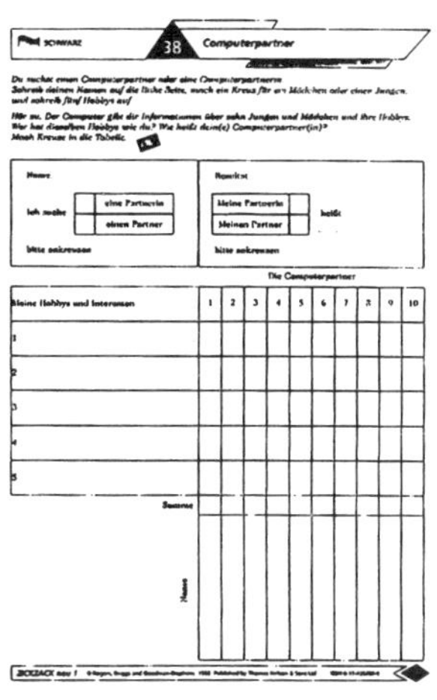

They will need the form from copymaster 38 on which they write down their name, whether they would like a male or female partner, and five of their hobbies or spare-time activities. Play the cassette and ask them to place a cross in the appropriate column each time there is a match between what the speaker says and the activities they have listed for themselves.

Finally, tell the students that the computer will read out in order the names of the teenagers who have been speaking. The students should copy the names in the appropriate columns and then from their totals work out who their partner is.

Teacher: *Hier sind zehn Jungen und Mädchen. Einer oder eine wird euer Computerpartner oder eure Computerpartnerin.* (Hand out the worksheets.) *Hier ist ein Fragebogen. Bitte, schreibt auf der linken Seite: hier, euren Namen; hier, macht ein Kreuz für ein Mädchen oder einen Jungen; hier, schreibt ihr fünf Hobbys auf — zum Beispiel ‚Ich gehe gern schwimmen'.*
(After they have finished:) *Hört gut zu. Der Computer gibt euch jetzt Informationen über die zehn Jungen und Mädchen und ihre Hobbys. Wer hat eure Hobbys? Macht Kreuze in die Tabelle.*

Computerpartner

— Guten Tag. Ich bin Compi, der Partnercomputer. Hier sind Informationen über zehn Partner oder Partnerinnen. Nummer eins.

— Ich gehe schwimmen, spiele Tennis, gehe in die Disco, spiele Fußball und höre Musik.

— Nummer zwei.

— Ich spiele Basketball, treffe mich mit Freunden, gehe spazieren, spiele mit dem Computer und sehe fern.

— Nummer drei.

— Ich spiele Klavier, fahre mit dem Rad, gehe ins Kino, sortiere Briefmarken und gehe schwimmen.

— Nummer vier.

— Ich gehe mit dem Hund spazieren, gehe in die Disco, sehe fern, höre Musik und spiele Fußball.

— Nummer fünf.

— Ich lese, sehe fern, gehe ins Kino, reite und gehe spazieren.

— Nummer sechs.

— Ich gehe in die Disco, höre Musik, sehe fern, spiele Fußball und bummle in der Stadt.

— Nummer sieben.

— Ich gehe schwimmen, gehe spazieren, spiele Tennis, spiele Basketball und höre Musik.

— Nummer acht.

— Ich spiele mit dem Computer, gehe mit dem Hund spazieren, höre Musik, spiele Fußball und gehe ins Kino.

— Nummer neun.

— Ich sehe fern, treffe mich mit Freunden, höre Musik, bummle in der Stadt und spiele mit dem Computer.

— Nummer zehn.

— Ich spiele Tennis, gehe schwimmen, höre Musik, gehe mit dem Hund spazieren und gehe in die Disco.

Teacher (for totalling scores on the copymaster): *Wie viele Kreuze hat Nummer eins? Schreibt die Zahl hinter ‚Summe'* (demonstrate). *So, jetzt hört wieder gut zu. Der Computer gibt euch jetzt die Namen. Schreibt die Namen ganz unten hin.*

— Hier ist wieder Compi, euer Partnercomputer. Hier sind die Namen: Nummer 1 Torsten; Nummer 2 Anne; Nummer 3 Murat; Nummer 4 Raphaela; Nummer 5 Peter; Nummer 6 Asla; Nummer 7 Florian; Nummer 8 Brigitte; Nummer 9 Bernd; Nummer 10 Uschi.

> Students could extend this activity by producing their own version on cassette and sending it to another class who have completed the copymaster. They can then listen to the recordings and find genuine matches.

Teacher: *Jetzt seid ihr dran. Macht eine Aufnahme wie Compi. Wir schicken dann die Kassette an die Klasse 7b.*

Revision of language (gern)

Listening
Speaking

Revise the use of *gern* in the context of food and drink and/or leisure activities. Use the flashcards to cue responses.

Teacher: *Was ißt du gern zum Mittagessen? Ißt du gern Brötchen mit Marmelade? Ich esse nicht gern Fisch. Und du? Trinkst du gern Kaffee? Spielst du gern Fußball/Basketball/Tennis ...*

Partnerarbeit. Was machst du gern/nicht gern?

An activity that provides pairwork revision in the use of *gern* in relation to leisure activities. Ask each partner to indicate by marking with a cross five things which he/she likes doing, and five or six things which he/she does not like doing. Each partner must then try to discover what the other has written by asking *Was machst du gern?* and *Was machst du nicht gern?* They could vary the questions by asking, for example, *Spielst du gern Fußball?* They should compare sheets afterwards.

Teacher: *Jetzt Partnerarbeit. Jeder Partner bekommt einen Arbeitsbogen. Jetzt, zum Beispiel: Ich spiele gern Fußball, und mache also ein Kreuz hier* (point). *Ich gehe nicht gern in die Disco, also ich mache ein Kreuz hier. Verstanden? Ihr macht jetzt fünf Kreuze in diese Spalte und fünf Kreuze in diese Spalte* (point). *Dann fragst du, Ann: ‚Was machst du gern?' und du, Mary, sagst: ‚Ich spiele gern Tennis.'*

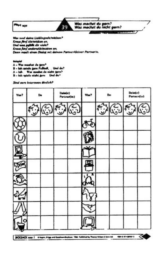

Beste Freunde

Listening
Speaking
Reading

A humorous poem about someone's best friends and their hobbies. Play the cassette version to students and ask them to recite it themselves, possibly learning it by heart.

Teacher: *Hört zu und seht euch das Gedicht an.*

Beste Freunde

Hab' einen Freund, der wohnt in Hof,
Furchtbar nett, furchtbar doof.

Hab' eine Freundin, die wohnt in Bern,
Hat keine Hobbys, guckt nur fern.

Hab' einen Freund, der wohnt in Kiel,
Trinkt wie ein Fisch und ißt zuviel.

Hab' eine Freundin, die wohnt in Trier,
Geht gern tanzen — nicht mit mir!

Hab' einen Freund, der wohnt in Essen,
Was macht er gern? Ich hab's vergessen.

Freunde und Freundinnen überall,
Wie sie sind, ist mir egal!

Jugendzentrum Pinneberg

Listening
Speaking
Reading
Writing

The programme of a youth club detailing the activities on offer during the course of a week. Ask students to look at the statements and the information and decide which of the statements are true and which are false.

Solution:

1 falsch **2** richtig **3** falsch **4** falsch **5** richtig **6** richtig **7** falsch **8** falsch

Students may now attempt the *Lernziel 1* activities in the *Selbstbedienung* section on page 82 of the students' book. See page 107 of this book for more details.

Partnerarbeit. Fernsehsendungen

Listening
Speaking
Reading

Present the TV programme types in groups of three or four using the screen visuals in the students' book. Once the students are confident in their pronunciation, ask them to identify some of the programmes, using the numbers. As soon as possible, hand the activity over to the students to perform in pairs.

Teacher: *Seht euch die Bilder und Texte an. Das sind Fernsehsendungen. Wie heißt das auf englisch? ... Richtig. Wiederholt ... Welche Fernsehsendung ist das: Nummer eins? ... Gut. Und Nummer sechs? ...* (continue). *Jetzt Partnerarbeit. Stellt einander die Frage: ‚Welche Fernsehsendung ist das — Nummer ... ?* (Write up the question for support.)

The pairwork activity could also be continued as a memory game, with one student having to answer with the book closed.

Im Fernsehen

Listening
Speaking
Reading
Writing

A copymaster providing opportunities for students to practise TV programme names. You can play some of the games listed in the ***Games cupboard*** on pages 8–12 and give students the opportunity to cut out and label the screens.

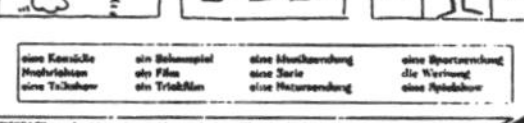

Welche Sendung?

Listening
Speaking

A series of extracts from TV programmes.
Ask the students to deduce or speculate about which programmes they are.

Teacher: *Hört zu. Das sind deutsche Fernsehsendungen. Aber Welche? Nummer eins:* (play and complete the first one).

Solution:

1 Nachrichten **2** Musiksendung **3** Trickfilm
4 Werbung **5** Sportsendung **6** Spielshow

Ich sehe gern fern

Listening
Speaking
Reading
Writing

A series of short statements relating to the TV programmes illustrated in the students' book. Ask the students to listen and match the programmes mentioned to the number of the programme shown in the book. Alternatively, they could write down the programme type in full.

Teacher: *Hört gut zu. Welche Sendungen sind das? Schreibt die Zahlen/die Sendungen auf.*

**Ich sehe gern fern**

1 — Ich sehe sehr gern fern. Meistens Filme und Serien.

2 — Ich sehe gern Natursendungen und Schauspiele.

3 — Ich sehe gern fern. Normalerweise Musiksendungen und Trickfilme.

4 — Meine Lieblingssendungen sind Spielshows und Talkshows.

5 — Ich sehe gern Nachrichten und Werbung.

Solution:

1 = 3, 7 **2** = 5, 8 **3** = 1, 10 **4** = 11, 12 **5** = 6, 4

Wie findest du Trickfilme?

Listening
Writing
Speaking

A number of dialogues expressing views on television programmes. Ask the students to listen to the cassette and note whether the comments are positive or negative. Write up the programmes to be discussed in a grid, and ask the students to copy it and record their answers by ticking the appropriate column. Alternatively, the activity could be completed orally with the whole class. In this case you will need to pause the cassette after each dialogue and check answers immediately. See whether they can hazard guesses as to the meaning of terms such as *doof* or *blöd.*

Teacher: *Hört gut zu. Diese Teenager sprechen über Fernsehsendungen. Ist das positiv oder negativ? Zum Beispiel:* (play and complete the first one on your grid).

Teacher (after playing the relevant extracts): *Wie heißt blöd/doof auf englisch?*

Wie findest du Trickfilme?

1 — Wie findest du die Werbung im Fernsehen?
— Die Werbung? Sie ist blöd.

2 — Siehst du gern Nachrichten?
— Nee. Ich finde sie stinklangweilig.

3 — Wie findest du die Talkshows im Fernsehen?
— Talkshows sind alle so blöd!

4 — Wie findest du die Natursendungen im Fernsehen?
— Meistens interessant. Ich sehe gern Natursendungen.

5 — Siehst du gerne Trickfilme?
— Oh ja. Sie sind toll!

6 — Wie findest du die Spielshows?
— Spielshows find' ich doof.

Solution:

	Positiv	Negativ
1 Werbung		✘
2 Nachrichten		✘
3 Talkshows		✘
4 Natursendungen	✘	
5 Trickfilme	✘	
6 Spielshows		✘

Partnerarbeit. Und du?

Listening
Speaking
Reading

A model dialogue to provide practice in commenting on types of television programme. If necessary refer the students to the TV screens in the book, and ask them questions before they start the pairwork. They could continue the activity in a chain game, taking it in turns to answer a question about a TV programme and then ask their immediate neighbour a different question.

Teacher: *Wie findest du Sportsendungen? Prima? Langweilig? Doof?*

Student: *Doof.*

Teacher (to the whole class): *Wer findet Sportsendungen doof? Hebt die Hand.*

(For the chain game:) *Jetzt ein Kettenspiel.*
(To one student:) *Stell eine Frage an deinen Nachbarn — zum Beispiel: ‚Wie findest du Fernsehfilme?'*

Student 1: *Wie findest du Fernsehfilme?*

Student 2: *Prima.*

Teacher (to student 2): *Jetzt stellst du eine andere Frage ...*

(For the pairwork:) *Jetzt Partnerarbeit. Macht Dialoge. Zum Beispiel:* (perform the model dialogue).

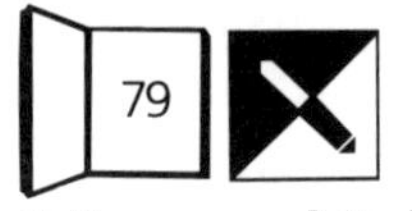

Hören und Sehen

Listening
Speaking
Reading
Writing

An extract from a TV magazine showing programmes for late afternoon/early evening. Ask the students to study the extract and classify the programmes, by title, under the headings listed below. Point out that some categories may have no entries at all, and that they should then write *keine.*

Teacher: *Seht euch diese Sendungen an. Was für Sendungen gibt es hier? Könnt ihr zum Beispiel eine Sportsendung finden? Und eine Natursendung? Schreibt diese Kategorien auf und macht Listen. Vorsicht. Wenn ihr keine Sendungen in einer Kategorie findet, dann schreibt ihr ‚keine'.*

Solution:

Kindersendungen: *baff, Dick und Doof, Trick 7, Dschungelbuch*

Musiksendungen: keine

Sportsendungen: *Sport heute, Sporthelden, Tennis, Step-Aerobic*

Filme: *Kidnapping in New York, Durch dick und dünn*

Natursendungen: keine

Schauspiele: keine

Talkshows: keine

Spielshows: *Geh aufs Ganze, Hopp oder Topp, Ruck Zuck*

Nachrichten: *Tagesschau, 5 vor 5*

Dokumentarfilme: *Nie mehr nach Hause, Alles klar*

Komödien: *Tante Trude aus Buxtehude*

Students' analyses could also be based on a full evening's viewing, if authentic magazines can be made available. Their findings could be displayed and/or stored in a database, showing percentages of TV time devoted to various categories of programme.

Streit

Listening
Speaking
Reading
Writing

Tell the students that Rifat and Cigden cannot agree about the programmes they want to see. Ask them to listen to the argument and list under the two names the programmes they mention.

Teacher: *Rifat und Cigden haben immer Streit. Rifat sagt: ‚Ich will „baff" sehen.' Cigden sagt: ‚Nein, das „Dschungelbuch" ist besser.' Rifat sagt: ‚Ach, das ist doch kindisch.' Was will Rifat sehen? Was will Cigden sehen? Schreibt die Sendungen unter die Namen.* (Write up the two names.)

Streit

Rifat: Ich will *baff* sehen.

Cigden: Nein, das *Dschungelbuch* ist besser.

Rifat: Ach, das ist doch kindisch.

Cigden: Dann sehen wir *Geh aufs Ganze.*

Rifat: Nein. Das Tennisturnier in Kiel ist besser.

Cigden: Ach, das ist doch blöd!

Rifat: Wie wäre es mit *Tante Trude aus Buxtehude*?

Cigden: Nein, der Film *Durch dick und dünn* ist viel besser.

Rifat: Auf keinen Fall — das ist echt doof!

Solution:

Rifat	Cigden
baff	*Dschungelbuch*
Tennisturnier	*Geh aufs Ganze*
Tante Trude	*Durch dick und dünn*

Was willst du sehen?

Listening
Speaking
Reading
Writing

A groupwork activity requiring the students to plan and negotiate an evening's viewing, using the TV magazine extracts. First get the students to practice *Ich will ... sehen* around the class in a chain game, in order to fix in their minds the different word order required. Then ask them to write down the programmes that they would choose from the TV page. Practise with them the vocabulary required to express opinions. You may wish to remind them of the comments they made on school subjects. Quote some of the TV programmes listed and ask them what they think of them.

They should then divide into groups, and take it in turns to say what they want to watch. The others in the group can comment positively or negatively. Finally, they should write out the group's decision, making sure that the programme times don't overlap! This could lead to some entertaining drama work for presentation to the class.

Teacher: *Seht euch die Sendungen an. Wie findet ihr zum Beispiel das ‚Dschungelbuch'? Prima? Toll? Kindisch? Blöd? Was wollt ihr sehen?*
(To one student:) *Du, zum Beispiel: ‚Ich will ...'*

Student: *Ich will ‚baff' sehen.*

Teacher: *Toll! Und du? Schreibt jetzt die Sendungen auf, die ihr sehen wollt. Zum Beispiel: ‚Ich will „baff" sehen.* (Write up the time and the programmes in order.) *Schreibt eine Liste. Jetzt Gruppenarbeit. Ein(e) Schüler(in) sagt, zum Beispiel: ‚Ich will „baff" sehen', und die Anderen sagen ‚Ja prima'/‚Toll!' oder ‚Ach nein, das ist doch doof/blöd/kindisch' ... Schreibt zum Schluß die Sendungen auf, die ihr alle sehen wollt.*

Wann ist der Film?

Listening
Speaking
Reading

A series of short dialogues about the times of the TV programmes listed in the book.
Revise times with the students, and introduce the 24-hour clock, to enable them to produce their own dialogues. Emphasise the position of *Uhr* in times such as *17 Uhr 15.* If necessary, provide a number of 12-hour times on the board/OHP, and ask the students to convert them, in pairs or groups, into 24-hour times.

Play the cassette, and pause it *after* the programme has been named but *before* the time is given. Students can take on the role of the person replying, and have their answers confirmed or corrected by the rest of the dialogue.

Teacher: *Die Uhrzeiten. Wie spät ist es jetzt? ... Gut.* (Use a clockface or drawings to cue more 12-hour times). *Drei Uhr nachmittags ist auch ... ?* (Point to or write up 15.00.) *Ja, fünfzehn Uhr. Und das ... ?* (Choose another programme time.) *Viertel nach fünf oder siebzehn ... ?*

Student: *Siebzehn Uhr fünfzehn.*

Teacher: *Genau. Prima! Hier sind noch mehr Uhrzeiten. Was paßt wozu?*

Write up 12-hour and 24-hour times jumbled, and ask the students to find and say both versions of each time. Encourage them to continue in pairs.

Teacher (for the listening activity): *Jetzt hört ihr ein paar Dialoge. Wann sind diese Sendungen? Hört zu:* (play the first one and pause as suggested before the time is given). *Gut, um ... oder um ... Uhr.*

Wann ist der Film?

1 — Wann ist der Film?
— Meinst du *Kidnapping in New York*?
— Ja.
— Warte mal ... *Kidnapping in New York* ist um ... sechzehn Uhr.

2 — Wann ist *Hopp oder Topp*?
— *Hopp oder Topp* ist um fünfzehn Uhr dreißig.

3 — *Sport heute* ist um achtzehn Uhr, oder?
— Warte mal ... *Sport heute* ... Ja, um achtzehn Uhr. Genau.

4 — Wann ist das Fitnessprogramm?
— *Step-Aerobic*? Um siebzehn Uhr.

5 — Willst du *Dick und Doof* sehen?
— Wann denn?
— Um fünfzehn Uhr dreißig.
— Ja, OK!

6 — Wann ist die Spielshow heute abend?
— Welche? *Geh aufs Ganze*?
— Nein, *Ruck Zuck*.
— Moment ... Um sechzehn Uhr dreißig.

Solution:

1 16.00 **2** 15.30 **3** 18.00 **4** 17.00 **5** 15.30 **6** 16.30

Partnerarbeit. Wann ist die Sportschau?

Listening
Speaking
Reading
Writing

An information-gap activity based on a TV magazine extract. Ask the students to interview each other and find out the missing information on their sheets. Practise the pronunciation of the programme titles before starting the communicative activity.

Teacher: *Partnerarbeit. Seht euch den Arbeitsbogen an. Das sind Fernsehsendungen. Aber beide Partner(innen) haben Lücken. Stellt einander Fragen, und füllt die Lücken aus. Zum Beispiel:* (complete one example and write it up).

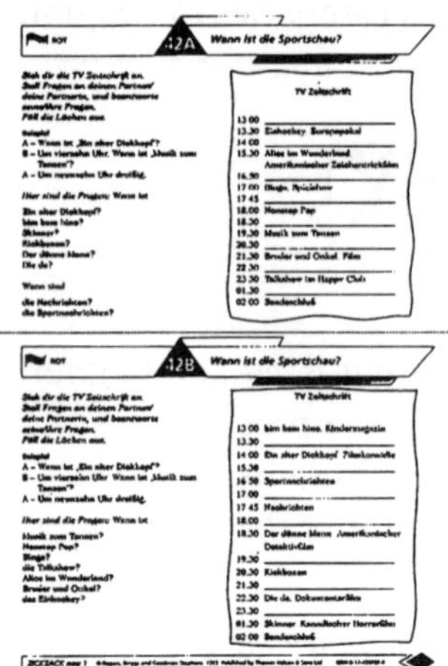

Superglotzer der Woche

Listening
Speaking
Reading

An opportunity for the students to compare their viewing habits. Teach them the term *ungefähr* by asking a student roughly how many hours a week he/she spends watching TV. Then ask the students to interview each other in pairs, using the model dialogue in the students' book, and to find out how long they spend each day watching. Ask them to report back with their findings, and nominate the *Superglotzer(in) der Woche.*

Teacher (to one student): *Wie lange siehst du fern? Montags?* (Write up the days and insert the details for the first one or two.) *Eine Stunde? Ungefähr zwei Stunden? Zwei bis drei Stunden?*

Student: *Zwei Stunden.*

Teacher: *Und dienstags? ... usw. Macht Interviews miteinander und schreibt die Stunden für jeden Tag auf — so ... Dann addiert die Stunden für die ganze Woche* (demonstrate on the board).

Teacher (when the students have finished): *Wer sieht über 12 Stunden fern? Hebt die Hand. Wer sieht über 13 Stunden fern? ... Wer sieht unter 5 Stunden fern? ...*

The students may now attempt the *Lernziel 2* activities in the *Selbstbedienung* section on page 83 of the students' book. See page 107 of this book for more details.

Presentation of language (am liebsten)

Listening
Speaking

Introduce *am liebsten*, both through known vocabulary and in a familiar context such as school subjects and leisure activities. Refer the students to ***Tip des Tages*** on page 80 of the students' book for support throughout the activity.

Teacher: *Was machst du gern in der Schule? Und was machst du am liebsten in der Schule? Was ist dein Lieblingsfach?*
(Continue with the following sequence:) *Ich gehe gern schwimmen. Ich spiele gern Squash. Ich sehe gern fern. Ich höre gern Musik. Am liebsten höre ich Musik.*

Go through the same list again in a different order, always transforming the last item into *Am liebsten ...* Continue until all the expressions in the sequence have been inverted.

Distribute a selection of flashcards or other pictures, and encourage students to display their cards, in turn, in order to elicit from other students *Was machst du am liebsten?* — to which they should reply *Am liebsten ...*

Student: *Am liebsten spiele ich Tennis.*

Teacher (to student): *Zeig deine Karte.* (To class:) *Wie stellt man die Frage? Was trinkst du am ... ?*

Student: *Was trinkst du am liebsten?*

Sonja und Max

Listening
Speaking
Reading
Writing

Two interviews with teenagers focusing on things they like to eat and drink. Ask the students to listen and note only the favourite foods and drink for both Sonja and Max.

Teacher: *Hört gut zu. Was trinkt Sonja am liebsten?* (Write this up.) *Und was ißt sie am liebsten? Und Max?*

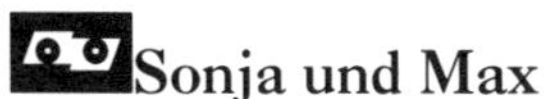**Sonja und Max**

— Was trinkst du gern, Sonja?

— Das ist schwer zu sagen. Zum Frühstück trinke ich gern Kaffee. In der Pause trinke ich gern Milch, aber abends trinke ich gern Cola oder Tee.

— Was trinkst du am liebsten?

— Naja, ich glaube, ich trinke Tee am liebsten.

— Und was ißt du gern?

— Was ich gern esse? Zum Frühstück esse ich gern Brötchen, ganz frisch und warm und knusprig, mit Butter und Marmelade.

— Was ißt du am liebsten?

— Das ist einfach. Am liebsten esse ich Schokolade.

— Danke, Sonja. Und du, Max. Was trinkst du gern?

— Ich trinke gern Limonade, Cola und auch Wasser.

— Und was trinkst du am liebsten?

— Am liebsten trinke ich Limonade.

— Und was ißt du gern?

— Ich esse gern Steak, Pommes frites, Wurst und Käse.

— Und was ißt du am liebsten?

— Am liebsten esse ich Steak.

— Vielen Dank, Max.

Solution:

Sonja ißt am liebsten Schokolade und trinkt am liebsten Tee; Max ißt am liebsten Steak und trinkt am liebsten Limonade

Statistik: Jugendliche in der Freizeit

Listening
Speaking
Reading

A simple reading comprehension exercise dealing with the overall popularity of out-of-school activities among a sample of one hundred 13- to 14-year-olds. The students could convert the statistics in the piechart into a bar graph. You could then conduct a class survey and ask them to present the results in a similar way, calling it *Freizeit-Statistik der Klasse.*

Teacher: *Seht euch die Statistik an. Was machen die Jugendlichen am liebsten in ihrer Freizeit? Wieviel Prozent hören am liebsten Musik? Und wieviel spielen am liebsten Fußball? Und jetzt ihr. Wer hört am liebsten Musik? Hebt die Hand* (write up the statistics). *Könnt ihr diese Statistik so darstellen?* (Draw a bargraph.)

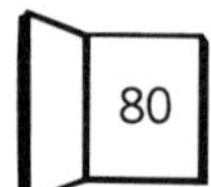

Britta Tell — ein Profil

Reading
Writing

This profile about the fictitious popstar Britta Tell continues the idea of favourite activities, extending the concept to other areas. The students have already encountered *Lieblingsfach*, and should be able to work out most of the other compound nouns.

IT suggestion

Students could then produce their own profiles, using word-processing or desktop-publishing software, and perhaps leaving out the *Lieblingsmotto*. Their final versions could be left anonymous and circulated for other students to guess the identity of the authors!

Was für Musik hörst du am liebsten?

Listening
Speaking
Reading
Writing

A number of teenagers stating their preferences in music. Ask the students to look at the photographs and separate texts and speculate as to who says what. Once they have decided, let them listen to the cassette to see whether they have guessed correctly.

Teacher: *Seht euch die Fotos und Texte an. Diese Teenager sagen, was für Musik sie am liebsten hören. Wer sagt wohl was? Was meint ihr? Wer sagt zum Beispiel ,Am liebsten höre ich klassische Musik'? Murat? Sonja? Hört zu: hier sind die Antworten.*

Follow this up by asking students to express their own views on types of music .

Was für Musik hörst du am liebsten?

1 — Hallo. Mein Name ist Murat. Meine Lieblingsmusik? Naja, am liebsten höre ich Popmusik.

2 — Ich heiße Stefan. Ich bin in einer Rockgruppe. Die Gruppe heißt Metal Hammer. Meine Lieblingsmusik ist natürlich Rock!

3 — Hallo. Ich bin Sonja. Ich spiele in einem Orchester. Am liebsten spiele ich klassische Musik.

4 — Tag. Ich heiße Hatice. Ich gehe oft in die Disco. Am liebsten höre ich Tanzmusik.

5 — Grüß dich. Ich bin Florian. Ich spiele kein Instrument, aber ich höre gern Musik. Am liebsten höre ich Jazz oder Chansons.

Solution:

Murat — Popmusik; Stefan — Rock;
Sonja — klassische Musik; Hatice — Tanzmusik;
Florian — Jazz/Chansons.

In meiner Freizeit

Listening
Speaking
Reading

A song bewailing the fact that, even if you have lots of hobbies, you've always got homework to tie you down. Encourage the students to learn the words by heart and sing the song as a class, in groups and/or with alternate verses/chorus sung by different groups.

In meiner Freizeit

Was machst du nach der Schule?
Naja, es tut mir leid.
Ich möchte gerne kommen,
Doch hab' ich keine Zeit.

Eine Stunde Hausaufgaben,
Manchmal zwei.
In meiner Freizeit
Bin ich niemals frei!

Ich spiele gern Gitarre,
Hab' jedoch wenig Zeit.
Ich gehe gern spazieren,
Doch ich komme nie sehr weit.

Eine Stunde Hausaufgaben,
Manchmal zwei.
In meiner Freizeit
Bin ich niemals frei!

Ich gehe nicht mehr schwimmen,
Und ich schwimme doch so gern.
Ich gehe nie ins Kino.
Ich sehe selten fern.

Zwei Stunden Hausaufgaben,
Manchmal drei.
In meiner Freizeit
Bin ich niemals ...
Bist du niemals ...
Bin ich niemals frei!

Students may now attempt the *Lernziel 3* activities in the *Selbstbedienung* section on page 83 of the students' book. See page 107 of this book for more details.

sb Selbstbedienung

Lernziel 1

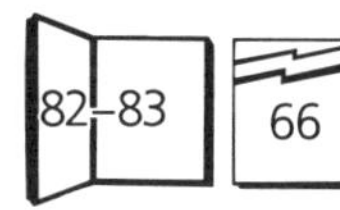

Was machst du?

Incomplete drawings of leisure activities. Students must write down what each person would say to describe the activity.

Solution: **1** Ich fahre mit dem Rad. **2** Ich spiele Fußball. **3** Ich gehe mit dem Hund spazieren **4** Ich spiele Tennis. **5** Ich spiele mit dem Computer. **6** Ich treffe mich mit meinen Freunden.

Treffpunkt

Students are asked to note what they would look for in a penfriend in terms of their age and hobbies. They must then read the penpal advertisements, and find a boy and a girl who comes closest to their requirements. They are also invited to advertise themselves in similar fashion for *Treffpunkt* magazine.

Lernziel 2

Was machst du gern nach der Schule?

A series of statements to match to the places illustrated.

Solution: **1** e **2** a **3** c **4** d **5** b

Stimmt das?

A 'true or false?' activity based on the TV guide extracts on page 79.

Solution: **1** richtig **2** falsch **3** falsch **4** richtig **5** richtig **6** falsch **7** falsch

Lernziel 3

Aber am liebsten ...

The students should complete the sentences using *am liebsten*, amending the subject/verb order accordingly.

Solution: **1** ... aber am liebsten spielt sie Klavier. **2** ... aber am liebsten geht er schwimmen. **3** ... aber am liebsten geht er in die Disco. **4** ... aber am liebsten geht sie mit dem Hund spazieren.

Mein Freizeitwappen

The students are asked to design their own leisure activities shield, using the one illustrated as a model.

Bildvokabeln

Musikinstrumente

A collection of labelled musical instruments. Students can use the copymaster to label the illustrations themselves.

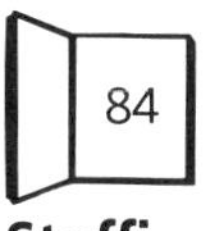

Steffi

Further adventures of Steffi — not intended for detailed exploitation.

Grammar exercises 14–15, on copymaster 75, is based on the material covered in this chapter.

After completing work on this chapter, check whether any further reinforcement is appropriate from the video material, Activity Box cards and Assessment Support Pack tasks.

9 Was kostet das?

Main teaching points

Lernziel 1: Talking about money and prices

Grammar presented: Third person singular present tense

Vocabulary presented:

der Arme	*fein*	*könnte*	*der Pfennig*	*der Sticker*
der Bettler	*fing ... an*	*leben*	*das Poster*	*das Stückchen*
bezahlt	*das Geld*	*der andere*	*der Preis*	*das T-Shirt*
einige Leute	*die Geldsumme*	*der Millionär*	*der Rappen*	*wäre*
der eine	*der Groschen*	*die Münze*	*reich*	*die Welt*
Franken	*die Hand*	*nie*	*der Schein*	
der Fußball	*der Kreis*	*ohne*	*Schillinge*	

Grammar revised:

Numbers

Countries

Lernziel 2: Talking about snacks and ice creams

Grammar presented: *einmal, zweimal*

Vocabulary presented:

die Bratwurst	*das Eis*	*das Erdbeereis*	*nimmst du?*	*Vanille*	*die Wurstbude*
einmal	*die Eisbude*	*ich habe Hunger*	*Schaschlik*	*das Vanilleeis*	*zweimal*

Grammar revised: Interrogatives

Lernziel 3: Saying what you spend your money on

Grammar presented:

geben für + accusative

Separable verb (*ausgeben*)

wofür?

fahren mit + dative

Vocabulary presented:

die Achterbahn	*gibst du ... aus?*	*kommst du mit?*	*sparst du?*
der Autoscooter	*das Jahrmarkt*	*das Make-up*	*das Theater*
fährst du?	*das Karussell*	*das Riesenrad*	*wofür*
die Geisterbahn	*Kleider*	*die Schiffschaukel*	*die Zeitschrift*

Grammar revised:

gern

zum

am liebsten

Before beginning work on this chapter, check where the video material, Activity Box cards and Assessment Support Pack tasks will be most appropriate.

Revision of language (numbers 1–100)

Listening
Speaking

Revise the numbers 1 to 100 in a variety of ways:

1 Ja oder nein?

Write a selection of numbers (about 20) at random on the board/OHP. Then read out a series of numbers, only some of which are on the board. The students must call out *Ja* when they hear a number that is written up, and *Nein* when the number does not feature. This could also be done in competing groups.

2 Umgekehrt

Name a student, who has to say any number in German between 10 and 99. That student then challenges someone else of his/her choice to reverse the figures and give the German for that number — for example:

Student A: *Vierundzwanzig* (24). *Sarah.*

Sarah: *Zweiundvierzig* (42).

3 Jede Menge

Write 100 on the board and say *hundert.* Now write 2 on the board and elicit *zwei.* Add two noughts to give 200 and elicit *zweihundert.* Write 300, 400 and so on up to 900. Finally give *tausend.*

4 Wieviel?

Some simple adding or subtracting could be attempted as practice in dealing with prices. Dictate the sum and ask for the answers in German.

Teacher: *Zweihundert minus acht* (repeat) *macht ... ?*

Teacher: *Hundertzwanzig plus sechsundzwanzig* (repeat) *macht ... ?*

5 Zählt mal

An effective way of showing the students how to understand (very) high numbers easily. Draw columns for units, tens, hundreds, thousands and tens of thousands, as shown below. Then ask the students to follow your example, thus:

Choose a high number, e.g. 55,631; point in turn to the 50,000 in the tens-of-thousands column, the 5,000 in the thousands column, the 600 in the hundreds column, the 30 in the tens column and the 1 in the units column.

Although the system does not appear to circumvent the problem of inverted numbers (e.g. *fünfundzwanzig-tausend* = 25,000), students soon learn to select the numbers quickly from the appropriate columns. Some may decide to point to the columns in 'German' order (e.g. for *fünfundfünfzigtausend*, column B, then column A). Hand the activity over to students gradually, until they can play it in groups.

A	B	C	D	E
90 000	9 000	900	90	9
80 000	8 000	800	80	8
70 000	7 000	700	70	7
60 000	6 000	600	60	6
50 000	5 000	500	50	5
40 000	4 000	400	40	4
30 000	3 000	300	30	3
20 000	2 000	200	20	2
10 000	1 000	100	10	1

Geld

Listening
Speaking
Reading

Introduce the students to the concept of currencies by comparing different countries.

Teacher: *In Großbritannien haben wir Pfund und Pence.* (Demonstrate:) *Dies hier ist das Geld in Großbritannien. Das ist ein Pfund. Das sind zehn Pence. In Frankreich gibt es Francs und Centimes. In den USA gibt es Dollars und Cents. Wieviel Cents hat ein Dollar? Wieviel Pence hat ein englisches Pfund? Wieviel Centimes hat ein Franc? Wie ist das in Deutschland? Was gibt es dort? Wie ist das in Österreich? Was gibt es dort? Wie ist das in der Schweiz? Was gibt es dort?*

It is likely that some of the currencies will already be known. If not, introduce them orally. Ensure that *Mark* or *D-Mark* is used, not *Deutschmark.* Give the students some time to familiarise themselves with the pictures of the coins and notes, then help them with the pronunciation. Ensure that they appreciate the difference between *Münzen* and *Scheine.*

Teacher: *Seht euch das Geld an. Das ist ein Geldschein* (show a note, then point to the notes in the book) *und das ist ein Fünfzigmarkschein, und das ist ... ?*
(For the coins:) *Also, das ist ein Schein, aber das hier ist eine Münze.* (Point to the coins in the book:) *Man sagt: ‚Das ist ein Fünfmarkstück'. Und das ... ?*

Now tell students that they are going to hear people mentioning prices, and that they must decide which country they are in. Emphasise that they are listening only for the currency and not the price or the items bought.

Teacher: *Ihr hört gleich einige Leute, die über Geld reden. Sie sagen manchmal ‚Franken' und ‚Rappen' — dann sind sie in der Schweiz. Manchmal sagen sie ‚Mark' und ‚Pfennig'. Wo sind sie dann?*

Student: *In Deutschland.*

Teacher: *Gut. So, jetzt hört gut zu. Wo sind die Leute?*

Geld

1 — Eine Cola, bitte.
— Hier, bitte schön. Zwei Mark fünfzig.

2 — Ein Schokoladeneis, bitte.
— Zu 10 Schilling?
— Ja, genau.
— Also, hier. Danke.

3 — Was kostet das?
— 10 Franken, 50 Rappen.

4 — Was macht das?
— 25 Mark.

5 — Hast du Geld dabei?
— Nur 20 Schilling. Wieso?
— Ich möchte noch eine Postkarte kaufen.

6 — Was kostet dieses T-shirt?
— 20 Franken.
— Oh, dann nein, danke.
— Bitte schön.

7 — Wieviel Taschengeld kriegst du?
— 20 Mark die Woche. Und du?
— Ich auch.

8 — Guck mal, die Kassette kostet nur hundert Schilling!
— Mensch, das ist ja billig. Kaufen wir die?
— Natürlich!

Solution:

1 Deutschland **2** Österreich **3** Schweiz **4** Deutschland **5** Österreich **6** Schweiz **7** Deutschland **8** Österreich

Wieviel Geld hast du dabei?

Listening
Speaking

Introduce the question *Wieviel Geld hast du dabei?* by counting some of your money in front of the class, and then ask individual students how much money they have on them. If or when the need arises, teach *Ich habe kein Geld dabei* and write it up with the key question just introduced.

Teacher: *50 Pence, ein Pfund ... zwei Pfund dreißig. Ich habe zwei Pfund dreißig dabei. Wieviel Geld hast du dabei?*

Student: *40 Pence.*

Students could continue the activity in pairs, using either the actual amount of money they have or sums they have invented and written down. It may prove helpful to start this game using pounds and pence first. To make it still more of a guessing game, you could teach them *Hast du mehr/weniger als ... Mark?* Ask the students to say how much they think a Mark is worth, in order to give them a clear idea of the amount of money the teenagers on the cassette have (see below).

Wieviel Geld haben sie dabei?

Listening
Speaking
Writing

A number of short recorded dialogues in which people talk about how much money they have on them. Ask the students to listen to the recording and note how much money each person has.

Teacher: *Hört gut zu. Wieviel Geld hat Metin? Wieviel Geld hat Leila? Ralf? Brigitte?* (Write up the names.)

Wieviel Geld haben sie dabei?

1 — Brigitte, wieviel Geld hast du dabei?
— 30 Mark. Meine Oma hat mir 30 Mark gegeben.

2 — Und wieviel Geld hast du dabei, Leila?
— 10 Mark. Ist das genug?
— Naja, das geht schon.

3 — Und du, Ralf? Wieviel Geld hast du dabei?
— Nur 20 Mark.

4 — Hast du Geld dabei, Metin?
— Ja, ziemlich viel. 35 Mark.

Solution:

Brigitte — 30 Mark; Leila — 10 Mark; Ralf — 20 Mark; Metin — 35 Mark

Partnerarbeit. Was kostet das?

Listening
Speaking
Reading

An activity designed to help students get used to German money. The visuals show variously priced articles. Familiarise the students with the new items of vocabulary (most of which are at least near-cognates) before asking them the price of each.

Teacher: *Seht euch diese Artikel an. Das ist eine Tafel Schokolade ... eine Kassette ...* (list the various items). *Was kostet ein T-Shirt? Und was kostet ein Tennisschläger? Und eine Cola?*

As a variant you could give the price but not the name of the item — thus:

Teacher: *Was kostet ... Mark?*

Hand the activity over to the students to perform in pairs as soon as possible.

The second stage of the activity assumes that the students are buying these items and are paying with various notes. Tell them what they have to pay with — for example, a 100-Mark note — and ask them what change they expect to receive.

Teacher (to one student): *Ich kaufe mir ein Eis. Ich bezahle mit einem Zehnmarkschein. Was bekomme ich zurück? Oder ich bezahle mit einem Zwanzigmarkschein — was bekomme ich zurück?*

Ask the students to continue the activity in pairs, choosing whichever item and denominations they wish.

Teacher: *Partnerarbeit. Wählt einen Artikel — zum Beispiel, ein T-Shirt. Partner(in) A sagt: ‚Ich kaufe mir ein T-Shirt mit einem Tausendmarkschein. Was bekomme ich zurück?'*

Partnerarbeit. Sechs Unterschiede

Listening
Speaking
Reading

A communicative activity based on 'spot the difference'. Ask the students to question each other about the items shown on their sheets, and to find the six differences in prices shown. Perform the model dialogue with a student.

Teacher: *Seht euch die Bilder und Preise an. Was kosten die Artikel? Partner(in) A hat diesselben Bilder wie Partner(in) B, aber sechs Preise sind anders. Stellt und beantwortet Fragen, und findet die Unterschiede heraus. Zum Beispiel: Ich bin Partner/in A ...*
(To a student:) *Was kostet das T-Shirt?*

Student: *DM 12,50.*

Teacher: *OK. Und der Fußball?*

Student: *(Er kostet) DM 20.*

Teacher: *Nein, dreißig Mark. Das ist ein Unterschied. Ihr schreibt* (write the following up):

	A	B
der Fußball	DM 30	DM 20

Jetzt Partnerarbeit.

Solution:

	A	B
die Kassette	DM 17,50	DM 17
der Tennisschläger	DM 150	DM 160
der Aufkleber	DM 1,50	DM 1,60
die Cola	DM 2,20	DM 2,50
der Fußball	DM 30	DM 20
der Kuli	DM 10	DM 11

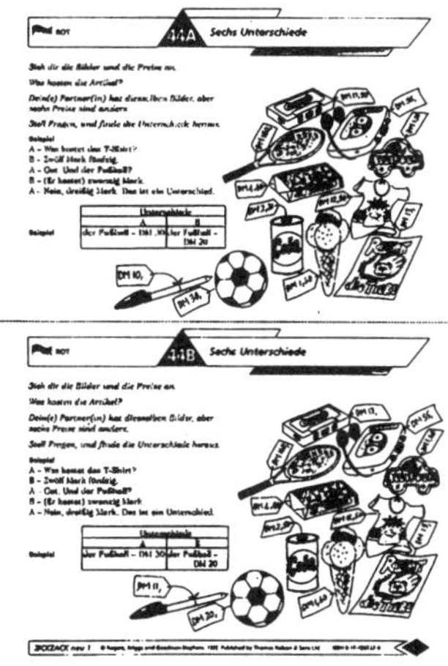

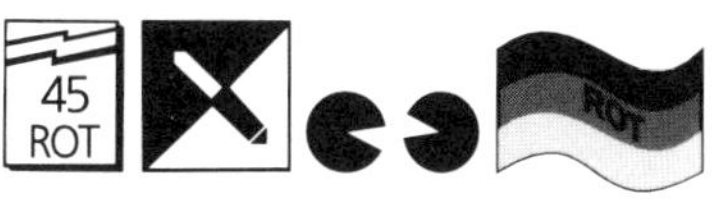

Partnerarbeit. Hast du mein Portemonnaie?

Listening
Speaking
Reading

A whole-class communicative game based on different amounts of money lost by Partner A but found by Partner B. Ask Partner-A students to find out who has found their purse/wallet by comparing the amounts of money shown on their cards. (If you have fewer than 32 students in your group, make sure that you reduce the number of cards consistently so that everybody can find a match. If there are 30 students, for example, remove the last item on each of the two halves.)

Teacher: *Partnerarbeit.*
(To all Partner-A students:) *Ihr habt euer Portemonnaie verloren. Seht euch die Geldsumme an, die drin ist* (point to the copymaster). *Findet heraus, wer euer Portemonnaie gefunden hat.*
(To all Partner-B students:) *Ihr habt ein Portemonnaie gefunden. Seht euch die Geldsumme an, die drin ist. Wer hat dieses Portemonnaie verloren? Macht Dialoge.*

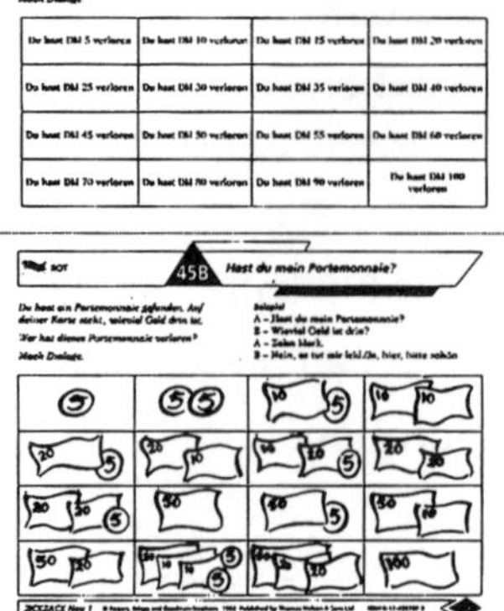

Perform a the model dialogue with three or four students in turn.

Auf der Bank

Listening
Speaking
Reading
Writing

A number of transactions in a bank. Play the recording, asking the students to write down how much money each customer wants to change and into which currency.

Teacher: *Hört gut zu. Diese Leute sind auf der Bank. Sie wollen Geld wechseln — zum Beispiel, Pfund in Mark, oder Pfund in Schilling oder in Franken* (write this up). *Wie heißt ‚wechseln' auf englisch? Wieviel Geld wollen sie wechseln?* (Complete the first one or two with the class, thus:)

1 10 Pfund → DM

2 25 Pfund → DM

Auf der Bank

1 — Guten Tag.
— Guten Tag.
— Ich möchte bitte zehn Pfund in D-Mark wechseln.
— Zehn Pfund? Ja, gerne. Bitte schön. Sie bekommen Ihr Geld da rechts an der Kasse.

2 — Guten Morgen.
— Kann ich hier Geld wechseln?
— Ja, sicher.
— Ich möchte fünfundzwanzig Pfund in D-Mark umwechseln, bitte.
— So? Moment bitte.

3 — Kann ich hier Pfund gegen D-Mark wechseln, bitte?
— Ja, natürlich. Wieviel wollen Sie wechseln?
— Fünfunddreißig Pfund.
— Danke schön. Fünf, zehn, zwanzig, dreißig, fünfunddreißig. Stimmt.

4 — Guten Tag.
— Ich möchte gern hundert Pfund in Schweizer Franken umwechseln, bitte.

5 — Kann ich Ihnen helfen?
— Ja, ich möchte etwas Geld wechseln, bitte.
— Ja, gerne. Was möchten Sie denn wechseln?
— Vierzig Pfund in D-Mark, bitte.

6 — Guten Morgen.
— Guten Morgen. Ich möchte diesen Reisescheck einlösen, bitte.
— Das sind fünfzig Pfund, ja?
— Ja.
— So, fünfzig Pfund gegen Schillinge, bitte hier unterschreiben.
— Danke schön.

7 — Können Sie mir dreißig Pfund in Schillinge umwechseln, bitte?
— Ja, gerne.

Solution:

1 £10 → DM **2** £25 → DM **3** £35 → DM
4 £100 → Franken **5** £40 → DM 6 £50 → Schilling
7 £30 → Schilling

Welt ohne Geld

Listening
Speaking
Reading
Writing

A song about how much more pleasant it would be to live in a world where money was not all-important.

Welt ohne Geld

Von Hand zu Hand, von Land zu Land,
Geht es in einem Kreis.
Jedoch der Arme auf der Welt,
Der bezahlt den Preis.

Eine Welt ohne Geld,
Da könnte man leben.
Eine Welt ohne Geld,
Nun das wäre fein!
Eine Welt ohne Geld,
Das wird es nie geben.
Eine Welt ohne Geld,
So wird es nie sein.

Der eine gibt zehntausend aus,
Das ist nur ein Spiel.
Der andere braucht ein Stückchen Brot,
Ihm kostet das zuviel.

Eine Welt ohne Geld,
Da könnte man leben.
Eine Welt ohne Geld,
Nun das wäre fein!
Eine Welt ohne Geld,
Das wird es nie geben.
Eine Welt ohne Geld,
So wird es nie sein.

Der eine war ein reicher Mann,
Heute hat er nichts mehr.
Der andere fing als Bettler an
Und ist jetzt Millionär.

Eine Welt ohne Geld,
Da könnte man leben.
Eine Welt ohne Geld,
Nun das wäre fein!
Eine Welt ohne Geld,
Das wird es nie geben.
Eine Welt ohne Geld,
So wird es nie sein.

Students may now attempt the *Lernziel 1* activities in the *Selbstbedienung* section on page 92 of the students' book. See page 119 of this book for more details.

An der Eisbude

Listening
Speaking
Reading

Introduce and practise ice-cream flavours using the price list in the students' book. Familiarise the students with the abbreviated forms of the various flavours, including the notation for *zweimal*, *dreimal* etc. Then ask the students to listen to and repeat the first dialogue.

Teacher: *Das ist eine Eisbude. Da kauft man Eis. Nun seht auf die Preisliste, und hört zu ... Hört nochmal zu und wiederholt.*

Now ask the students how someone asks for a vanilla ice-cream.

Teacher: *Ich möchte ein Vanilleeis. Was sage ich?*

Student: *Einmal Vanille.*

Repeat for *ein Schokoladeneis*, then play the second dialogue and do the same for *zweimal.*

Finally, read through the transcripts of the dialogue in the students' book.

An der Eisbude

1 — Einmal Vanille und einmal Schokolade, bitte.
— Hier, bitte, einmal Vanille und einmal Schokolade. Zwei Mark.

2 — Zweimal Erdbeer und zweimal Schokolade, bitte.
— So. Zweimal Erdbeer und zweimal Schokolade. Vier Mark.

Einmal Vanille

Listening
Speaking
Reading
Writing

Further dialogues at an ice-cream stand. Ask the students to listen to the recording and make notes of what they can understand. Use 'S' for *Schokolade*, 'V' for *Vanille*, 'H' for *Himbeer*, and so on.

Teacher: *An der Eisbude. Was kaufen die Leute? Ihr hört ‚Einmal Vanille' und schreibt hier ein ‚V' hin. Und hier schreibt ihr den Preis hin. Nummer eins:* (write up *Eis* and *Preis*, and complete the first one with the class).

Einmal Vanille

1 — Einmal Vanille und einmal Schokolade, bitte.
— Hier, bitte. Zwei Mark.

2 — Einmal Himbeer und zweimal Erdbeer.
— Drei Mark.

3 — Einmal Zitrone und einmal Erdbeer, bitte.
— Das macht zwei Mark.

4 — Zweimal Schoko und zweimal Zitrone, bitte.
— Vier Mark.

5 — Ich hätte gern ein Eis — Mokka und Vanille.
— Das macht dann zwei Mark.

6 — Zweimal Erdbeer und einmal Himbeer, bitte.
— Drei Mark, bitte.

7 — Eine Kugel Himbeer und eine Kugel Vanille, bitte.
— Bitt' schön. Zwei Mark.

8 — Zweimal Mokka und zweimal Zitrone, bitte.
— Vier Mark, bitte.

Solution:

	Eis	Preis
1	V, S	DM 2
2	H, E(×2)	DM 3
3	Z, E	DM 2
4	S(×2), Z(×2)	DM 4
5	M+V	DM 2
6	E(×2), H	DM 3
7	H, V	DM 2
8	M(×2), Z(×2)	DM 4

Presentation of language (snacks)

Listening
Speaking
Reading
Writing

Present the flashcards of other snacks one by one — for example: *Das ist ein Hamburger* — asking the students to repeat after you. After the first three, hold up one of the flashcards and ask: *Was ist das?* Continue with the next three in the same way until the students have seen and said the names of all of them. Make sure the students are clear about the difference between *Chips* and *Pommes frites*. Alternatively, copymaster 46 could be used.

Teacher: *Schaut auf die Karten und wiederholt: (der) Hamburger, (das) Schaschlik, usw.*

Practise using various games, such as:

1 Stimmt das?

A 'true or false?' game.

Teacher: *Schreibt eins bis zehn in euer Heft. Ich halte eine Karte hoch, so* (hold up *Bratwurst*) ... *und ich sage ‚ein Hamburger'. Stimmt das? Nein! Dann schreibt ihr ‚N' für ‚nein'. Wenn ‚ja', dann schreibt ihr ‚J'.*

2 Gedächtnisspiel

Stand the cards in a row with their backs to the class on a table or shelf, or blu-tack them to the board, naming each one as you position it. Don't work from left to right, but dot them about randomly, filling the gaps with the last ones. Now either divide the class into teams or choose individuals, and ask where they think the nominated items of food are. The individual or team representative comes up and chooses a card, which is removed if he/she is right and replaced if he/she is wrong.

Teacher: *Wo ist das Schaschlik? Wo sind die Chips?* ...

Was ißt du gern?

This worksheet can be used in a variety of ways: as reinforcement or as a possible homework activity, especially for students with learning difficulties; as an OHP Master providing an alternative way of presenting and practising different foods; or cut up into cards to play various word games.

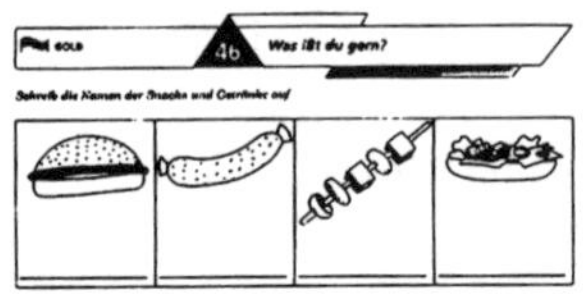

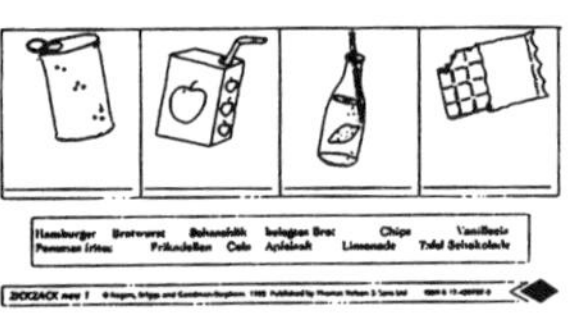

Was nimmst du?

Listening
Speaking
Reading

Dialogues at a *Wurstbude*. Ask the students to write 1 to 8 in their books. Explain that they are going to hear eight conversations. The pictures labelled A to H show what the people in the conversations are buying. Students must write a letter next to each number to show who buys what. Do the first one together as an example.

Teacher: *Ihr hört gleich acht Gespräche. Hier kaufen die Leute etwas zu trinken oder zu essen. Jetzt seht euch das Buch an, Seite 88. Da seht ihr, was die Leute kaufen. Aber wer bestellt was? Zum Beispiel, Nummer eins. Hört gut zu!* (Play the first conversation.) *Nun, was kaufen sie?*

Student: *Eine Bratwurst und zwei Cola.*

Teacher: *Richtig. Und wo ist das im Buch?*

Student: *Hier. C.*

Teacher: *Gut.* (Write '1C' on the board/OHP.) *Und jetzt Nummer zwei.*

Was nimmst du?

1 — Was nimmst du, Regina?
— Ich nehme eine Cola.
— Martin?
— Eine Bratwurst, bitte.
— Und ich nehme auch eine Cola, also zwei Cola und eine Bratwurst, bitte.

2 — Einmal Bratwurst mit Ketchup, bitte. Und ... was nimmst du?
— Hmm ... Eine Portion Pommes für mich.
— Also eine Portion Pommes und einmal Bratwurst mit Ketchup.

3 — Ja, bitte?
— Zweimal Schaschlik und einmal Bratwurst, bitte.
— So, zweimal Schaschlik und einmal Bratwurst. Sonst noch etwas?
— Was trinkt ihr denn alle?
— Cola, bitte.
— Ja, ich auch.
— Ich nehme eine Limo.
— Also, zweimal Schaschlik, einmal Bratwurst, zweimal Cola und eine Limo.
— Ja, genau.

4 — Ich hätte gern einen Hamburger und eine Currywurst.
— Ist das alles?
— Und zweimal Apfelsaft, bitte.
— Bitte sehr.

5 — Ein belegtes Brot mit Käse, bitte.
— Etwas zu trinken?
— Nein, danke.

6 — Du, ich habe Hunger. Essen wir etwas?
— Ja, klar. Guck mal, da ist eine Imbißbude. Was willst du? Pommes frites?
— Ja, gut. Und ich trinke einen Apfelsaft dazu.
— Zwei Portionen Pommes frites, eine Cola und einen Apfelsaft, bitte.

7 — Bitte schön?
— Einmal Schaschlik und ... Karin?
— Zwei Frikadellen, bitte.
— Also — zwei Frikadellen, einmal Schaschlik und zweimal Limo, bitte.

8 — Mensch, bin ich durstig! Ich kaufe mir eine Cola. Nimmst du auch etwas?
— Ja, gute Idee.
— Zwei Cola, bitte.
— Ich glaub', ich kaufe mir auch etwas zu essen.
— Die haben hier Chips.
— Also, zweimal Chips und zwei Cola.

Solution:

1 C **2** F **3** B **4** H **5** A **6** D **7** G **8** E

Partnerarbeit. An der Wurstbude

Listening
Speaking
Reading

A photo of a price list at a *Wurstbude*. Ask the students to look at the price list and answer a few questions. When they are confident, ask them to continue in pairs.

Teacher: *Schaut auf die Preisliste. Was kostet hier eine Bratwurst? Kann man hier Chips kaufen? Jetzt Partnerarbeit. Stellt einander Fragen. Zum Beispiel:* (perform the model dialogue).

Follow up the activity by asking students to produce their own dialogues based on the price list and the language in the ***Tip des Tages***. These could be word-processed.

Teacher: *Jetzt seid ihr an der Wurstbude. Macht Dialoge mit einem Partner/einer Partnerin. Zum Beispiel:* (demonstrate).

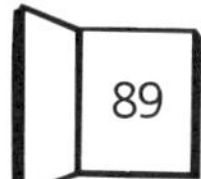

Die neue Kellnerin

Reading

This reading activity is intended to reinforce the students' recognition of snacks and drinks. They simply need to decide from the visuals whether the waitress has brought the correct order each time.

Solution:

a richtig **b** falsch **c** falsch **d** richtig

IT suggestion

The dialogues could be 'written up' for homework using word-processing software.

Students may now attempt the *Lernziel 2* activities in the *Selbstbedienung* section on pages 92–93 of the students' book. See pages 119–120 of this book for more details.

Ich gebe mein Geld für CDs aus

Listening
Speaking
Reading

A piechart to illustrate the results of a survey of young people on ways in which they spend their money. Read through the introductory text with the students, and practise pronunciation of the question *Wofür gibst du dein Geld aus?* Go through the various categories named, clarifying what each one means. Then ask individual students what they spend their money on.

Teacher: *Seht euch das Diagramm an. Das ist das Resultat einer Umfrage. Die Frage ist: ‚Wofür gibst du dein Geld aus?' Wie heißt das auf englisch? Zwanzig Prozent geben ihr Geld für Kleider aus. Wieviel Prozent geben ihr Geld für Make-up aus? ... Und ihr?*
(To one student:) *Wofür gibst du dein Geld aus?*

Student: *(Für) Hobbys.*

Now the students should be able to listen to the cassette and note how people spend their money.

Teacher: *Hört gut zu. Wofür geben diese Teenager ihr Geld aus? Schreibt die Kategorien auf. Zum Beispiel:* (complete the first one with the class).

Ich gebe mein Geld für CDs aus

1 — Wofür gibst du dein Geld aus?
— Meistens für meine Hobbys.

2 — Wofür gibst du dein Geld aus?
— Naja, für Bonbons und Snacks.

3 — Und du?
— Ich gebe mein ganzes Geld für Kleider aus.

4 — Wofür gibst du dein Geld aus?
— Meistens für Make-up und CDs.

5 — Wofür gibst du dein Geld aus?
— Ich gehe oft aus ... ins Theater, ins Kino oder in die Disco.

6 — Und du?
— Ich lese sehr gern. Ich gebe mein Geld für Zeitschriften und Bücher aus.

Solution:

1 Hobbys **2** Bonbons und Snacks **3** Kleider **4** Make-up und CDs **5** Ausgehen **6** Zeitschriften und Bücher

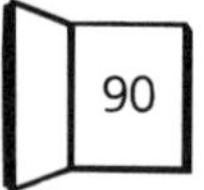

Umfrage

Speaking
Listening

Finally, the students could carry out a survey, working in groups and asking each other what they spend their money on. Collate the results of all the groups, and convert them into percentages for (some of) the students to record either on a bar graph or a piechart for display. The information could also be stored in a database.

Teacher: *Gruppenarbeit. Macht jetzt eine Umfrage. Stellt einander die Frage ‚Wofür gibst du dein Geld aus?' und schreibt die Kategorien auf.*
(For collating the results:) *Wieviel in der Gruppe geben ihr Geld für Make-up aus? ...*

Write up *Make-up* and all the other categories, together with the totals for conversion to percentages.

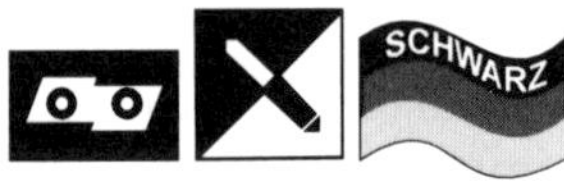

Sechs junge Leute

Listening
Writing

Tell the students they are going to hear six young people talking about how they spend their money. Ask them to make a note of what each person buys. Write up the list of names.

Teacher: *Hört zu. Sechs junge Leute sagen, wie sie ihr Geld ausgeben. Was kaufen sie? Hier sind die Namen.*

Sechs junge Leute

1 — Inga, wofür gibst du dein Geld aus?
— Naja, ich gehe gern aus. Ich gehe immer am Wochenende aus, ins Kino oder so. Und ich kaufe mir auch mal eine Zeitschrift.

2 — Omar, wofür gibst du dein Geld aus?
— Tja, für Kleider, und für Bücher und Hefte für die Schule. Und dann brauche ich auch zehn Mark die Woche für den Bus.

3 — Matthias, wofür gibst du dein Geld aus?
— Ich gehe in die Disco. Wenn man auch noch eine Cola trinken will, dann ist das Geld schnell alle.

4 — Bianca, gibst du dein Geld aus oder sparst du es?
— Ich gebe es aus.
— Wofür?
— Eine ganze Reihe Zeitschriften. Und Schulsachen.
— Auch für Make-up?
— Ja, so fünfzehn Mark im Monat für Make-up.

5 — Thomas, wofür gibst du dein Geld aus?
— Für mein Hobby. Das ist Tennis. Ich kauf' mir ziemlich viele Sachen dafür.

6 — Susanne, wofür gibst du dein Geld aus?
— Ja, wenn ich abends ausgehe — wenn ich zum Beispiel ins Kino gehe ... oder ein Eis essen gehe.

Solution:

1 Ausgehen + Zeitschrift **2** Kleider, Bücher und Hefte für die Schule + Bus **3** Disco + Cola **4** Zeitschriften + Schulsachen + Make-up **5** Tennis **6** Kino + Eis

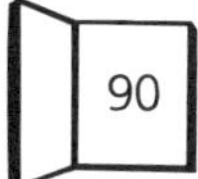

Wofür sparst du dein Geld?

Listening Speaking Reading Writing

A number of people talking about what they are going to buy or what are saving up for. Ask the students to listen to the cassette and decide who will be buying what. Practise the vocabulary with the students before playing the cassette.

Teacher: *Seht euch die Bilder an und wiederholt. Das ist ein Computer, ein Computerspiel, ein Rad, ein T-Shirt und eine Gitarre ... und das sind Turnschuhe. Hört gut zu. Wer kauft was, oder wer spart wofür? Zum Beispiel: Nummer eins ...*

Wofür sparst du dein Geld?

1 — Wofür sparst du?
— Für einen Computer.

2 — Und du? Wofür sparst du?
— Für ein Fahrrad.

3 — Und du?
— Ich spare für eine Gitarre. Ich spiele in einer Band.

4 — Ich spare für ein Computerspiel. Es kostet 150 Mark.

5 — Ich spare für Kleider. Ich kaufe mir einen neuen Pullover und ein T-Shirt.

6 — Wofür sparst du denn?
— Ich spare für ein Paar neue Turnschuhe.

Solution:

1e (einen) Computer **2f** (ein) Fahrrad **3a** (eine) Gitarre **4b** (ein) Computerspiel **5c** (einen) Pullover + (ein) T-Shirt **6d** Turnschuhe

Billig oder teuer?

Listening Speaking Reading Writing

An activity in which the students are asked to express their opinions on the prices attached to the items listed, and then to compare their views with those of a number of German teenagers. Talk them through one or two examples, and make sure they understand the meaning of *teuer* and *billig*.

Teacher: *Seht euch die Bilder und die Preise an. DM 4 für eine Flasche Cola. Ist das zuviel?*

Student: *Ja.*

Teacher: *Ja, das ist teuer! Wie heißt ‚teuer' auf englisch? ... Gut. 200 Mark für ein Fahrrad. Ist das teuer?*

Student: *Nein.*

Teacher: *Nein, das ist billig. Wie heißt das auf englisch?*

Tell the students that they are going to hear people commenting on the prices of the things shown. Play the cassette, pause and ask for the students' views on the price, then play the rest of the extract. Ask them to note whether the speakers find the prices cheap or expensive. Complete the first one or two with the class, thus:

	billig	teuer
Computer	✗	
Cola		✗

Billig oder teuer?

1 — 400 Mark für einen Computer. Wie findest du das?
— Das ist billig.

2 — 4 Mark für eine Flasche Cola. Wie findest du das?
— Das ist viel zu teuer.

3 — 200 Mark für das Rad! Das ist billig!

4 — 4 Mark für die Bonbons. Was meinst du?
— Tja, ein bißchen teuer.

5 — Guck mal. 2 000 Mark für den Ring.
— Das ist teuer!

6 — Hier ist eine CD für 14 Mark 50. Wie findest du das?
— Das ist billig.

7 — Wieviel kostet das?
— Das T-Shirt? 50 Mark.
— Nein, das ist viel zu teuer.

8 — Du, nur 2 Mark für die Ohrringe!
— Mensch, das ist ja billig!

9 — 12 Mark für einen Stadtplan? Ein bißchen teuer.

10 — Eine Stereoanlage für 3 000 Mark.
— Das ist ja teuer!

11 — 60 Pfennig für ein Eis!
— Das ist billig.

12 — 150 Mark für die Turnschuhe. Wie findest du das?
— Das ist ein bißchen teuer.

Solution:

	billig	**teuer**
Computer	✘	
Cola		✘
Rad	✘	
Bonbons		✘
Ring		✘
CD	✘	
T-Shirt		✘
Ohrringe	✘	
Stadtplan		✘
Stereoanlage		✘
Eis	✘	
Turnschuhe		✘

Some students could make a collage of items from magazines, newspapers etc. for which they know the German, and then make a separate price list in German currency. The collages could then be used as prompts for pairwork. Make sure the students doing these activities have practised both singular and plural forms of the verb (e.g. *kostet* + *kosten*) before they complete the activities.

A (looking at B's collage): *Was kostet das? Was kostet der Computer? Was kosten die Ohrringe?*

B: *Der Computer? Zweitausend Mark.*

A: *Das ist ein bißchen teuer.*

Monitor the students' performance, and invite a few pairs to perform in front of the class.

Kommst du mit zum Jahrmarkt?

Listening
Speaking
Reading

An introduction to the language of funfairs. Funfairs are very common in Germany, especially in spring and autumn. The visuals introduce the topic and clarify the vocabulary so that the students should be able to cope with the questions that follow and give their personal reactions.

Teacher: *Geht ihr gern zum Jahrmarkt?* (Point to the photos:) *Das ist ein Jahrmarkt in Deutschland. Das ist ein Karussell ... Bitte, wiederholt.*

Now you can play the cassette, and ask the students to note which rides the people interviewed like and which they like best of all. Start by asking one or two students which rides they like (best).

Teacher (to one student): *Fährst du gern mit dem Karussell?*

Student: *Nein.*

Teacher: *Mit der Geisterbahn?*

Student: *Ja.*

Teacher: *Fährst du am liebsten mit der Geisterbahn?*

Student: *Nein, mit dem Autoscooter.*

Teacher: *Ausgezeichnet. Hört gut zu.* (Write up two columns for the students to copy.)

gern **am liebsten**

Teacher: *Was machen die Leute gern und am liebsten? Schreibt die Antwort in die richtige Spalte. Zum Beispiel ...*

Kommst du mit zum Jahrmarkt?

1 — Was machst du gern am Jahrmarkt?
— Naja, ich fahre gern mit dem Riesenrad, aber am liebsten fahre ich mit der Geisterbahn. Das find' ich fantastisch.

2 — Fährst du gern mit dem Autoscooter?
— Ja natürlich, aber am liebsten fahre ich mit dem Riesenrad.

3 — Wie findest du die Schiffschaukel?
— OK ... Ja, ich fahre gern mit der Schiffschaukel, aber am liebsten fahr' ich mit dem Karussell.

4 — Kommst du mit auf die Geisterbahn?
— Nee.
— Du fährst aber doch gern mit der Geisterbahn?
— Ja, aber am liebsten fahre ich mit dem Autoscooter.

5 — Fährst du gern mit dem Karussell?
— Ja, aber am liebsten fahre ich mit der Schiffschaukel. Kommst du auch mit?
— Nein, ich habe keine Lust.

Solution:

	gern ✓	am liebsten ✓✓
1	Riesenrad	Geisterbahn
2	Autoscooter	Riesenrad
3	Schiffschaukel	Karussell
4	Geisterbahn	Autoscooter
5	Karussell	Schiffschaukel

IT suggestion

As a conclusion to this *Lernziel*, students could produce two lists: *Ich gebe mein Geld für ... aus* and *Ich spare für ...* Encourage them to try to produce accurate accusative articles, but at the same time persuade them to use their imagination and enlist the help of dictionaries.

Students may now attempt the *Lernziel 3* activity in the *Selbstbedienung* section on page 93 of the students' book. See page 120 of this book for more details.

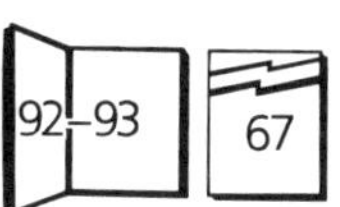

Lernziel 1

Wieviel ist das zusammen?
Illustrations of different amounts of money in coins and notes. Students are asked to choose the correct total from the three alternatives given.

Solution:

1 a **2** c **3** c **4** b **5** a **6** b

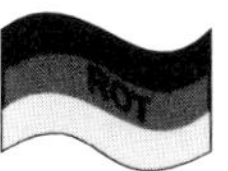

Kostet? Kosten?
The students must read the sentences, each of which have the verb — *kostet* or *kosten* — missing. They must first decide which form is correct, and then look at the illustrations of the items and write out the cost.

Solution:

1 kostet — (Der Computer kostet) tausend Mark.
2 kostet — (Die Kassette kostet) sechzehn Mark.
3 kosten — (Die Turnschuhe kosten) hundert Mark dreißig.
4 kostet — (Das Eis kostet) eine Mark fünfzig.
5 kosten — (Die Bonbons kosten) zwei Mark vierzig.
6 kostet — (Der Film kostet) siebzehn Mark achtzig.

Lernziel 2

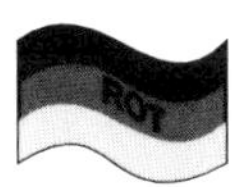

Zweimal Cola, bitte
Students must look at the illustrations of snacks and drinks and write down what they would say if they were ordering them.

Possible solution:

a Zweimal Cola, bitte
b Einen Hamburger, bitte
c Einen Apfelsaft und eine Limonade, bitte
d Zweimal Eis, bitte
e Eine Limonade, eine Cola und einmal Pommes frites, bitte
f Dreimal Apfelsaft, bitte
g Dreimal Eis, bitte
h Zweimal Limonade, einen Hamburger, eine Bratwurst, eine Tafel Schokolade und ein Eis, bitte

Am Schnellimbiß
The students read what the customers and stallkeepers say, and must deduce the prices on the signboard. They

can then work out and fill in how much the other four customers will have to pay.

Solution:

Schaschlik DM 3,20; Pommes frites DM 2,20; Bratwurst DM 2,50; Cola DM 2,00.

The customers pay (from left to right): DM 6,40; DM 14,20; DM 4,50; DM 12,80.

Lernziel 3

Wofür gibst du dein Geld aus?

The students must do two things. First they must unjumble the sentences, and then they have to match them to the five statements, to find out who says what.

Solution:

1 Ich gebe mein Geld meistens für Bücher und Kassetten aus. (Barbara)

2 Ich gebe mein Geld für meine Hobbys aus. (Dieter)

3 Ich gebe mein Geld für Kleider und Make-up aus. (Marga)

4 Ich gebe nicht viel aus. (Kirsten)

5 Ich gebe ziemlich viel Geld beim Ausgehen aus. (Anton)

Bildvokabeln

Im Wilden Westen

Reading
Writing

Items of clothing vocabulary. The copymaster version gives students the opportunity to label the drawing.

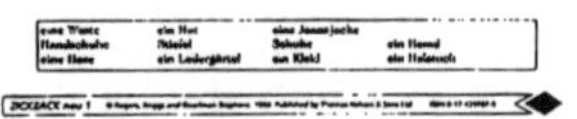

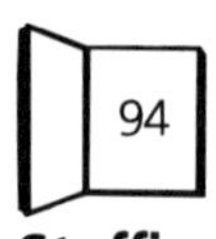

Steffi

Reading

A cartoon for comprehension and practice. No detailed exploitation is intended, but you could point out the practice of students buying their own school books in most parts of Germany.

> Grammar exercises 16 and 17, on copymasters 75 and 76, are based on the material covered in this chapter.

> After completing work on this chapter, check whether any further reinforcement is appropriate from the video material, Activity Box cards and Assessment Support Pack tasks.

10 Wie schön!

Main teaching points

Lernziel 1: Talking about the weather and the seasons

Grammar presented:
Impersonal verbs present tense — Adjectives — Interrogatives

Vocabulary presented:

alles gute, *Athen*, *es regnet*, *es schneit*, *Ferienpostkarten*, *im Frühling*, *fast*, *der Grad*, *im Herbst*, *heiß*, *ich fahre ... Ski*, *ich surfe*, *die Jahreszeit*, *Nizza*, *neblig*, *im Sommer*, *die Sonne*, *der Strand*, *scheint*, *im Winter*, *wie ist das Wetter?*, *wieviel Grad ist es?*, *windig*

Lernziel 2: Talking about holidays

Grammar presented:
Prepositions — Verbs in the present tense

Vocabulary presented:

allein, *an der Ostsee*, *an die See*, *aufs Land*, *das gefällt uns*, *deshalb*, *ein paar Tage*, *das Ferienhaus*, *Ferienpläne*, *fliegen*, *Griechenland*, *das Hotel*, *ich fahre nicht weg*, *im Schwarzwald*, *in den Alpen*, *ins Ausland*, *ins Gebirge*, *die Jugendherberge*, *mieten*, *mit wem fährst du?*, *mitten in*, *nach Spanien*, *nächstes Jahr*, *Süditalien*, *Touristen*, *treiben*, *übernachten*, *verbringen*, *der Wintersport*, *der Winterurlaub*, *der Wohnwagen*, *wo fährst du hin?*, *das Zelt*

Grammar revised:
Prepositions — Interrogatives

Lernziel 3: Impressions of other countries

Grammar presented: Adjectives

Vocabulary presented:

alle 10 Minuten, *amerikanisch*, *an*, *auf Urlaub*, *der Badeanzug*, *das Badetuch*, *der Berg*, *der große Boß*, *erst*, *fantastisch!*, *fürchterlich*, *gleich aussehen*, *kurz*, *die Luftmatratze*, *länger*, *läuft*, *die Meinung über*, *man darf nicht*, *meint ihr uns?*, *der Sand*, *die Sandburg*, *das Segelboot*, *die Sonnenbrille*, *die Sonnencreme*, *der Sonnenschirm*, *die Soße*, *der Strandkorb*, *das Surfbrett*, *streng*, *der Tierfilm*, *ununterbrochen*, *überhaupt nicht*, *von sieben bis elf*, *vor dem Fernseher*

Grammar revised:
Adjectives — Verbs in the present tense

> Before beginning work on this chapter, check where the video material, Activity Box cards and Assessment Support Pack tasks will be most appropriate.

Presentation of language (weather vocabulary)

Listening
Speaking

Presentation of weather vocabulary. Make an OHP transparency or an enlargement of the weather cards on copymaster 49. Following the usual approach, present the expressions in groups of two or three. The area offers much scope for the use of mime and gesture.

Teacher: *Wie ist das Wetter?* (Show rain card:) *Ach nein! Es regnet!* (Pointing to sunshine card:) *Super! Die Sonne scheint. Fantastisch!*

Continue the activity, encouraging students to vary their intonation to show pleasure and/or disappointment in their answers: *Furchtbar!! Es ist neblig ... Toll! Es schneit! ...*

Hand over the question-and-answer activity to the students once they are confident about the new vocabulary.

Teacher: *Jetzt seid ihr dran.* (Show a card:) *Bist du glücklich?* (Draw a smiling face ☺.) *Wie ist das Wetter?*

Student: *Toll! Es ist windig!*

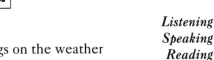

Schönes Wetter?

Listening
Speaking
Reading

Eight short recordings on the weather for the students to identify. Ask them to listen to the recording and to write down the corresponding letters.

Teacher: *Hört gut zu, und seht euch die Bilder an. Wie ist das Wetter? Wie ist die richtige Reihenfolge?* (Do the first one as an example.)

Schönes Wetter?

1 — Es ist kalt heute. Willst du einen Kaffee?
— Oh ja. Das ist eine gute Idee.

2 — Oh nein. Es ist windig. Wir können nicht Tennis spielen.

3 — Hallo Dieter. Wie geht's?
— Hallo Frank. Mir geht's gut, danke. Wo bist du denn?
— In Hamburg.
— Wie ist das Wetter?
— Sehr neblig.

4 — Gehst du in die Stadt?
— Nein. Es regnet.

5 — Es ist heiß heute. Ich gehe ins Schwimmbad. Kommst du mit?
— Oh ja!

6 — Toll! Es schneit. Bauen wir einen Schneemann?

7 — Gehen wir an die See? Die Sonne scheint.

8 — Wie ist das Wetter dort?
— Das Wetter? Es ist schön im Moment.

Solution:

1 D 2 G 3 A 4 F 5 C 6 B 7 H 8 E

Follow up the activity by asking students to work in pairs, using mimes to cue answers from each other about the weather. Perform one or two examples to illustrate.

Teacher (miming by holding up an umbrella): *Wie ist das Wetter?*

Student: *Es regnet.*

Teacher: *Gut.*

Encourage the students to come to the front and make up their own mimes for the class to guess, then ask them to continue in pairs.

Teacher: *Jetzt seid ihr dran. Partnerarbeit.*

Wetterspiel

Listening
Speaking
Reading

A matching game for students to practise their reading comprehension of the weather. They should work in groups of two or three, taking it in turns to turn over a text card and an illustration. The winner is the player holding the most matching pairs at the end of each round.

Teacher: *Gruppen/Partnerarbeit. Was paßt wozu? Das hier sind die Bilder, und das sind die Texte. Ich drehe sie so um:* (demonstrate).
(To one student:) *Nimm zwei Karten. Was hast du gewählt? ‚Es regnet' und dieses Bild — passen die zusammen? Nein. Schade! Du legst die wieder hin.*
(Continue until a match is found:) *Das ist ein Paar. Der Text paßt zum Bild. Du behältst das Paar. Jetzt macht ihr weiter ...*

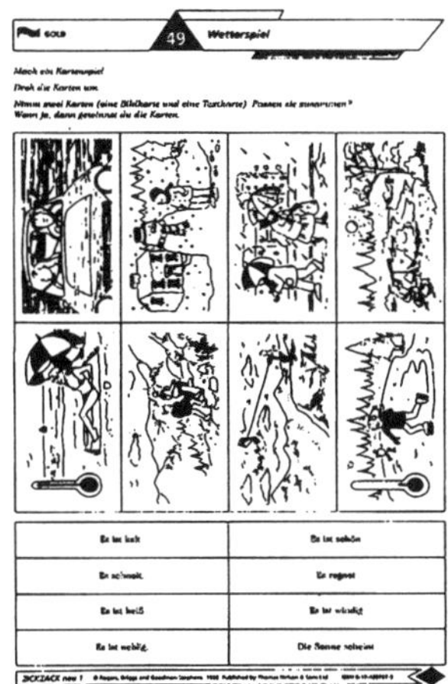

Drei Telefonate aus den Ferien

Listening
Speaking
Writing

Three phone calls made by young people on holiday to their friends, all of which include comments about the weather. Ask the students to listen only for the comments on the weather and to make a note of them.

Teacher: *Hört gut zu. Diese Jugendlichen sind am Telefon. Sie beschreiben das Wetter. Was sagen sie? Wie ist das Wetter?*

Drei Telefonate aus den Ferien

1 — Hallo, Evi.
— Hallo, Birgit! Wo bist du denn?
— Am Meer. Tolles Wetter haben wir hier. Die Sonne scheint, und es ist so heiß!
— Was machst du denn die ganze Zeit?
— Ich gehe schwimmen, ich gehe spazieren, und abends gehe ich in die Disco.
— Toll. Und wann kommst du zurück?
— Am Samstag. Also, tschüs. Bis dann, ja?
— Ja, tschüs. Danke für den Anruf.

2 — Bernd, du?
— Ja. Hallo, Ingrid. Wie geht's dir denn in England?
— Nicht gut. Das Wetter hier ist schrecklich. Es regnet, und es ist so kalt.
— Was machst du denn die ganze Zeit?
— Ich lese, höre Musik und gehe ins Kino.
— Das kannst du doch auch hier zu Hause machen. Wann kommst du denn zurück?
— Montag.
— Gut. Also, tschüs, dann. Bis Montag.
— Ja. Tschüs.

3 — Hallo Martin!
— Hallo, Michael. Wo bist du denn?
— In Saas Fee, in der Schweiz.
— Du läufst doch nicht Ski?
— Doch, ich laufe Ski. Aber ich gehe auch spazieren, und abends gehe ich in die Disco.
— Und ist das Wetter gut?
— Fantastisch. Nachts schneit es, und am Tag scheint die Sonne.
— Und wann kommst du zurück?
— Am Freitag.
— Also, viel Spaß noch.
— Danke. Tschüs.

Solution:

1 die Sonne scheint + es ist heiß **2** es regnet + es ist kalt **3** es schneit + die Sonne scheint

Wieviel Grad ist es?

Listening
Speaking
Reading
Writing

Ask the students to look at the small outline map of Europe, and then to listen to the 'weather forecast'. They have to write down the name of the capital and the temperature. Clarify the meaning of *Grad*, and quickly revise numbers up to 30. If necessary, you could write up a grid for the students, with the capitals listed in the correct order and a column headed *Grad*, for example:

	Hauptstadt	Grad
1	London	21
2	Paris	...

Teacher: *Seht euch die Karte an. Hier sind Hauptstädte in Europa: London, Paris usw. Wieviel Grad ist es? Grad — das heißt die Temperatur. Wie heißt das auf englisch? Wieviel Grad ist es in London? Zwanzig? Fünfundzwanzig? Dreißig? Hört gut zu.*

Wieviel Grad ist es?

— Hier sind die Temperaturen für heute in Europa:
London: 21 Grad.
Paris: 24 Grad.
Berlin: 25 Grad.
Rom: 32 Grad.
Brüssel: 23 Grad.

Wien: 28 Grad.
Bern: 29 Grad.
Athen: 33 Grad.
Madrid: 30 Grad.
Warschau: 22 Grad.

Solution: see tapescript.

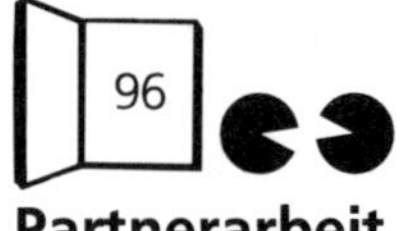

Partnerarbeit

Speaking
Listening
Reading

The students can now use the map, complete with weather symbols, to question each other about the temperature and the weather in any of the locations shown. Use the model dialogue in the book to demonstrate. As the temperatures are not marked on the map, students will either have to use their memories or refer to their answers from the previous activity. For a more demanding exercise, the activity could also be developed into a memory game in which one of the students is not allowed to look at the map when answering the question about the weather.

Teacher: *Partnerarbeit. Stellt einander Fragen über die Temperatur und das Wetter. Zum Beispiel ...* (For the memory game:) *Ein Gedächtnisspiel: Partner(in) A macht das Buch zu, und Partner(in) B stellt Fragen* (demonstrate with the whole class).

Partnerarbeit. Telefongespräche

Listening
Speaking
Reading

An information-gap activity for pairs of students. Each partner has a map of the German-speaking countries with twelve towns marked. Partner A has weather symbols on half of these towns, while Partner B has weather symbols on the other half. The students pretend to phone each other to find out precisely where their partner is and what the weather is like there, so that they can each mark the information on their map (or make a separate note in their exercise books). They are free to choose each time which town they are in, so the information may be exchanged in any order. As each partner has information on six towns, both their maps should reach completion at the same time. Go through one dialogue with the students as an example.

Teacher: *Ihr telefoniert miteinander. Ihr seid in Deutschland, in Österreich oder in der Schweiz. Partner(in) A ist in einer Stadt — zum Beispiel Bern — und Partner(in) B ist in einer anderen Stadt — zum Beispiel Stuttgart. Ihr sagt etwas über das Wetter.* (Perform the model dialogues). *Jetzt Partnerarbeit.*

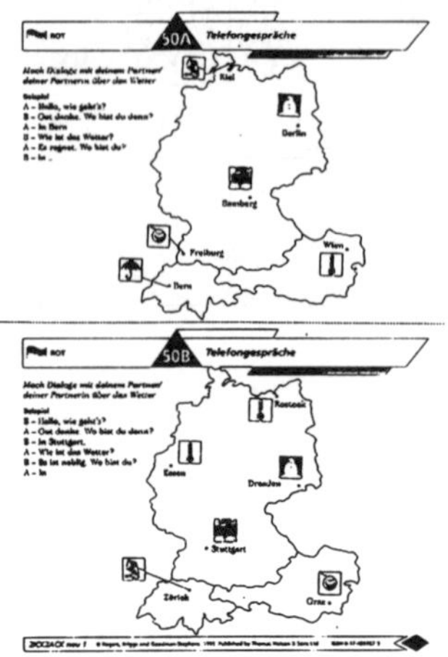

Ferienpostkarten

Listening
Speaking
Reading
Writing

An opportunity for students to revise the months and leisure activities alongside weather expressions. Ask them to read the holiday postcards and make notes under the following headings:

	Monat	Wo?	Wetter	Aktivitäten

Teacher: *Hier sind drei Ferienpostkarten. Wie heißt ‚Ferien' auf englisch? Gut. Was wissen wir über diese Ferien? Macht Notizen, so:* (write up the headings and complete one or two details).

Solution:

	Monat	Wo?	Wetter	Aktivitäten
1	März	Zermatt	die Sonne scheint + es schneit	Ski, Disco
2	Oktober	Berlin	kalt + es regnet	Lesen, Fernsehen, Kino
3	Juli	Nizza	heiß	Schwimmen, Surfen, Volleyball

Some students may now be able to compose their own imaginary holiday postcard in German, using the three postcards as models.

Partnerarbeit. Die Jahreszeiten in Europa

Presentation
Listening
Speaking
Reading

Present the seasons by referring the students to the months of the year, grouped according to season. Once the students are familiar with the seasons, display the weather cards and ask them to assign these to different seasons. Finally, ask them to work in pairs, using the model dialogue together with the visual in the students' book showing the seasons and months of the year.

Teacher: *Die Jahreszeiten. Die vier Jahreszeiten sind: der Winter, der Sommer, der Frühling und der Herbst. Wie heißt ‚Jahreszeit' auf englisch? Ist Dezember im Sommer oder im Winter? Welche Monate sind im Sommer? Wie ist das Wetter meistens im Herbst? Und im Frühling? ... Partnerarbeit. Seht euch das Bild an und stellt einander Fragen. Zum Beispiel:* (perform the model dialogue with a student).

As a follow-up activity, some students might like to produce for display either a poster-sized version of the students' book visual or their own idea for representing the weather and seasons.

Students may now attempt the *Lernziel 1* activities in the *Selbstbedienung* section on page 104 of the students' book. See page 131 of this book for more details.

Wo fährst du hin?

Listening
Speaking
Reading

Five young people talking about where they are going and/or what they are going to do in the holidays. Play the cassette and ask the students to decide who is speaking.

Teacher: *Hört gut zu, und seht euch die Bilder und die Texte an. Wer spricht? Schreibt die Namen auf. Zum Beispiel:* (complete the first one with the class).

Wo fährst du hin?

1 — Wohin fährst du in den Ferien?
— Ich fahre nach Südfrankreich — ans Meer. Ich schwimme sehr gern.

2 — Fährst du wieder aufs Land?
— Nein, dieses Jahr nicht. Ich fahre ins Gebirge. Ich mache eine Bergtour.

3 — Im Sommer fahre ich nicht weg. Ich bleibe zu Hause. Wir haben ein neues Haus, und ich helfe ein bißchen im Garten.

4 — Ich fahre im Juli weg — aufs Land. Wir machen einen Campingurlaub.

5 — Wo fährst du denn hin?
— Ich? Naja — ich fahre mit meiner Familie nach Spanien. Wir mieten einen Wohnwagen im Süden.

Solution:

1 Ulla **2** Dirk **3** Beate **4** Udo **5** Britta

Partnerarbeit

Reading
Speaking
Listening

Follow up the previous activity by asking the students to recap on what each person says about his or her holidays. This activity lends itself to pairwork.

Teacher: *Was sagt Ulla? ‚Ich fahre ans Meer'? ... Oder ‚Ich fahre aufs Land'?*

Equally, students could play *Wer bin ich?* simply by taking it in turns to make a statement and ask the question — for example: *Ich fahre ins Gebirge — wer bin ich?*

Partnerarbeit. Ferienpläne

Listening
Speaking
Reading

Ask the students to look at the flowchart on page 98, and ask them to choose their answers from the boxes. Revise the names of the countries, using spelling games and ***Ich denke an ein Land — es beginnt mit B.*** Practise the questions and the new items of vocabulary with the whole class. It will help to reinforce the students' grasp of the new structures if you write up the questions in four columns and ask several students the questions in turn. Write in their answers so that the whole class has a visual record of the types of answers required for each of the questions.

Teacher: *Seht euch Seite 98 an. Wiederholt die Fragen: Wohin fährst du in den Ferien? ... Mit wem fährst du? ... Wie lange bleibst du dort? ... Wo wohnst du?*

Once the students are confident about the new language, get them to work in pairs, taking it in turns to ask the questions and answer them, using the flow diagram. (The information could be used for reference, like a ***Tip des Tages***.)

Teacher: *Partnerarbeit. Stellt einander die Fragen, und findet heraus, was für Ferienpläne dein(e) Partner(in) hat.*

Wir fahren nach Spanien ans Meer

Listening
Speaking
Reading
Writing

A number of teenagers talking about their holiday plans. Talk the students through the names and the printed extracts from the tapescript, then ask them to listen and identify the order in which the teenagers speak. Then provide them with copies of the table below (or ask them to copy it down). Play the cassette again and ask the students to fill in the missing information. If necessary provide a menu of possible answers on the board/OHP. If a piece of information is not supplied, tell them in advance.

	Name	Wohin?	Mit wem?	Wie lange?	Was für Unterkunft?
1	Lisa				
2	Rudi				
3	Frauke				
4	Kai				
5	Jochen				
6	Karola				
7	Gina				
8	Rainer				

Teacher: *Seht euch Seite 99 an. Wie heißen die jungen Leute? Was sagen sie? Jetzt hört gut zu. Wer ist das? Rudi? Frauke?* (Play the first recording.) *Richtig, es ist Lisa.* (Write her name up and continue.) *Schreibt jetzt diese Tabelle in euer Heft. Ihr hört jetzt alles noch einmal. Hört gut zu: Wohin? Mit wem? Wie lange? Was für Unterkunft? Zuerst Lisa.* (Play the first recording again and complete the first line.)

Continue the process, and collate all the results on the board/OHP.

Wir fahren nach Spanien ans Meer

1 — Meine Eltern, mein Bruder und ich fahren nach Spanien ans Meer. Wir bleiben da 14 Tage in einem Hotel.

2 — Ich fahre mit ein paar Freunden für eine Woche nach Österreich — auf einen Campingplatz. Hoffentlich regnet es da nicht.

3 — Ich fahre mit meinen Eltern nach Holland ans Meer — in ein Ferienhaus. Für zwei Wochen.

4 — Ich fahre nach England, und wohne drei Wochen bei meinem Brieffreund in Leeds. Ich war letztes Jahr auch da.

5 — Ich fahre nicht weg. Ich habe nämlich einen Job im Supermarkt.

6 — Meine Freundin und ich fahren nach Dänemark. Wir bleiben 10 Tage in verschiedenen Jugendherbergen.

7 — Ich fahre mit meinen Eltern nach Mallorca — ans Meer. Jedes Jahr dasselbe! Zwei Wochen ohne Computer!

8 — Wir fahren dieses Jahr ins Gebirge — meine Eltern, meine Schwester und ich — leider nur für 14 Tage.

Solution:

	Name	Wohin?	Mit wem?	Wie lange?	Was für Unterkunft?
1	Lisa	nach Spanien	Eltern + Bruder	14 Tage	Hotel
2	Rudi	Österreich	ein paar Freunden	eine Woche	Campingplatz
3	Frauke	Holland	Eltern	zwei Wochen	Ferienhaus
4	Kai	England	allein	drei Wochen	bei Brieffreund
5	Jochen	—	—	—	—
6	Karola	Dänemark	Freundin	10 Tage	Jugendherbergen
7	Gina	Mallorca	Eltern	zwei Wochen	?

8	Rainer	ins Gebirge	Eltern + Schwester	14 Tage	?

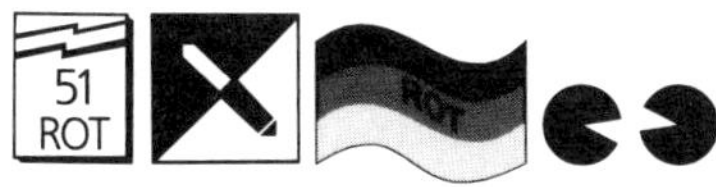

Partnerarbeit. Ich fahre nach ...

Listening
Speaking
Reading

Cue cards providing further practice in the use of language relating to holiday plans. Refer the students to the questions in ***Wir fahren nach Spanien ans Meer*** for support and/or to provide a menu of possible answers on the board/OHP. Divide the students into groups of eight, and ask them to interview each other in pairs about their holiday plans as given on the cue cards. Once a pair have interviewed each other, they should each find another partner in the group to interview.

Teacher: *Hier sind Zettel für die Partnerarbeit. Macht Interviews. Das sind eure Ferienpläne ... Seid ihr fertig? Jetzt interviewt andere Partner.*

Finally, the students could interview each other about their own (real or imaginary) holiday plans. Results could then be collated.

Was paßt zusammen?

Listening
Speaking
Reading

Seven spoken extracts about people's holiday plans, which the students have to match to visuals of the holidays described. Ask them to listen to the recordings and follow the texts in the book.

Teacher: *Hört gut zu und lest die Texte. Welches Bild paßt zu welchem Text?* (Complete the first one with the class.)

Was paßt zusammen?

Gisela: Ich fahre mit drei Freundinnen ins Gebirge. Wir übernachten in Jugendherbergen.

Ali: Ich fahre sehr gern mit meiner Familie weg. Diesen Sommer zum Beispiel fliegen wir nach Griechenland, und wir wohnen in einem Hotel.

Michael: Meine Schwester und ich treiben sehr gern Wintersport — meine Eltern auch — deshalb machen wir nächstes Jahr einen Winterurlaub in den Alpen.

Konstanze: Wir haben ein Ferienhaus in Süddeutschland. Da verbringen wir zwei Wochen im Juli. Mein Onkel und seine Kinder fahren auch hin.

Birgit: Dieses Jahr fahren wir zu einem Campingplatz mitten in der Natur im Schwarzwald.

Stefan: Wir fahren dieses Jahr ins Ausland und wie immer in den Süden. Warme Sonne, klares Wasser und nicht zu viele Touristen — das gefällt uns. Diesen Sommer mieten wir ein Ferienhaus in Süditalien.

Susanne: Ja, wir verbringen vierzehn Tage in einem Wohnwagen an der Ostsee. Es ist ganz schön — wir waren auch letztes Jahr dort.

Solution:

Gisela **g** Ali **d** Michael **a** Konstanze **e** Birgit **b** Stefan **f** Susanne **c**

Ein Brief über Ferienpläne

Speaking
Reading
Writing

Using this copymaster, the students write a letter detailing their holiday plans. Ask them to write the letter by choosing sentences from the boxes.

Teacher: *Schreibt einen Brief über eure Ferienpläne. Wählt die Sätze aus den Kästchen* (demonstrate).

IT suggestion

The letters could finally be reproduced using word-processing software.

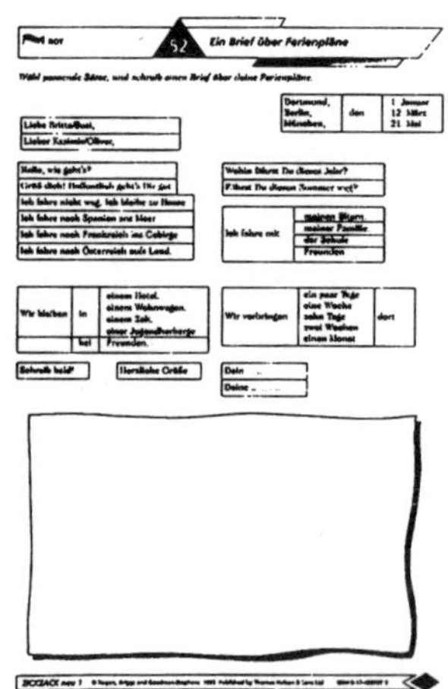

Students may now attempt the *Lernziel 2* activities in the *Selbstbedienung* section on page 105 of the students' book. See page 131 of this book for more details.

This final *Lernziel* focuses on the views and impressions of German teenagers who are spending time with British families. Sometimes they make generalisations or incorrect statements. The intention is that these statements should promote discussion among the students, and make them aware of the dangers involved in generalisations based on limited experience or knowledge. Although the students are encouraged to agree or disagree with the statements made, most of the language is intended to be for receptive purposes. Consequently there is a good opportunity here for students to exercise their dictionary skills.

Häuser und Wohnungen

Listening
Speaking
Reading

Some young Germans give their opinions about houses in the UK. Ask the students to look at page 100, listen to the cassette and discover what these Germans think about British housing.

Teacher: *Hört zu und lest den Text. Was sagen die Deutschen über britische Häuser? Stimmt das?*

Häuser und Wohnungen

— Meistens sind die Häuser klein.

— Die Häuser sehen alle gleich aus.

— Viele Engländer haben ein Haus mit Garten. In Deutschland wohne ich in einer Wohnung.

— Die Häuser sind sehr alt.

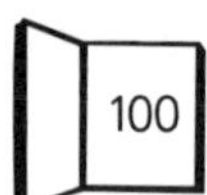

Wie ist das bei dir?

Listening

The students should answer all the questions given under ***Wie ist das bei dir?*** Collate their answers on the board/OHP, and help them to form their own conclusions about the generalised statements.

Teacher: *Lest jetzt* ***Wie ist das bei dir?*** *und schreibt ‚ja' oder ‚nein'. Zum Beispiel, Nummer eins: hebt die Hand, wenn euer Haus oder eure Wohnung alt ist.* (Count and record all the 'yes' and 'no' answers.)

Schmeckt das?

Listening
Speaking
Reading
Writing

What some young Germans think about food in the UK.

Tell the students that you are going to play a recording of German teenagers talking about food in the UK. Ask them to look in their books and listen to the recording. Then refer them to the copymaster or write up a list of the names and the categories. Ask them to put a plus or a minus sign in the appropriate boxes, and answer the two questions.

Teacher: *Hört zu und lest den Text. Was sagen die Leute über das Essen in Großbritannien? Schreibt ein Plus oder ein Minus in die richtigen Spalten. Zum Beispiel:* (complete the first one).

Alternatively, for a SCHWARZ approach, ask the students to draw up two lists covering positive and negative comments under the headings *schmeckt gut* and *schmeckt nicht gut*.

Teacher: *Macht zwei Spalten: positiv und negativ. Zum Beispiel* (demonstrate):

schmeckt gut	schmeckt nicht gut
die Marmelade	das Toastbrot

Schmeckt das?

1 — Bonbons, Kekse und Schokolade schmecken toll. Die Kuchen schmecken nicht so gut, finde ich.

2 — Das Frühstück schmeckt gut, aber das Essen in der Schule ist fürchterlich! Die englischen Kuchen schmecken toll.

3 — Das Essen schmeckt immer gut. Fisch mit Pommes ist fantastisch!

4 — Das Toastbrot zum Frühstück schmeckt mir nicht. Die Marmelade schmeckt aber gut. Die Cornflakes schmecken auch gut.

5 — Ja, das Essen geht, aber ich kriege nicht genug. Nach dem Abendessen bin ich immer noch hungrig und gehe zu McDonald's.

6 — Es ist immer so ein Berg auf meinem Teller — acht Kartoffeln, dann noch Gemüse, Fleisch und Soße!

7 — Das Brot schmeckt mir überhaupt nicht. Der Tee schmeckt gut, aber der Kaffee ist grauenvoll!

Solution:

	Birgit	Jens	Wiebke	Jürgen	Harald	Sabine	Margit
Frühstück		+					
Bonbons	+						
Fisch mit Pommes			+				
Tee							+
Cornflakes				+			
Brot							–
Schokolade	+						
Marmelade				+			
Kekse	+						
Kuchen	–	+					
Schulessen		–					
Kaffee							–
Toastbrot				–			

a Harald **b** Sabine

Solution:

schmeckt gut	**schmeckt nicht gut**
Frühstück	Brot
Bonbons	Kuchen
Fisch mit Pommes	Schulessen
Tee	Kaffee
Cornflakes	Toastbrot
Schokolade	
Marmelade	
Kekse	
Kuchen	

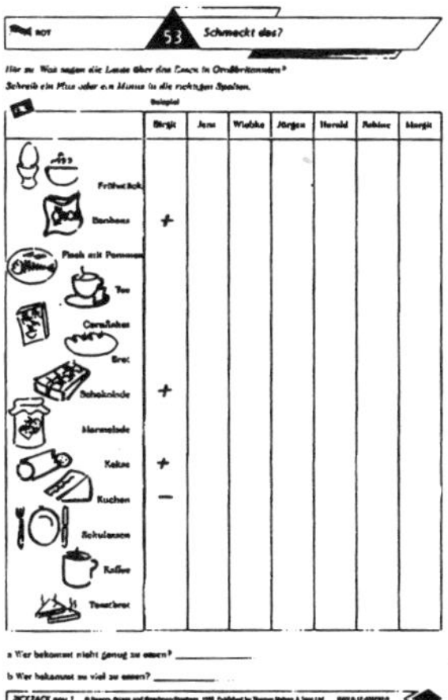

Fernsehen und Radio in Großbritannien

Listening
Speaking
Reading
Writing

Some German teenagers' views on British listening and viewing habits.
Play the first set of comments on the cassette, and ask the students to agree or disagree with them. The copymaster gives students the opportunity to analyse their own viewing and listening habits. If their answers are collated, this may produce some surprising results.

Teacher: *Hört zu und lest den Text. Was meint ihr? Zum Beispiel:* (play the first one). *Stimmt das? Ja oder nein?*

(For the copymaster:) *Wie ist es bei euch? Beantwortet die Fragen.*

Fernsehen und Radio in Großbritannien

- Der Fernseher ist den ganzen Tag an.
- Sie haben ein Radio im Badezimmer.
- Die Familie sitzt von sieben bis elf vor dem Fernseher.
- In der Küche steht ein Fernseher.
- Sie gucken fern zum Frühstück.
- Das Radio in der Küche läuft ununterbrochen.
- Auch im Eßzimmer gibt es einen Fernseher.
- Sie sehen fern im Bett.

Das Fernsehprogramm

Listening
Speaking
Reading
Writing

The German teenagers go on to express their views on British TV programmes. Play the second set of comments on the cassette, and ask the students to identify them (some are ambiguous and open to interpretation). The students can then give their own opinions on the second half of the copymaster.

Teacher: *Was finden die deutschen Jugendlichen gut im britischen Fernsehprogramm? Und was finden sie nicht so gut? Schreibt es auf ... Und ihr? Was findet ihr gut?*

Das Fernsehprogramm

- Es gibt viele Musikshows.
- Die Serien sind gut.
- Es gibt viele Sendungen für junge Leute.
- Die Filme sind meistens amerikanisch.
- Es gibt viele Tierfilme.
- Die Nachrichten bringen wenig Informationen über Deutschland und über Europa.
- Es gibt viele Komödien.
- Die Nachrichten sind nicht so gut.
- Es gibt zuviel Werbung. Sie kommt alle 10 Minuten.

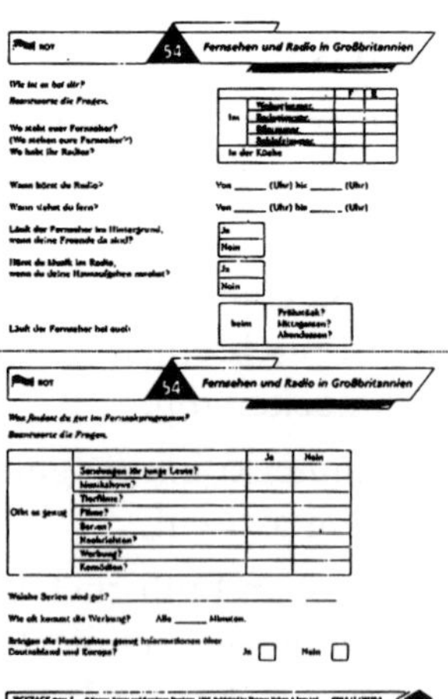

ROT 54 *Fernsehen und Radio in Großbritannien*

Wie ist es bei dir?
Beantworte die Fragen.

Wann hörst du Radio? Von ____ (Uhr) bis ____ (Uhr)

Ja / Nein

Frühstück? Mittagessen? Abendessen?

ROT 54 *Fernsehen und Radio in Großbritannien*

Was findest du gut im Fernsehprogramm?
Beantworte die Fragen.

		Ja	Nein
Oft	Sendungen für junge Leute?		
	Musikshows?		
	Tierfilme?		
	Filme?		
	Serien?		
	Nachrichten?		
	Werbung?		
	Komödien?		

Welche Serien sind gut? ____

Wie oft kommt die Werbung? Alle ____ Minuten.

Ja ☐ Nein ☐

Die Schule in Großbritannien

Listening
Speaking
Reading

What some young Germans think about school in the UK. Ask the students to say whether they agree with the comments.

Teacher: *Hört gut zu. Was sagen diese deutschen Teenager über die Schulen in Großbritannien? Stimmt das?*

Die Schule in Großbritannien

- Ich kann länger schlafen als in Deutschland.
- Der Schultag ist zu lang. Es gibt zu viele lange Pausen.
- Die haben samstags keine Schule. Das finde ich toll.
- Nachmittags Schule? Ich finde das nicht gut.
- Sie haben zu wenig Freizeit.
- Der Lehrer ist der große Boß in Großbritannien.
- Die Lehrer sind sehr streng. Man muß ‚Yes, Miss' oder ‚Yes, Sir' sagen.
- Viele kommen mit dem Schulbus zur Schule. Es gibt sehr laute Popmusik im Bus.

IT suggestion

If the students in your class have been to Germany on an exchange or similar visit, they may have their own views on German customs. Produce a wall chart using pictures of German food/houses etc., with the students' word-processed comments and views pasted on.

Students may now attempt the *Lernziel 3* activity in the *Selbstbedienung* section on page 105 of the student's book. See page 131 of this book for more details.

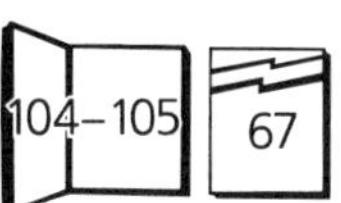

Lernziel 1

Welcher Planet ist das?

A number of imaginary planets and weather types. Students must match the statements to the visuals.

Solution:

1 Plark **2** Zark **3** Tark **4** Gark **5** Mark **6** Nark

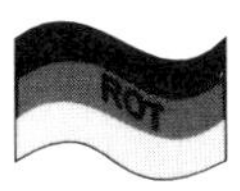

Alles Gute!

Four postcards and four photographs jumbled.

Solution:

1 C **2** D **3** A **4** B

Lernziel 2

Wohin fahren sie?

A map of Europe and a series of statements to enable students to identify who is going where.

Solution:

Brigitte — Bern; Jürgen — Neapel; Ulla — Nizza; Petra — Lourdes; Karl — Tarragona; Werner — Sylt; Kirsten — Leipzig; Anke — Loch Ness; Georg — Graz.

Ich fahre ans Meer

Five sentences, each containing an illustration in place of the key words.

Solution:

1 Meer **2** Land **3** Gebirge **4** einem Hotel **5** zwei Wochen **6** meiner Familie

Lernziel 3

Mein Problem

A humorous account of a German student failing to recognise the house of his host family.

Solution:

Er kann das Haus nicht finden.

Bildvokabeln

Am Strand

Reading
Writing

Further items of vocabulary related to holidays. The copymaster version gives students the opportunity to label the illustration.

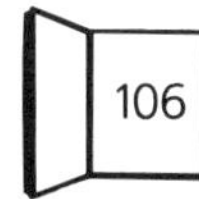

Steffi

Reading

Steffi and her family on holiday. The cartoon is not intended for detailed exploitation.

WIE SCHÖN!

Grammar exercise 18, on copymaster 76, is based on the material covered in this chapter.

After completing work on this chapter, check whether any further reinforcement is appropriate from the video material, Activity Box cards and Assessment Support Pack tasks.

Zickzack neu and the National Curriculum

Attainment targets

	Listen	Speak	Read	Write
	AT1	AT2	AT3	AT4
Kapitel 1				
CM Wie sagt man?	1a 2a	1b 2a	1a 2a	
Partnerarbeit	1a	1a		
Hallo!	1a	1ab	2a	
Wie heißt du?	1a	1a		
Hier ist dein Deutschbuch	1a	1ab	1a	
Partnerarbeit	1a	1a	2a	
Im Sportklub	1b 2a	1a	2a	1a
Fotoquiz	1a	1ab	2a	
Partnerarbeit	1a	1b	2a	
Namenlied	1a	1b	2ab	
Feuer	1a	1b	2a	
Partnerarbeit. Was ist das?	1a	2b	1a	
Was läuft?	2b	1a	2a	
CM Dominozahlen	2a	1a	1a	
Die Hitparade	1b	1b	2ab	
Partnerarbeit	2a	2b	2a	
CM Eine Woche später	2a	2b	2a	
Zahlreich	2a	1a	2a	1a
Wie heißt du? Wie alt bist du?	2b	1a	2a	1a
Was sagen Asaf und Anne?	2a	2ab	2a	
Partnerarbeit. Was sagen sie?	2a	2ab	2a	
Partnerarbeit. Wie alt sind sie?	2a	2ab	2a	
Das Alphabet	1a	1a		
Das Alphabetlied	1a	1b	2ab	
Wie sagt man das?	1b	1b		
Wie schreibt man das?	2a	1b	2a	
Internationales Leichtathletikfest	2a	2b	2a	1a
Welcher Buchstabe fehlt?	2a	1a	1b	
Buchstabensalat			1a	1a
Spiegelbild			1a	1a
Wieviel ist das?			2a	2a
Welche Zahl ist das?			2a	2a
Zahlenrätsel			2a	1a
Frage und Antwort			2a	2a
Bildvokabeln: Im Klassenraum			1a	
CM Bildvokabeln: Im Klassenraum			1a	1a
Kapitel 2				
Europa	2ab	1ab	1a, 2ac	
Welches Land ist das?	1a	1a		
1. Ich denke an ein Land	2a	1a		
2. Länderlotto	1a	1a		1a
3. Buchstabenquiz	2a	1a		
4. Was hast du geschrieben?	2ab	1a	1a	1a
Was ist die Hauptstadt?	2a	1b, 2b	1a	
Partnerarbeit. Buchstabenrätsel	1a	1a	1a	
CM Europa			1a	1a
CM Finde die Städte	2a		1a	1a
Städte und Länder (Galgenspiel)	1a	1a, 2b	1a	1a
Auf dem Campingplatz	2ab	1a	2a	
Partnerarbeit. Wer bin ich?	2a	2b	2a	
CM Ich komme aus Österreich/wohne in Linz	2a	2b	1a	
Partnerarbeit. Ich wohne in Köln	2b	2b	2a	
CM Wie heißt dein Partner? (x2)	2b	2b	1a	
Zungenbrecher	2a	1b	2c	2ab, 3ab
Steffi			2a	
Wo ich wohne	3a	1b	2ac	

Wer ist das?	2a		2a	
Wo wohne ich?	2ab	1a	1a	
Partnerarbeit	2a	2b	2a	
Das liegt im Osten	2ab	1ab	1a, 2a	
In der Nähe von _	2a	1b		
Richtig oder falsch?	2ab	1a	1a, 2a	1a
Partnerarbeit. Wo liegt Zirl?	2a	2b	2a	
Länderquiz			1a	1a
Die Hauptstadt von Italien ist Rom.			2a	1a
Das Auto kommt aus _			1a	2a
Purzelwörter			1a	1a
Zahlenrätsel			2a	1a, 2a
Alphabeträtsel			2a	1a
Wo liegt Grasdorf?			2ab	2a
Auch wir sprechen Deutsch!		1b	2ab, 3ab	
Kapitel 3				
Wie heißen sie?	2ab	1a	2a	1a
Hast du Geschwister?	2a	2ab	2a	
Wieviel Geschwister hast du?	2ab	1a	1a	1a
Familienumfrage	2ab	2ab		1a
CM Ich habe eine Schwester	1b	1a	1a	1a
Partnerarbeit. Welche Familie ist das?	2ab	2ab	2a	
CM Und du? Wie heißt du?	2ab	2ab	1a, 2a	1a
Mein Stammbaum	2a	1ab	1a	
Wie sind die Namen?	1b, 2a	1ab		
Partnerarbeit	2a	2ab	2a	
Meine Familie	2ab	2ab	2a	2ab
Junge oder Mädchen?	1ab	1a, 2a	1a	1a
Zwei Briefe	2a	1b	3ab	
Schreib einen Brief auf Deutsch!	2a	2a	3a	3ab
CM Lieber oder Liebe?	2a	2a	2a	2a
Steffi				2a
Hast du ein Haustier?	2ab	1a	1a, 2a	
CM Tiere			1a	1a
Ich habe einen Hund	2ab	1a	1a, 2a	
Klaus hat eine Maus	2a	1b	2ac	1a
CM Lauter Tiere	2a	2a	2a	2a
CM Tierisch kompliziert			3a	1a
Umfrage	2a	2ab	1a	1a
Wie heißt der Hund?	2a	2ab	2a	
Tanjas Haustiere			2a	2ab
Hast du kein Haustier?	2a	1b	2a	
Und du?			2a	2a
Hallo!			2a	1a
Graf Draculas Familie			2a	2a
Was ist das?			1a	2a
Suche die Tiere			2b, 4a	2a
Bildvokabeln: Ungewöhnliche Haustiere			1a	
CM Bildvokabeln: Ungewöhnliche Haustiere			1a	1a
Wie viele Flöhe?	2a	1b	2b, 3a	
Kapitel 4				
Ich wohne in _	2a	2ab	1a	
Presentation of language	2a	1b		
Ich wohne in einem Dorf	2ab	1b, 2ab	2a	1a
CM Wo wohnen sie?	2ab	1a	2a	1a
Wo denn?	2a	2ab	2a	
CM Welches Zimmer ist das?	2a	1a	1a	1a
CM Was für Zimmer habt ihr?	2a	2ab	3a	
Das ist das Wohnzimmer	2ab	2a	1a, 2a	
Partnerarbeit	2a	2ab	2a	
Krabbi	2a	1b	2b, 3a	
Zu verkaufen	2a	1a	2a	
Mein Traumhaus	2a	2ab	2ab	2ab
Meine Adresse	2ab	1a	2a	1a
Wie sind die Adressen?	2a	1ab	2ab	2a
Partnerarbeit. Wer bin ich?	2ab	2ab	2a	
Computerliste	2ab	1a	2a	
Alter Mann	2a	1b, 2a	4ab	
Meine Familie			3a	2a
Welches Zimmer ist das?			1a	1a
Der Immobilienmarkt			2b, 4ab	
Wie bitte?			2a	2a
Komm zu uns!			3a	1a, 2a, 4b
Bildvokabeln: Im Haus			1a	

CM Bildvokabeln: Im Haus			1a	1a
Kapitel 5				
CM Die Uhrzeit	1a	1a	1a	
Es ist ein Uhr	1b, 2a	1b	1a	
Partnerarbeit. Zeig auf die Uhr	2a	1a, 2ab	1a	
CM Zeitdomino	2a	2b	2a	
Entschuldigung. Wieviel Uhr ist es?	2ab	1a	2a	
Partnerarbeit. Zehn Minuten später	2a	2ab	2a	
Was zeigt deine Uhr?	2ab	2ab		
Wie spät ist es in New York?	2a	2ab	2a	
Wann beginnt der Film?	3ab	2b		
Martina beschreibt ihren Alltag	2ab	2ab	2a	
CM Martina beschreibt ihren Alltag	2a	2ab	2a	
CM Das Verb bleibt sitzen	2a	2ab	2a	
Und du?	2ab	3ab, 4ab		
Katzenalltag	2ab	2ab	2ab	
Presentation of language:				
1. Von Januar bis Dezember	2ab	2ab		
2. Welcher Monat ist das?	2a	1a		
3. Ich denke an einen Monat	2a	1a		
4. Nicht alle zusammen!	2a	1a		
5. Wann hast du Geburtstag?	2ab	2ab		
Presentation of language	2a	1b		
Wann hast du Geburtstag?	2ab	2ab	2a	
CM Geburtstagsumfrage	2a	2ab	2a	1a
Wann ist es?	2ab	2ab		2a
Ein Geburtstag in der Familie	2ab	1a	2a	
Wann sind die Feiertage?	3a	2ab	2ab	
Steh auf!	2a	1b, 2a	2ab	
Wieviel Uhr ist es?			2a	2a
Wo sind sie?			2a	1a
Füll die Lücken aus!			2a	1a, 2b
Evi Bamms Tagesroutine			2a	2ab

Was fehlt?			2ab	1a
Wann denn?			2b, 3a	2ab
Zum Lesen: Was machst du an deinem Geburtstag?	2a		2ab	
Und du?	2a	2ab	2a	2ab
Kapitel 6				
Presentation of language	2a	1ab		
CM Was ißt man zum Frühstück?	1a	1a	1a	1a
Das Frühstück bei der Familie Braun	2ab	1a	2b	1a
Die Frühstückspalette	2ab	2ab	2a	
Eine Umfrage in einer Schule in Deutschland	2a	1a	2a	1a
CM Zum Frühstück	2ab	2ab	3a	
Frühstücksgedicht	2a	1b, 2a	2a	
Frühstücksposter	2a			2ab
Was ißt du gern zum Mittagessen?	2ab	2ab	2ab	
Das Abendessen. Ein Interview mit der Klasse 6c	2a	2a	2a	
Partnerarbeit. Und du?	2ab	2ab	2a	
Kantine-Wochenplan			2ab	2a
In der Pizzeria	2ab	1a	2a	1b
CM Interviews/Kreuzworträtse 1	2a	1a	2a	1a, 2b
Was heißt ‚gesund essen'?	2a, 3b	2ab	2b, 3a	3a, 4b
Kalorientabelle	2a	2ab	1a, 2ab	2ab
CM Ißt du gern Süßes?	2a	2ab	2ab	
Frühstückskarte			2ab	1a
Müsli, oder _			2a	1a
Namengedicht			2a	1a, 2ab
Briefe aus Spanien, Frankreich und Italien			2a, 3a	1a
Picknickzeit			2a	1a, 2b
Poster für gesundes Essen			2ab	2ab
Bildvokabeln: Zu Tisch			1a	
CM Bildvokabeln: Zu Tisch			1a	1a
Kapitel 7				
CM Welches Fach ist das?	2a	1ab	1a	1a
1. School subject bingo	1b, 2a	1a		

2. Pairwork	2a	2ab		
3. Guessing game	2a	2ab		
Welche Fächer hast du heute?	2ab	1a	1a	1a
Purzelwörter	2a	1a	1a	1a
Schulaufgaben	2a	2ab	2a	
Und du?	2a	2ab	1a	1a
Interviews über Schulaufgaben	3ab	2ab	2a	2ab
Eine gute Ausrede	2a	3ab	2b, 3a	4b
Deutsch ist mein Lieblingsfach	2b, 3a	1a	1a	1a
Was ist dein Lieblingsfach?	2a	2ab	2a	
Wie gefällt dir Deutsch?	2ab	2ab	2a	
CM Schuldomino	2a	2a	2a	
Hast du heute dein Lieblingsfach?	2a	2ab	2a	
Sag mal	2ab	2ab	2a	1a
Eine schlechte Note	2ab	1a	2a	
Steffi			2a	
Kirstens Stundenplan	3a	1ab	2a	
Richtig oder falsch?	2a	1a	2a	1a
Partnerarbeit. Welcher Tag?	2a	2ab	2a	
CM Kreuzworträtsel			2a	1a
CM Stundenplan-Lotto	2a		2a	1a
CM Die Klasse 7c	2a	2ab	2a	
Die erste Stunde fällt aus!	2ab	2ab	2a	
Großbritannien oder Deutschland?	2a	1a	3a	1a
Was haben sie auf?			2a	1a
Kochen? Köstlich!			2a	1a
Fragen und Antworten			2a	
Lieblingsfächer, oder _?			2a	2a
Hauptschule, Realschule _?			2b, 3a	1a
Bildvokabeln: In der Schule			1a	
CM Bildvokabeln: In der Schule			1a	1a
Kapitel 8				
Was machst du in deiner Freizeit?	2a	1b, 2a	2a	

Interviews nach der Schule	2ab	1a		
CM Freizeitaktivitäten	2a	2ab	2a	2a
Was machen sie nach der Schule?	2a, 3b	2a	1a	1a
Eine Freizeitumfrage	2a	2ab	2a	2a
Wer ist das?	2a	1a	2a	2a
CM Computerpartner	2b, 3a	1a	3a	2a
CM Was machst du gern/nicht gern?	2a	2ab	2a	
Beste Freunde	2ab	1b	3a	
CM Jugendzentrum Pinneberg	2ab	2ab	4a	1a
Partnerarbeit. Fernsehsendungen	2a	1ab	2a	
CM Im Fernsehen	1ab	1a	1a	1a
Welche Sendung?	2a	1a		
Ich sehe gern fern	2ab	1a	1a	
Wie findest du Trickfilme?	2a	1a	1a	
Und du?	2ab	2ab	2a	
Hören und Sehen	3a	1a	2ab	1a
Streit	2ab	1a	2a	1a, 2a
Was willst du sehen?	2a	2ab	2a	1a, 2a
Wann ist der Film?	2ab	2ab	2a	
CM Wann ist die Sportschau?	2a	2ab	2ab	1a
Superglotzer der Woche	2a	2ab	2a	
Sonja und Max	2ab	2ab	2a	1a
Statistik: Jugendliche in ihrer Freizeit	2a	2ab	2a	2ab
Britta Tell — ein Profil			2b, 3a	4b
Was für Musik hörst du am liebsten?	2ab	2ab	2a	3ab
In meiner Freizeit	2a	1b, 2a	2b, 3a	
Was machst du?			2a	2ab, 3a
Treffpunkt			3a	3a, 4b
Mein Freizeitwappen			2a	2ab
Was machst du gern nach der Schule?			2a	
Stimmt das?			3a	1a
Bildvokabeln: Musikinstrumente			1a	
CM Bildvokabeln: Musikinstrumente			1a	1a
Steffi			2a	

Aber am liebsten			2a	2a

Kapitel 9				
Revision of language:				
1. Ja oder nein	1a	1a		
2. Umgekehrt	2ab	2ab		
3. Jede Menge	1a	1a		
4. Wieviel?	2a	1ab		
5. Zählt mal	2ab	2ab		
Geld	2a	2a	2a	1a
Wieviel Geld hast du dabei?	2a	2ab		
Wieviel Geld haben sie dabei?	2ab	1a		1a
Partnerarbeit. Was kostet das?	2a	1a	1a, 2a	
CM Sechs Unterschiede	2a	2ab	2a	
CM Hast du mein Portemonnaie?	2ab	2ab	2a	
Auf der Bank	3ab	1a		1a
Welt ohne Geld	2a	1b, 2a	2b, 4a	
An der Eisbude	2ab	1ab	2a	
Einmal Vanille	2ab	1a	1a	
Presentation of language:				
1. Stimmt das?	2a	1a		
2. Gedächtnisspiel	2a	1a		
Was nimmst du?	2a	2ab	2a	
Partnerarbeit. An der Wurstbude	2a	2ab	2a	
Die neue Kellnerin			2a	
CM Was ißt du gern?			1a	1a
Ich gebe mein Geld für CDs aus	2b, 3a	1a	2a	
Umfrage	2a	2ab	1a	2a
Sechs junge Leute	2a, 3b	2a		1a, 2a
Wofür sparst du dein Geld?	2ab	1a	2a	
CM Billig oder teuer?	2ab	1b	2a	1a
Kommst du mit zum Jahrmarkt?	2ab	1a	2ab	1a
Wieviel ist das zusammen?			2a	
Kostet? Kosten?			2a	1a
Zweimal Cola, bitte			2a	2a
Am Schnellimbiß			2a	1a
Wofür gibst du dein Geld aus?			2a	2a
Bildvokabeln: Im Wilden Westen			1a	
CM Bildvokabeln: Im Wilden Westen			1a	1a
Steffi (Auf dem Flohmarkt)			3a	
Kapitel 10				
Schönes Wetter?	2ab	1a, 2ab	2a	
CM Wetterspiel	2a	1a	2a	
Drei Telefonate aus den Ferien	2a, 3b	2a		2a
Wieviel Grad ist es?	2ab	1a	2a	
Partnerarbeit	2a	2ab	2a	
CM Telefongespräche	2a	2ab	2a	
Ferienpostkarten	2a	2a	2a	
Partnerarbeit. Die Jahreszeiten in Europa	2a	2ab	2a	
Wo fährst du hin?	2ab	1a	2a	1a
Partnerarbeit	2a	2ab	2a	
Partnerarbeit. Ferienpläne	2a	2ab	2a	
Wir fahren nach Spanien ans Meer	2ab	2a	2a	2a
CM Ich fahre nach _	2ab	2ab	2a	
Was paßt zusammen?	2a	2a	3a	
CM Ein Brief über Ferienpläne	2a		2a	2a
Häuser und Wohnungen	2a, 3a	2a	2b, 3a	
Wie ist das bei dir?	2a, 3a	2a	3a	
CM Schmeckt das?	2ab	1a	2a	1a
Fernsehen und Radio in Großbritannien	2a, 3b	2a	3a	
Das Fernsehprogramm	2a	2a	3a	
Die Schule in Großbritannien	2a, 3b	2a	3a	
Welches Planet ist das?			2a	1a
Alles Gute			3a	
Wohin fahren sie?			2a	1a
Ich fahre ans Meer			2a	1a
Mein Problem			4a	3a
Bildvokabeln: Am Strand			1a	
CM Bildvokabeln: Am Strand			1a	1a
Steffi			3a	

Areas of Experience

Chapter	Areas of Experience (see key below)
1: Hallo! Wie heißt du?	B C F G
2: Wo wohnst du?	B C E F G
3: Meine Familie	B C F G
4: Bei mir zu Hause	B C D F G
5: Mein Alltag	A B C D F G
6: Wie schmeckt's?	A B C D F G
7: Schule	A B C D E F G
8: Meine Freizeit	A B C E F G
9: Was kostet das?	B C D F G
10: Wie schön!	A B C D E F G

Key

A Everyday activities
B Personal and social life
C The world around us
D The world of education, training and work
E The world of communication
F The international world
G The world of imagination and creativity

Opportunities offered to students in *Zickzack neu* Stage 1

- Communication
- Skills and strategies
- Learning
- Materials and equipment
- Attitudes

Zickzack neu and the SOED 5–14 guidelines

We have selected a single example from the different components of *Zickzack neu* Stage 1 to demonstrate how the course matches up to the SOED 5–14 guidelines for each Attainment Target, at each of the three Levels of Attainment and across the various strands.

Strands	Elementary	Intermediate	Level E
Listening			
Classroom language	Show understanding, through an appropriate response, of simple and familiar words and short phrases in the form of simple instructions and requests, given visual support, repetition, rephrasing.	Show understanding, through an appropriate response, of familiar words and phrases in the form of instructions, requests and simple explanations, given visual support, repetition, rephrasing if necessary.	Show understanding, through an appropriate response, of familiar words and phrases in the form of instructions, comments, information and explanations, where these form a more routine part of the everyday language of the classroom.
	Examples from *Zickzack neu*: From the very beginning, the Teacher's Notes for *Zickzack neu* 1 recommend using German for introducing and preparing classroom activities. For each activity, appropriate language is suggested, beginning with simple instructions and requests and gradually moving towards more complex comments and explanations. Further support for the student is provided on Copymaster 1, which gives a list of common classroom language. Example: Teacher's Book, Kapitel 1, Lernziel 1 **Teacher:** *Kommt bitte 'rein. Setzt euch ...* Teacher's Book, Kapitel 8, Lernziel 2 (Wann ist der Film?) **Teacher:** *Genau. Prima! Hier sind noch Uhrzeiten. Was paßt wozu? ... Jetzt hört ihr ein paar Dialoge.*		

Listening to establish relationships with others	Listen to others while working in pairs or groups and/or with the teacher; and show understanding of familiar words and short phrases by taking part in simple exchanges in familiar contexts. Example: Students' Book, Kapitel 1, page 7, Partnerarbeit: Wer ist das?	Listen to others while working in pairs or groups and/or with the teacher and show understanding of familiar words and short phrases embedded in longer utterances, by taking part in simple conversations in familiar contexts. Example: Teacher's Book, Kapitel 3, Lernziel 3, Umfrage	Listen to others while working in pairs or groups and/or with the teacher and show understanding of familiar words and phrases, embedded in utterances which might contain new language, by taking part in simple conversations in a widening range of familiar contexts. Example: Teacher's Book, Kapitel 5, Lernziel 3, Presentation of how to say your birthday
Listening for information	Show understanding of familiar words and short phrases, from a live or recorded source, supported by repetition and a structured task. Teacher's Book, Kapitel 3, Lernziel 1 Wieviel Geschwister hast du?	Show understanding of short items from a widening range of familiar material, from a live or recorded source, supported by repetition and a structured task. Students' Book, Kapitel 7, Lernziel 2, Deutsch ist mein Lieblingsfach	Show understanding of material from a live or recorded source, supported, if required, by repetition and a structured task. This material may contain some items of unfamiliar language. CM Kapitel 5, Lernziel 1, Zeitdomino
Speaking			
Classroom language	Use simple and familiar words and phrases as part of classroom activities, with teacher support	Use the target language readily, to participate in familiar classroom activities, with some teacher support if required.	Use the target language to participate in and contribute to most classroom activities.
	Copymaster 1 provides students with a list of useful classroom language and encourages them to ask for help, explain problems and organise classroom activities in German. Example: CM1, Kapitel 1 Darf ich auf die Toilette? Ich habe keinen Bleistift. Du bist dran.		
Speaking to establish relationships with others	Take part in simple exchanges using familiar words. Example: Students' Book, Kapitel 2, Lernziel 3, page 21, Partnerarbeit Wo liegt Zirl?	Take part in simple conversations in familiar contexts, occasionally initiating as well as responding, with support as necessary.	Take part in conversations and simple discussions, initiating and responding and going beyond the minimum response where appropriate.
		Example: Students' Book, Kapitel 8, Lernziel 2, Superglotzer der Woche	
Speaking on a topic	Say a few short sentences about oneself with preparation and prompting. Example: Teacher's Book, Kapitel 3, Lernziel 3, Meine Familie und meine Haustiere	Say a few sentences on a familiar topic with preparation and prompting. Example: Students' Book, Kapitel 4, Lernziel 2, Mein Traumhaus	With preparation and prompting as required, talk on a familiar topic from a widening range. Example: as Intermediate

Asking for support	Use familiar words and phrases to ask for help with the language, in a restricted range of familiar circumstances.	Use familiar words and phrases to ask for help with the language in a wider range of familiar circumstances.	Use familiar words and phrases accurately and fluently to ask for help with the language, in the context of a range of activities, using appropriate register.
	Copymaster 1 provides students with a list of useful classroom language and encourages them to ask for support in German. Example: CM1, Kapitel 1, Wie sagt man das (auf englisch)? Ich verstehe nicht		
Pronunciation and intonation	In all of the above targets, speak with increasingly accurate pronunciation and intonation. Throughout *Zickzack neu* 1 students are encouraged to use correct pronunciation and intonation through listening to and repeating rhymes, tongue-twisters, etc. Example: Students' Book, Kapitel 2, Lernziel 2, page 19, Zungenbrecher		
Knowledge about language	Use an increasing knowledge of the language structure and register to communicate with clarity and courtesy in a range of circumstances. During the course of *Zickzack neu* 1, students are introduced to the conventions of du and Sie and are encouraged to use conventions such as bitte, Entschuldigung/Entschuldigen Sie and danke/danke schön.		
Reading			
Reading for information	Understand words, phrases and simple sentences of familiar language, presented in a familiar context. Example: Students' Book, Kapitel 2, Selbstbedienung, page 22, Das Auto kommt aus ...	Understand short, straightforward texts, consisting of familiar language, in a familiar context. Example: Students' Book, Kapitel 3, Selbstbedienung, page 32, Hallo!	Understand straightforward texts which may include some unfamiliar language, though in a familiar context. Example: Students' Book, Kapitel 3, Selbstbedienung, page 32, Such die Tiere
Reading for enjoyment	Read words, phrases and simple sentences, with the support of illustrations, word lists and help from the teacher. Example: Students' Book, Kapitel 1, Lernziel 1, page 7, Namenlied	Read short, straightforward texts with growing confidence, using as necessary word lists and help from the teacher. Example: Kapitel 6, Lernziel 3, page 60, Steffi	Read a variety of materials with increasing confidence and independence, checking on new words and phrases as necessary. Example: as Intermediate
Pronunciation and the written word	Show a developing understanding of the relationship between the printed word, pronunciation and meaning:		
	read aloud familiar words, phrases and short sentences. Example: Students' Book, Kapitel 1, Lernziel 1, page 6, Partnerarbeit	read aloud familiar words, phrases and short sentences, pronouncing them sufficiently accurately so as to convey their meaning readily. Example: Students' Book, Kapitel 6, Selbstbedienung, page 62, Namengedicht	read aloud familiar text with fluency; scan and read aloud a short unfamiliar text, with accent and intonation sufficiently accurate so as to convey meaning readily. Example: Students' Book, Kapitel 3, Lernziel 3, page 31, Hast du kein Haustier?

Using reference sources	Make use of word lists, glossaries and dictionaries with increasing accuracy and independence, to check the meaning of new words and phrases introduced in the context of a unit of work or personal reading activities. Throughout *Zickzack neu* 1 students are encouraged to make use of the comprehensive German-English, English-German glossary at the back of the Students' Book. In addition, the Students' Book contains advice on using a simple bilingual dictionary, with practice activities provided on copymasters.

Writing			
Copying	Copy familiar words and phrases. Example: CM13, Kapitel 3, Welches Wort paßt?	Copy words and phrases, including new material, with increasing accuracy. Example: CM30, Kapitel 6, Bildvokabeln: Zu Tisch!	
Writing from memory			Write familiar words and phrases from memory, using the correct written form with increasing consistency. Example: CM34, Kapitel 7, Mein Stundenplan
Continuous writing	Write a few familiar words within a guided framework. Example: Students' Book, Kapitel 3, Lernziel 3, page 30, Klaus hat eine Maus	Write a few words or simple sentences, with support, guidance and reference materials. Example: CM52, Kapitel, Ein Brief über Ferienpläne	Write a few simple sentences with support, guidance and reference materials if required, using the correct written form with increasing consistency. Example: as Intermediate